THE CIVILIZATION OF THE OLD SOUTH

The Civilization of the Old South

Writings of Clement Eaton

Edited with an introduction by

ALBERT D. KIRWAN

University of Kentucky Press

Grateful acknowledgment is made for permission to reprint the following excerpts from the works of Clement Eaton:

Chapters 1 and 7. From *A History of the Old South,* chapters 10 and 18. Copyright © 1966 by The Macmillan Company. By permission of the publishers.

Chapters 2 and 3. From *Henry Clay and the Art of American Politics,* chapters 5 and 6. Copyright © 1957 by Clement Eaton. By permission of Little, Brown and Company, publishers.

Chapters 4, 9, and 13. From *The Mind of the Old South,* chapters 6, 9, and 12. Copyright 1964 by Louisiana State University Press. By permission of the publishers.

Chapters 5 and 6. From *The Growth of Southern Civilization, 1790-1860,* chapters 6 and 3. Copyright © 1961 by Clement Eaton. By permission of Harper & Row, publishers.

Chapters 8 and 10. From *The Freedom-of-Thought Struggle in the Old South,* chapters 14 and 13. Copyright 1940 by The Duke University Press. New material copyright © 1964 by Clement Eaton. By permission of Harper & Row, publishers.

Chapters 11 and 12. From *A History of the Southern Confederacy,* chapters 1 and 13. Copyright 1954 by Clement Eaton. By permission of The Macmillan Company, publishers.

MANUFACTURED IN THE UNITED STATES OF AMERICA
LIBRARY OF CONGRESS CATALOG CARD NO. 68-29638

CONTENTS

INTRODUCTION

After twenty years of distinguished service at the University of Kentucky, Clement Eaton will pass a milestone in a scholarly career devoted to the study of the American South. At the end of the 1967-68 academic year he will reach the age of retirement. The University of Kentucky is marking the occasion by publishing a volume of selections from his writings. This book is the product of that venture. It will serve as a demonstration of the affectionate regard of his colleagues for "a true gentleman of the Old South" as well as their esteem for an eminent scholar who has been an inspiration to them.

Winston, North Carolina, was already a thriving, tobacco-manufacturing town in the piedmont when Clement Eaton was born there in 1898. It was situated close by the quaint Moravian town of Salem, to which it would soon be joined. Like most American cities, Winston-Salem was a class-structured community where Clement's father, the longtime mayor, occupied a patriarchal relationship with the large Negro population; and some of Clement's earliest recollections are of warm, affectionate associations with many of his dark-skinned fellowtownsmen. There was, for instance, Emma who lived in a cottage on his father's farm and who served as a wet nurse for Clement's baby sister; there was lame, grizzled Milus who preached eloquent sermons and who fathered numerous progeny; there was Milus's grandson, Clement's sometime playmate, whose summer wardrobe consisted of a cap of many colors; there was Joe, the half-Negro, half-Indian janitor of the school, who was loved by all the children; there was Frank, the Eaton's intelligent yardboy, whose mother was white. There were, of course, other friends and neighbors, both white and black, but Emma and Milus and Joe and Frank were personalities of Clement's earliest childhood that have lingered in his memory.

As a boy Clement showed an inclination toward scholarship. It was quite natural that he should have a partiality for literature, for his father, although a successful businessman, had a feeling for the arts and was an avid reader. According to Clement's brother, himself a professor of English, their father "could quote more poetry from the entire English tradition than anyone I have ever met." Indeed, there was a tradition of interest in the arts that was very much alive in the family: Clement's mother and sister were accomplished painters, and Clement himself tried his hand at landscape painting during summer vacations. In this attempt, as in all his intellectual and artistic pursuits, Clement had great encouragement from his parents. But the boy was no bookworm. Although a brilliant student with an interest in music and painting, he played an unusually good game of tennis and participated in the other school sports.

Clement was only seventeen when he left home in 1915 to enter college at the University of North Carolina at Chapel Hill. It was at the height of a period of great intellectual ferment at the university, and Chapel Hill was an exciting place for the students, most of whom were unsophisticated country lads. There were perhaps fewer than twelve hundred students enrolled at the time and it was possible for them to develop close personal relationships with members of the faculty, many of whom stimulated inquiry and a liberal view and encouraged dissent. Clement had been indoctrinated by his parents with a curious mixture of stern Calvinism in religion and liberal principles in politics. Although he had deep respect and affection for both parents, he was closer to his mother, who was of an exceptionally warm and affectionate nature and who had great belief in the potential of her children. She was a South Carolina gentlewoman of a Cavalier temperament, and she balanced for her children the more direct and disciplined nature of their father. Clement never ceased to hold his father in deep respect and admiration; indeed it was his father, he believes, who inspired his strong competitive spirit, "the desire for distinction, for winning honor rather than devoting my life to the acquisition of money or to the pursuit of pleasure." Nevertheless, at the university he was released from the dominating influence of his father and was free to develop his own philosophy and make his own decisions for the future.

Of his seven brothers and sisters Clement was especially close to his brother Clifton. Although a year younger than Clement, Clifton had started to school with him, and the two brothers entered the university together. Clifton, too, was a brilliant student, a poet, a fine public speaker, and a good athlete. The two brothers competed with each other for academic honors and were considered the most brilliant members of their class at Chapel Hill; indeed, at the end of their junior year Clifton ranked first in class standing just a fraction above his older brother, who was second. But though they competed for the same honors they were unselfishly devoted to each other, and there was never friction between them. The brothers were inseparable and were known throughout the university community as "Jonathan and David." Clifton's untimely death at the end of their junior year severed these extraordinarily strong bonds of brotherly love.

Among the faculty at Chapel Hill who influenced Eaton's commitment to scholarship was Edwin Greenlaw, professor of English. Greenlaw "had a vast scorn for superficial thinking and sloppy work"; and from him Eaton not only learned Shakespeare but also developed much of his latent skill in writing. There was Frederick Koch, professor of drama, under whose guidance Eaton wrote a play about Daniel Boone. It was this experience which persuaded the fledgling dramatist that his talents lay in some other direction. At Chapel Hill, too, he came to know Horace Williams, professor of philosophy, whose cryptic questions stirred deep thoughts in the young scholar and encouraged him to skepticism. But perhaps the Chapel Hill professor who had the most lasting influence on Eaton was Norman Foerster, who taught American literature. It was Foerster who instilled in him great respect for the New England transcendentalists. He became an ardent admirer of Henry David Thoreau, read him exhaustively, and resolved like him to become an individualist.

In his senior year at Chapel Hill Clement lived in the ramshackle "Old Inn" in the room next to Thomas Wolfe's and close by those of Paul Green, Luther Hodges, and Albert Coates. The five of them ate together at the same table. Wolfe had a voracious appetite, and Eaton today has a much clearer recollection of their passing food to Wolfe than he has of the brilliance of the conversation that must have prevailed among this remarkable quintet. Meanwhile, Eaton had decided to pursue graduate study in history, and in the autumn of 1920 he and Tom Wolfe set out for Harvard.

Lyman Kittredge was in his heyday at the time, and Eaton took his celebrated course in Shakespeare. Kittredge taught him to appreciate not only the genius of the great dramatist but also the value of precision in language. He attended also the scholarly and popular lectures of Professor Lowe who specialized in the English Romantic poets. These two courses in English literature were broadening influences on the young scholar and doubtless were significant factors in the development of his own literary style.

But it was to history that Eaton gave his concentrated attention, and the classes and seminars of Frederick Jackson Turner, Edward Channing, Samuel Eliot Morison, Roger Merriman, and Arthur M. Schlesinger opened new worlds to him. Here he had impressed upon him the value of factual detail as compared to superficial generalization. Great as was the intellectual debt he would owe these illustrious scholars, it was not they but a relatively young and as yet unknown disciple of Turner's who would exert the greatest influence on Eaton. Frederick Merk, now a distinguished professor emeritus but then an obscure associate of his more famous colleagues, directed the research and writing of Eaton's dissertation. A warm relationship developed between the young teacher and his younger scholar.

It was under Merk's guidance that Eaton perfected his clear, lucid style, with its cogent simplicity, its well-balanced sentences, its spontaneous power. It was Merk who advised him not to strain for effect, to scorn adorning adjectives, and to develop vigor through sentence structure. "The great masterpieces of art in whatever field," he wrote his student, "are magnificent in their simplicity and in the completeness of their fusion and ornament." He urged the study of John Stuart Mill as a model of clarity, logic, and organization in writing.

On completion of his residence at Harvard, Eaton taught at Clark University.[1] In 1930 he moved to Lafayette College, where he remained for sixteen years. Here he rose to professorial rank and also served as chairman of the history department from 1933 until 1946. In the latter year he moved to the University of Kentucky where he has remained until his retirement. During his tenure at Kentucky he has served as visiting professor at the University of Wisconsin, and as visiting Fulbright lecturer at the universities of Manchester, Innsbruck, and Bologna. He has taught summer courses at Princeton and Columbia. He has served as a member of the council of the American Historical Association and as president of the Southern Historical Association. He was a Guggenheim Fellow in 1945-46 and has received research grants from the

[1] The biographical material in this introduction is compiled from a letter from Clement Eaton's brother, Charles Edward, dated January 10, 1968; from Clement Eaton, "Student Days with Thomas Wolfe," *The Georgia Review,* XVII (Summer 1963), 146-55; and from conversations with Clement Eaton.

Huntington Library and from the Social Science Research Council. In 1968-69 he will serve as Pitt Professor of American history at Cambridge University.

In 1940 Eaton published his first major work, *Freedom of Thought in the Old South* (in a later edition the title was changed to *The Freedom-of-Thought Struggle in the Old South*). Basically it was his doctoral dissertation, but he had spent more than a decade since his Harvard days incorporating in it the results of new and broader research. Thus the original manuscript grew into an intellectual history of the Old South from the founding of the republic to the outbreak of the Civil War. Eaton saw the ante bellum period as composed of two eras of almost equal length, the dividing line being the death of Jefferson. In the earlier period when slavery had not become so thoroughly imbedded in southern society, dissent had been tolerated by the aristocratic leaders. In the second period liberalism had vanished and the urbane cosmopolitanism of the age of Jefferson was replaced by parochialism. Slavery and religious orthodoxy had become barriers to intellectual freedom, and this triumph of orthodoxy banished freedom of thought. To assault slavery now was tantamount to political and social suicide. Jacksonian democracy had elevated the largely illiterate common man who was politically and socially conservative.

Freedom of Thought was awarded the Duke University Press prize for 1939, and its great merit was all but universally acknowledged. One reviewer wrote, "Probably no previous writer has presented a clearer and more convincing analysis and interpretation of the economic, political, and social thought which made the Old South what it was." He praised the comprehensiveness of the volume, its meticulous diagnosis of the subjects treated, and the author's "calm and dispassionate analysis and interpretation." He thought the work "blazes the way which should be followed in rewriting Southern history as actuality." Another competent critic called the book "a fine specimen of historical writing." Herbert S. Doherty, writing a critique of the literature of the field a quarter of a century later, still thought the book "an historiographic land mark."[2]

It was almost a decade later when Eaton brought out his second book. Meantime, he had broadened his research into almost all facets of the society of the Old South: political, social, intellectual, economic. The result was the publication in 1949 of *A History of the Old South.* It was a penetrating exploration of the puzzling enigmas and class stratifications of the Old South. It won universal praise for its craftsmanship and style as well as for its balance and objectivity. One authority called it "the most satisfactory treatment now available" of the subject. Another thought the discussion of slavery "the most complete coverage to be found" in such a general work.[3]

Eaton's third book, *A History of the Southern Confederacy,* appeared in 1954. In just three hundred pages, almost half of them devoted to military affairs, the author discussed politics, diplomacy, economics, and almost all phases of civilian life. With admirable detachment and dispassionate judgment he weighed the evidence on both sides of controversial questions before coming to his own conclusions. Long-neglected aspects of civilian morale, the role of the Negro both as a southern slave and as a Union soldier, the part played by southern women, cultural activities in general and literary efforts in particular, all are treated in an enlightened and revealing

[2] W. M. Brewer, *The Journal of Negro History,* XXV (April 1940), 246-48; O. P. Chitwood, *William and Mary Quarterly,* XX (July 1940), 444-46; Herbert J. Doherty, "The Mind in the Ante-Bellum South," in *Writing Southern History: Essays in Honor of Fletcher M. Green,* ed. Arthur S. Link and Rembert W. Patrick (Baton Rouge, 1966), 201.

[3] *Journal of Negro History,* XXV (April 1950), 207-209; *American Historical Review,* LVI (Oct. 1950), 139-41; *Mississippi Valley Historical Review,* XXXVII (Dec. 1950), 512-13; *Journal of Southern History,* XVI (May 1950), 212-13. See also Bennett H. Wall, "African Slavery," in *Writing Southern History: Essays in Honor of Fletcher M. Green,* ed. Arthur S. Link and Rembert W. Patrick (Baton Rouge, 1966), 178-79.

manner. The decisive results of the western military campaigns are clearly shown, and a splendid balance is maintained between military and social history. Eaton's provocative conclusion that Confederate failure was due less to economic failure and more to ineffective propaganda and to the work of southern obstructionists drew praise from critics. Praised, too, was the "clear and restrained treatment of the war itself," the "spice and atmosphere" added to the work by the extensive use of manuscript sources, and the "excellent short sketches of the principal military commanders." David Donald called the book "an admirable account of the southern experiment in independence," combining "the merits of all its predecessors." Eaton's unusual mastery of sources and authorities enabled him to write of the South as it actually was. And Eaton's discussion of logistics, he added, was "the best analysis to be found anywhere of Confederate problems of supply."[4]

Eaton was named one of the authors to prepare the series in the Library of American Biography, and in 1957 his *Henry Clay and the Art of American Politics* made its appearance. Because of the limitations imposed (the volume was less than two hundred pages), together with Clay's long and eventful career and the voluminous materials concerning him, Eaton found it necessary to limit his biography to a series of sketches of Clay in each of his several roles: politician on the hustings, statesman laboring over compromise proposals, diplomat, lawyer, planter, husband, father. The result won high praise from critics. Bernard Mayo, himself an earlier biographer of Clay, hailed Eaton's skill in selecting "the pertinent matter from a huge mass," organizing and distilling it into a readable

[4] *Journal of Negro History,* XXXIX (July 1954), 227-29; Mary Elizabeth Massey, "The Confederate States of America: The Homefront," and John G. Barrett, "The Confederate States at War on Land and Sea," in *Writing Southern History: Essays in Honor of Fletcher M. Green,* ed. Arthur S. Link and Rembert W. Patrick (Baton Rouge, 1966), 257 and 289, respectively; *American Historical Review,* LX (Oct. 1954), 131-32; David Donald's review in *Journal of Southern History,* XX (Nov. 1954), 554-57.

and objective appraisal. Other competent reviewers were agreed on the author's objective balance and judicious evaluations of his subject.[5]

Four years after the publication of *Henry Clay,* Eaton brought out his fifth book, *The Growth of Southern Civilization.* In many ways this was a summary of the scholarly work of a lifetime. It was a comprehensive and detailed description of southern ante bellum society in all its facets. As always, Eaton's approach to his subject was specific and detailed rather than generalized. He portrayed the southern mind as more complex than other historians had believed. His mastery of detail surpassed all earlier efforts and won the universal admiration of reviewers. One of them saluted the work as a fresh and stimulating "book of many virtues and few faults." Avery Craven was greatly impressed by Eaton's thoroughness and the "richness of his illustrative material." He thought the treatment of slavery "remarkably well-balanced and sane." Eaton, he said, "steers an intelligent course between the distortions of [Kenneth M.] Stampp and the idealizing of [Ulrich B.] Phillips." He thought the book brought "a breath of fresh air to the prevalent emotional, but quite unhistorical treatment of slavery and the anti-slavery movement." Wendell H. Stephenson, another elder statesman among historians of the Old South, compared the book with Phillips's *Life and Labor in the Old South* and concluded that Eaton's book was more broadly conceived. Another critic thought Eaton's treatment of the yeoman and the poor white in this book was "as accurate a general account as can be found."[6]

[5] *American Historical Review,* LXII (April 1958), 748-49; *Mississippi Valley Historical Review,* XLIV (Sept. 1957), 356-57; *Journal of Southern History,* XXIII (Aug. 1957), 386-87.

[6] Avery Craven in *Mississippi Valley Historical Review,* XLIX (June 1962), 124-25; Wendell H. Stephenson in *American Historical Review,* LXVII (July 1962), 1058-59. See also Herbert J. Doherty, "The Mind of the Ante-Bellum South," and James C. Bonner, "Plantation and Farm: The Agricultural South," in *Writing Southern History: Essays in Honor of Fletcher M. Green,* ed. Arthur S. Link and Rembert W. Patrick (Baton Rouge, 1966), 202 and 159, respectively.

Eaton's most recent major work, *The Mind of the Old South,* was published in 1964. It was a greatly expanded revision of the Walter L. Fleming Lectures that he had delivered at Louisiana State University three years before. Through case histories of men whom he regarded as typical (although for the most part they were not the most famous of southerners), Eaton traced the development of the southern mind in the four decades preceding the Civil War. Purposely avoiding more celebrated figures—John C. Calhoun, Robert Toombs, Alexander C. Stephens, Jefferson Davis—and concentrating on such men as John Hartwell Cocke, Maunsel White, Hinton R. Helper, Joseph Le Conte, and several others, he attempted to trace the process of historical change in the Old South. The essays are rich and provocative. Fletcher Green thought the biographical material "interesting, enlightening, and worthwhile in themselves," and a "substantial contribution to our knowledge of these men." Walter Posey praised Eaton's scholarly research and his clear and perceptive writing.[7]

A volume that will soon be added to the list of Eaton's major works is *The Waning of Southern Civilization.* In addition to his major works, Eaton edited *The Leaven of Democracy: The Growth of the Democratic Spirit in the Time of Jackson* (New York, 1963). It is a volume of selected sources together with a scholarly and comprehensive essay on Jacksonian democracy. He was also editorial consultant for and wrote the introduction to *Green Mount: A Virginia Plantation Family During the Civil War* (Lexington, Ky., 1962). Eaton is the author of approximately a score of articles in leading historical journals.

Clement Eaton is generally regarded as the leading authority on the history of the Old South. Others have blazed new trails in monographic studies of special subjects: slavery, agriculture, politics, religion, literature, biography, the Civil War.

[7] *American Historical Review,* LXX (April 1965), 813-14; *Mississippi Valley Historical Review,* LI (Dec. 1964), 494-95.

None, however, it seems to me, has attained the comprehensive inclusiveness, the catholicity of view that he has achieved. There is not an element of southern thought or society, hardly a major movement of any kind, an event of any significance that has escaped his penetrating thought and skilled analysis.

Lexington, Kentucky Albert D. Kirwan
December 1967

CHAPTER ONE

THE GREAT GENERATION

HEROIC AND NOBLE QUALITIES are likely to lie dormant in men until a great occasion arises. It is this historic occasion that shakes them out of preoccupation with their private concerns and forces them to think and act in the interest of the nation. Ordinary individuals are like the plant that has been thwarted in its growth by being shaded but blossoms luxuriantly when strong sunlight pours upon it. The generation that fought in the Revolution, founded the Federal Constitution and the early republic, and then passed away with the death of Jefferson in 1826 was a remarkable generation. Yet the sage of Monticello (as Jefferson was called in his old age) has warned us against idealizing this unique generation. In 1816 he wrote to the Virginian historian Samuel Kercheval:

> Some men look at constitutions with sanctimonious reverence and deem them like the ark of the covenant, too sacred to be touched. They ascribe to the men of the preceding age a wisdom more than human, and suppose what they did to be beyond amendment. I knew that age well; I belonged to it, and labored with it. It deserved well of the country. It was very like the present, but without the experience of the present. . . .[1]

Since the great Virginia liberal was the most distinguished and versatile leader of that generation and moreover has left a prodigious correspondence,[2] a study of his life should afford a clue to the question "Why did the Southerners of the Revolutionary and early republican periods constitute the great generation in the entire history of the South?" The generation of Southerners that followed produced no great men, with the possible exception of Lee, and it blundered into the catastrophe of the Civil War.

An answer to this question may be found in examining the backgrounds of some of the political leaders, especially Jefferson and Madison. The Virginia background of Jefferson gave him an excellent preparation to become the leader of a democratic movement. His boyhood was spent on a plantation in the Piedmont region of the colony near Charlottesville, which in the eighteenth century was one of the newer settled areas, although it was not the crude frontier of Boone and Crockett. Influenced to some extent by this semi-frontier region, he was principally the product of the culture of the colonial aristocracy. Although his father was a self-made man, modern researches show that he came from good stock and was associated with the gentry.[3] Jefferson's mother, Jane Randolph, was a member of one of the first families of Virginia. When he was 17, he entered the College of William and Mary, where he displayed a passion for learning comparable to the zest for knowledge manifested by Goethe, the great European exponent of self-culture. Fully as important in educating the young Virginian as his college courses were his friendships with three cultivated men in Williamsburg, Professor William Small, who stimulated his interest in science, George Wythe, his law instructor, who influenced him in the direction of liberalism, and Governor Francis Fauquier, a charming man of the world and a freethinker, who often invited the young student to dinner.

[1] Lipscomb and Bergh (eds.), *Writings of Thomas Jefferson*, XV, 32-34.

[2] Jefferson carefully kept copies of his letters, and his preserved correspondence (much of it in the Library of Congress) is enormous. Julian Boyd is editing the *Jefferson Papers* (Princeton, 1950–). The last published volume carries the correspondence to July 4, 1790 (Vol. XVI).

[3] Marie Kimball, *Jefferson, the Road to Glory, 1743–1776* (New York, 1947), 138.

Jefferson was a violin player, and one of his great pleasures was to join Governor Fauquier and others in a quartette of chamber music.

In his early youth he developed an enduring passion for the study of the antique world. He mastered Greek and Latin so that he could read the classics in the original. In his notebooks (the so-called *Literary Bible*) he copied passages from the wisdom of Euripides, Cicero, Horace, Tacitus, and other classical writers. But his attitude toward the past was far from being uncritical and sentimental. Indeed, his study of the ancient world, as a modern scholar has observed, revealed to him "the dark side of humanity" and liberated him from a reverence for tradition. From his classical studies Jefferson derived many fruitful ideas of architecture, a lifelong interest in the growth of language, particularly through neologisms, and a passionate love of political and intellectual freedom. Jefferson's remarkable serenity, although partly the result of temperament and good health, was undoubtedly strengthened by his unceasing conversation with classical authors who taught the individual to become "impassible and unassailable by the evils of life, and for preserving his mind in a state of constant serenity."[4] Jefferson mingled his knowledge of antiquity with his daily experience in government, agriculture, and observation of people, each illuminating the other. His education in the classics did not stop with his college days at Williamsburg, but was continuously enriched by constant reading of the great literary works of Greece and Rome.

After completing seven years of study at the College of William and Mary and in the law office of Wythe, Jefferson began to practice law at Charlottesville. Although he obtained a good income from his profession, he disliked controversy and the necessity of making public speeches. His aversion to the legal profession was expressed in his statement that the

[4] Karl Lehmann, *Jefferson, American Humanist* (New York, 1947), 138.

lawyer's trade is "to question everything, yield nothing, and talk by the hour." Fortunately, Jefferson did not have to depend upon his profession for a living. He became a wealthy young man through inheritance from his father and by his marriage to a widow who owned considerable property. One of the large landed proprietors of the South, he owned 10,000 acres of land, divided into nine plantations, which were cultivated by 204 slaves. His income enabled him to satisfy his tastes in buying books, in acquiring musical instruments, and in enjoying the delights of a gentleman farmer without the sweat and toil of physical labor in the sun.

Returning from Philadelphia after he had composed the Declaration of Independence, he entered one of the most fruitful periods of his life when, as a member of the Virginia legislature, he worked for "the great reforms." He succeeded almost immediately in having the law of entails abolished, which he regarded as equivalent to cutting the roots of the tree of aristocracy in his native state. The repeal of the law of primogeniture came later, as well as his famous statute for religious freedom, which was not adopted until 1786. He made an important contribution in revising the legal code of Virginia with "a single eye to reason" and the public welfare.[5] He proposed abolition of capital punishment for all crimes except murder and treason, but this humanitarian measure was not adopted until nearly 20 years later. The legislature abolished the slave trade in 1778, a reform that he had urged, but the successful bill was introduced by another man. The two most basic reforms that he advocated, which would have revolutionized the state and probably have prevented the Civil War, the gradual emancipation and colonization of the slaves and a liberal system of free public education, were

[5] The best biography of Jefferson is by Dumas Malone, *Jefferson and His Time.* Vol. I, *Jefferson the Virginian* (Boston, 1948), covers the early period of his life to 1784, when he sailed as the American minister to France, chaps. 17-20.

rejected. It is a significant commentary on the evolution of his democratic thought that he proposed to retain the property qualification on voting in Virginia's first constitution but to give gratis to each adult male citizen 50 acres of land, which would enable him to qualify for the suffrage.

From June, 1779, to June, 1781, he was war governor of Virginia. In striving to furnish supplies and soldiers for the Continental army he neglected local defense, and the state was ravaged by invading armies. Accordingly, he was severely criticized for his administration of state affairs. So keenly was he hurt by these attacks that he resolved never again to hold public office. This period of bitterness was accentuated by grief over his wife's death, marking the nadir of his life. Despite his resolution of the renunciation of public office, we find him serving for six months in the Congress of the Confederation and in 1784 going to Paris as the American minister. Thus, for five years he was absent from the United States at a period when the Federal Constitution was being drafted and ratified. Nevertheless, he had a significant influence in securing the addition of the first ten amendments to the Constitution, known as the Bill of Rights. He advised his followers in America that he favored the ratification of the Constitution by nine states, insuring its acceptance, but that four states should withhold ratification until a bill of rights had been added. It is indicative of Jefferson's economic liberalism that he advocated the incorporation in this bill of rights of a provision outlawing monopolies, which was not adopted.

American politics has been characterized by an ebb and flow of conservatism and liberalism.[6] A flowing tide of liberalism reached a high point in the adoption of the Declaration of Independence and of such social reforms as the abolition of

[6] Arthur M. Schlesinger, "The Tides of National Politics," *Paths to the Present* (New York, 1949), 77-92.

primogeniture and entail and the disestablishment of the Anglican church. Following the Revolution a conservative reaction led to the framing and ratification of the Federal Constitution, in which many checks were placed on rabid democracy. For ten years after the new government went into operation the aristocratic and conservative class of society controlled the administration. During this period, however, a new party, the Republican, was gathering strength to overthrow the dominant Federalist faction.

Jefferson and Madison were the main organizers. Madison's role in the formulation of democratic theory and in the organization of the Republican party until recently has been greatly subordinated to Jefferson's role, but actually the work of the two men should be described as "the great collaboration."[7] Despite his idealistic theories and philosophic outlook, Jefferson was a practical politician. One of the first important examples of his willingness to engage in the art of practical politics to attain his objectives was his deal with Hamilton in the summer of 1791 over the assumption of the state debts. Hamilton proposed that the national government take over about $18 million of state debts and pay them at par. The Virginia legislature strongly opposed this proposal in a resolution drafted by Patrick Henry, pointing out the danger to liberty and "the prostration of agriculture at the feet of commerce" by the adoption of such an unconstitutional measure perpetuating an enormous debt upon the nation. Nevertheless, Jefferson agreed to secure enough votes to pass this measure if Hamilton would use his influence to locate the national capital on the banks of the Potomac after a ten-year period in Philadelphia. The deal went through, and the South thus obtained the seat of the nation's capital. The District of Columbia was created out of adjoining parts of Maryland and

[7] Adrienne Koch, *Jefferson and Madison, the Great Collaboration* (New York, 1964).

Virginia, but in 1846 the Virginia portion, containing the town of Alexandria, was retroceded to the Old Dominion.

In this same summer of 1791 Jefferson's skill as an adroit politician was demonstrated by his "botanizing trip" up the Hudson River. At that time he and James Madison went ostensibly on a botanical excursion, but actually for the purpose of forming political alliances in New York, where Governor George Clinton, the Livingston clan, and Aaron Burr, the manipulator of St. Tammany Society of New York City, were opposed to the Federalist administration. In 1792 Virginia, North Carolina, Georgia, and New York voted for George Clinton for Vice-President instead of for John Adams. Thus began the Virginia-New York Alliance, which has played such a significant role in the rise of the Republican and Democratic parties.[8]

After Jefferson resigned from Washington's cabinet in 1793, he devoted himself to organizing a political party of opposition. By a variety of means he built up the early Republican party. He gathered around him some of the most brilliant of the Southern leaders, particularly James Madison, who was converted from his strong Federalist allegiance. Realizing the need of propaganda and the fact that the newspapers were controlled by the Federalists, he gave Philip Freneau, the poet, a clerkship in the State Department, which enabled the latter partly to support himself while he was editing the *National Gazette*, the journal of the Republican party. Also Benjamin Franklin Bache, a grandson of Benjamin Franklin, edited the *Aurora* in Philadelphia, which violently attacked the Federalist policies. Jefferson hated to make public speeches, but he accomplished much in mobilizing his party by writing letters to key men in the states and by conversation. He and his cohorts continually attacked the Federalist party as having

[8] See Dumas Malone, *Jefferson and His Time.* III. *Jefferson and the Ordeal of Liberty* (Boston, 1962).

"monarchical" designs. In 1796 the Virginia leader was the candidate of the Republicans for President against John Adams, who won the election by the narrow margin of three electoral votes. Jefferson became Vice-President, which made him presiding officer of the Senate and gave him further opportunities quietly to organize his party.

A splendid opportunity to agitate for the advancement of the Republicans occurred in the autumn of 1798, when the Federalists in Congress secured the passage of the Alien and Sedition Acts. The Sedition Act was rightly regarded as a violation of the First Amendment of the Constitution, protecting the freedom of speech and of the press. Moreover, these laws were harshly enforced by partisan Federalist judges, and most of the persons prosecuted were Republican editors. Jefferson determined to arouse the people to protest against these arbitrary acts and at the same time to formulate a platform for his party. Since he was Vice-President, however, he felt that he should not take an open part in the attack. Consequently, his authorship of a strong protest against the arbitrary acts of the Federalists, called the Kentucky Resolutions, was concealed. These resolutions were introduced into the Kentucky legislature by John Breckinridge and adopted by that body on November 16, 1798. A month later the Virginia legislature passed similar, but less radical, resolutions drafted by James Madison but introduced by John Taylor of Caroline.

The political character of the Virginia and Kentucky Resolutions has been so emphasized that their significance as a restatement of civil liberties in America has not been properly recognized.[9] In the Kentucky Resolutions Jefferson made an important point that has relevance today, namely that the civil liberties are so closely related that whatever violates one

[9]Adrienne Koch and Harry Ammon, "The Virginia and Kentucky Resolutions . . . ," *William and Mary Quarterly*, Third Series, V (April 1948), 145-176.

"throws down the sanctuary which covers the others." Thus he stated the doctrine of "the entering wedge" in the assault on liberty, which he was later to cite in his criticisms of the Supreme Court for its gradual sapping and mining of the Constitution.

These documents were written at a time when Americans believed in a social compact, or contract, among citizens, as forming the true basis of government. According to this view, sovereignty was divided by the Federal Constitution between the states and the central government. The question who should determine the violations of the compact, the Constitution, whenever the Federal government should encroach upon the rights of the states had not yet been decided. Marshall's decision of *Marbury* v. *Madison*, establishing the right of judicial review by the Supreme Court, was not rendered until 1803. Jefferson and Madison maintained in their resolutions that in the absence of an umpire between the states and the Federal government, the states or the people had this power—in the words of the Kentucky Resolution, "That the government created by this compact was not made the exclusive or final judge of the extent of powers delegated to itself."[10]

The Virginia and Kentucky Resolutions restated the theory that the Federal government was a government of strictly limited and delegated powers. The Alien and Sedition Acts, they asserted, were unconstitutional and therefore null and void. They called upon the sister states, or "co-states," to remonstrate and secure the repeal of the obnoxious laws. These resolutions were a protest against the trend toward centralization, or a "general consolidated government." The Virginia and Kentucky Resolutions represented the appeal of a minority against the tyranny of a majority. They reflected the fear of the Southern states that the central government would be controlled by the commercial interests of the North, which

[10] See E. D. Warfield, *The Kentucky Resolutions of 1798* (New York, 1887).

would use their power to injure the agriculture interests of the South. This fight of Jefferson and Madison to preserve the federal character of the central government was not a disunion movement, for both men were loyal to the Union. Rather, the Republicans had a strong suspicion that the Federalists were trying to change the original character of the central government. The people should be aroused, they believed, to resist the first attempt to convert the Federal government into a highly centralized and powerful institution. Jefferson and Madison were therefore fighting for a limited national government, or constitutionalism.

None of the states responded favorably to the Virginia and Kentucky Resolutions. Several of the Northern states definitely said that the Supreme Court, and not the states, was the proper agency to determine when infractions of the Constitution had been made by Congress. In rebuttal, the Kentucky legislature, on February 22, 1799, passed some additional resolutions, in which for the first time the word *nullification* was used. The core of the second Kentucky Resolutions was the statement "That the several states who formed that instrument [the Constitution] being sovereign and independent, have the unquestionable right to judge of the infraction; and, *That a nullification of those sovereignties, of all unauthorized acts done under the color of that instrument is the rightful remedy.*"[11] The Virginia and Kentucky Resolutions are important documents in Southern political theory, for the compact theory of the Constitution that they expounded contained the germs of the South Carolina nullification movement and of the secession doctrines.

Although Jefferson, and Southerners in general, were fond of using constitutional arguments in defense of their positions, the Virginia leader was quite aware of the economic realities of politics. In a letter to Philip Mazzei in 1796, in which he shrewdly analyzed the economic alignment of the two parties,

[11] H. S. Commager (ed.), *Documents of American History*, I, 155, 184.

he described the Republican party as containing "the whole landed interest and a great mass of talents," and the Federalist group was portrayed as "an Anglican monarchial aristocratical party, merchants, speculators, holders of bank stock and government bonds, and timid men."[12] Jefferson's characterization of his own party as representing the whole of the agrarian interest was not strictly correct, for many of the aristocratic planters of the Tidewater were Federalists.

Nevertheless, the Republican party appealed powerfully to farmers and small planters in the Southern states. In Virginia, Jefferson had been a representative of the back country farming interest and of the dissenters against the conservative Tidewater planters. Hamilton's financial measures and his doctrine of the loose construction of the Constitution were regarded by these agricultural groups as hostile to their economic interests and as favoring a "moneyed aristocracy." Furthermore, Southern farmers had a reasonable distrust of centralizing power in a distant government (the program of the Federalists), which in a day of slow travel and communication could not have an adequate understanding of local conditions and needs, but which might exercise a dangerous power of interference with their lives. Such a limitation of the powers of government that the Jeffersonians advocated could be safely practiced at this time, for the United States was fortunate in having no powerful armed neighbors, whose menace would require a large degree of centralization of the powers of government.

Although the Republican party derived its greatest support from the South, it was powerfully aided by some Northern leaders of factions out of power and representatives of the underprivileged classes. In 1800 Jefferson and Aaron Burr were elected President and Vice-President over the Federalist candidates, John Adams and Charles C. Pinckney. Jefferson

[12] Lipscomb and Bergh (eds.), *Writings of Thomas Jefferson,* IX, 335-336.

was not a sectional leader; indeed, he abhorred geographical parties. In his Cabinet he appointed Albert Gallatin from Pennsylvania, and Levi Lincoln, Henry Dearborn, and Gideon Granger from New England. Jefferson had the wonderful power of phrasing the ideals of his youthful party, reminding one in this respect of Woodrow Wilson, but he also knew the practical art of organizing the forces of opposition into a victorious party. In truth, he was much more than the brilliant expounder of Southern economic interests, for he realized the dignity of human nature and the rights of personality of even the humblest individual. He has frequently been portrayed as a dreamer and a theoretical person, but in the long view of history he has proved to be more practical than Alexander Hamilton, the cynical "realist," for he based his political philosophy on a sounder and more optimistic view of human nature.

The election of 1800 has often been called a peaceful revolution. The Republicans believed that they had overthrown an aristocratic monarchical group in control of the government and restored a republican regime. Jefferson walked to the Capitol from his boardinghouse to be inaugurated instead of riding in state in a coach attended by liveried servants. Thus he symbolized his belief in republican simplicity as contrasted with Federalist ceremony and aristocratic attitudes. As President he discarded the practice of seating guests at the dinner table of the White House in accordance with their rank or importance and instituted the democratic principle of pellmell. Even in his negligence and simplicity of dress he dramatized his belief in republican simplicity. Once he offended the pompous English minister, Anthony Merry, who was dressed in diplomatic uniform, by receiving him clad in slippers without heels.[13] Jefferson's emphasis on the fact that clothes do not make the man was illustrated by

[13] Henry Adams, *History of the United States During the Administration of Thomas Jefferson* (New York, 1930), Book II, 366.

a vivid description of his appearance written by a New England Senator, William Plumer:

> In a few moments after our arrival a tall, high-boned man came into the room. He was dressed, or rather undressed, in an old brown coat, red waistcoat, old corduroy small-clothes much soiled, woolen hose, and slippers without heels. I thought him a servant, when General Varnum surprised me by announcing that it was the President.[14]

Yet Jefferson was an aristocrat, not of the European model, but a republican aristocrat. He had the tastes of an aristocrat. He gave elegant dinners at the White House, with the aid of his French chef. His generous hospitality is indicated by the fact that his wine bill for the first year in office was $2,800. The critical Senator Plumer has described a delightful dinner with the President in which eight different kinds of wine were served, including a Tokay that cost a guinea a bottle. Jefferson on this occasion was well dressed, with a new black suit, silk hose, clean ruffled linen, and hair highly powdered. Furthermore, the man presiding at the table (he was a widower at this time) was the most brilliant conversationalist in America. Jefferson loved music, architecture, and the collecting of fine books. Although he hated useless dogs, he loved birds—he brought to live with him in the White House a pet mockingbird that would perch on his shoulder or finger. Like most of the Southern gentry, he delighted in fine horses, frequently riding his beautiful saddle horse "Wildair" about the streets of Washington.[15]

Jefferson was the product primarily of the Enlightenment of the eighteenth century and of Virginia plantation influences.

[14] William Plumer, *William Plumer's Memorandum of Proceedings in the United States Senate, 1803-1807* (New York, 1923).

[15] Jefferson's private personality is charmingly portrayed in Sarah N. Randolph, *The Domestic Life of Thomas Jefferson* (New York, 1871); see also Daniel J. Boorstin, *The Lost World of Thomas Jefferson* (New York, 1960), for his scientific interests.

He was not unique among the plantation gentry, for many of the liberal aristocrats of his period were very much like him, differing from him principally in degree rather than in quality. It was the fashion in the eighteenth century for men to be versatile, and Jefferson became the most versatile of our Presidents. He was an accomplished violinist until in middle life he broke his right wrist, which caused him to give up his violin playing and to learn to write with his left hand. His talents included the art of practical invention, which enabled him to devise an improved type of plow, a polygraph for writing several copies of a letter, the swivel chair, later to become the throne of bureaucrats, and numerous gadgets for his home at *Monticello*. He was a collector of American Indian vocabularies and was one of the first paleontologists in the United States, studying the fossils of prehistoric animals. In politics, he was not only a skilled diplomat and a practical statesman, but America's leading political philosopher. He was also one of the finest amateur architects of this country. His literary skill was exhibited in his political pamphlets, his *Notes on Virginia* (1784), his inaugural addresses, his *Anas*, his *Parliamentary Manual,* and his enormous correspondence.[16]

His versatility, however, may not have been as deeply based as his extravagant admirers have claimed for him. We know that there was little originality in his composition of the Declaration of Independence, which was strongly influenced by the writings of John Locke. Indeed, Jefferson's mind was empiric and practical, which tended to make him an opportunist. His character and personality were so complex that, as a modern biographer has observed, his portrait cannot be painted in broad brush strokes of black and white. Perhaps the best insight into his many-sided nature is afforded by his epitaph, in which he wrote down the achievements for which he wished to be remembered.

[16] *Jefferson's Notes on the State of Virginia* [1784], edited by T. P. Abernethy (New York, 1963), was his only published book.

> Here was buried Thomas Jefferson,
> Author of the Declaration of American Independence,
> Of the Statute of Virginia for Religious Freedom,
> And Father of the University of Virginia.

The "revolution of 1800" was not so profound a change as has been depicted. Actually it was the transfer of the power of the central government from the control of a commercial aristocracy into the hands of a landed aristocracy. Jefferson formulated the theory of a republican form of government, but the practice of this theory was largely left to the succeeding generation. The psychology of the common man toward the government was not greatly changed until the Jacksonian movement of the 1820's and 1830's. The victory of the Republicans in 1800 arrested only temporarily the growing centralization of the Federal government, and it is significant that much of the Federalist program was retained. Indeed, Jefferson did not indiscriminately discharge Federal office-holders, but steered a middle course between preserving a nonpartisan civil service and the later spoils system.[17]

The theory of politics held by the agricultural South was admirably stated by Jefferson in his first inaugural address, March 4, 1801. In broad outlines he sketched the ideal of a laissez faire government—"a wise and frugal Government, which shall restrain men from injuring one another, shall leave them otherwise free to regulate their own pursuits of industry and improvement, and shall not take from the mouth of labor the bread it has earned." For the defense of the state he proposed to rely on the militia instead of the standing army, and he upheld the supremacy of the civil over the military authority. In foreign affairs the nation should pursue a policy of peace and no "entangling alliances." His first inaugural address was permeated with the spirit of reconciliation with

[17] See Leonard D. White, *The Jeffersonians, a Study in Administrative History, 1801-1829* (New York, 1951); and Noble E. Cunningham, Jr., *The Jeffersonian Republicans in Power, Party Operations, 1801-1809* (Chapel Hill, 1963).

the Federalists, who had so bitterly attacked him. He declared that although the will of the majority must prevail, the rights of minorities must be protected.

In his conduct of foreign affairs, despite his recommendation of avoiding foreign alliances, Jefferson was not isolationist. He had the modern concept that nations, having a common feeling for democracy and a similar ideology, should support each other by moral, political, and economic means short of war. When the French overthrew their absolute monarchy, Jefferson wrote to George Mason: "I look with great anxiety for the firm establishment of the new government in France, being perfectly convinced that if it takes place there it will spread sooner or later all over Europe. On the contrary a check there would retard the revival of liberty in other countries. I consider the establishment and success of their government as necessary to stay up our own and to prevent it from falling back to that kind of a half-way house, the English constitution."[18] Later he anticipated the Good Neighbor policy of Franklin Delano Roosevelt in proposing "a cordial fraternization" between the republics of Latin America and the United States.

Nevertheless, Jefferson was an ardent pacifist who neglected the navy, in contrast to Roosevelt, the advocate of building a more powerful navy to meet the dangers of a European war. A Jeffersonian aberration was a scheme of constructing a number of small gunboats and anchoring them in the ports and mouths of the rivers to be manned by the citizens of the surrounding country in case of an invasion. By this "mosquito fleet" he hoped to save money, but it proved totally impractical. When England and France violated our rights on the high seas and immediately after the British warship *Leopard* fired on our frigate the *Chesapeake,* in 1807, Jefferson restrained his country from a declaration of war. Instead, the Republican

[18] Gilbert Chinard, *Thomas Jefferson, the Apostle of Americanism* (Boston, 1946), 494-495.

Congress passed the Embargo Act, which prohibited American vessels from leaving the harbors of the United States for foreign ports.

Franklin Delano Roosevelt drew much of the support for his liberal program from the underprivileged classes of the cities. Jefferson, on the other hand, compared the mobs of large cities to sores on the body politic, unsuitable raw material to make good citizens in a republic. Pre-eminently the leader of the Southern agrarians, he placed great faith in the virtue and judgment of small, independent farmers, who were property owners as contrasted with the proletariat of the cities. He wished to keep America rural as long as possible in order to prevent the duplication of the unhappy conditions of the mature countries of Europe. American yeoman farmers and planters might temporarily be misled by propaganda, he believed, but the returning good sense of the people would correct their mistakes. Strangely, Jefferson seldom used the words *democratic* and *democracy,* but referred to the American experiment of government as "republican." The word *Democratic* as applied to the political party that Jefferson founded was first used alone as the party label in 1844.

The Southern planters and farmers, who desired a decentralized government, found a spokesman in Jefferson. If the South had possessed a more balanced economy, undoubtedly there would have been less emphasis on State rights in the history of that section. Over and over again crops up the fear of Southerners that a strong central government would be controlled by the Northern states, which would pass adverse legislation against Southern interests, particularly in regard to slavery and the tariff. The South, therefore, advocated a strict interpretation or construction of the Constitution to confine the Federal government to its delegated powers. In addition to this fear Jefferson had another strong reason for favoring localism in government. An ardent admirer of the New England town meeting, he urged the Southern states to divide their counties into wards, or "ward-republics" he called them, which would enable every citizen to participate in direct government. He believed that if political power was kept largely in the hands of the states and of the local communities the people would have an opportunity to watch their officials more closely and thus prevent corruption.

The democratic leader of 1800 and the democratic leader of 1936 found a Supreme Court hostile to their policies, and therefore they tried to curb its power. Jefferson's attempt to reform the judiciary by the initiation of impeachment proceedings was motivated particularly by his opposition to the centralizing tendency of the Supreme Court. This attack on the independence of the judiciary failed when the trial of Justice Samuel Chase in 1805 resulted in acquittal despite the fact that the Republicans had the requisite majority in the Senate to convict. Jefferson continued, however, to oppose a Supreme Court that was "independent of the Nation," and therefore he proposed that, instead of the tenure of the judges being for life, their appointments should be renewed every four or six years. Indeed, Jefferson's writings give strong support to a modern questioning of the wisdom of judicial review.[19]

The great Virginian was a firm advocate of majority rule, not merely of the original majority who drafted the Constitution, but of the continuing majority. He appealed to young men in all ages by declaring that "the earth belongs in usufruct to the living; that the dead have neither power nor rights over it. . . ." Literally, he held that each generation should make its own laws and not be bound by the dead hand of the past—a generation being 20 to 34 years. He was youthful in spirit also in his flexibility, in adapting himself to changed conditions. During the War of 1812 he became convinced that the United States must give up the ideal of a rural Arcadia and develop a more balanced economy by manufacturing

[19] See H. S. Commager, *Majority Rule and Minority Rights* (New York, 1943).

enough goods to be independent of Europe. On his plantation of *Monticello* he himself had erected a nail factory. He took great strides away from his former doctrine of the negative, laissez faire state by proposing that after the public debt had been liquidated the surplus Federal revenues should be used to build national roads and canals and to support a national university.

Jefferson's political philosophy was derived partly from his experience during the fermenting period of the American Revolution and partly from the insemination of liberal European thought. The works of the English democratic thinkers of the seventeenth and eighteenth centuries, such as those of John Locke, Algernon Sidney, and Bolingbroke, as well as the writings of the Scotsman Lord Kames, had a profound influence on the development of his political philosophy. With the exception of Montesquieu's *Spirit of the Laws,* French political writings do not seem to have greatly affected him. After he had matured his philosophy of life, he spent five delightful years as American minister to France, where he acquired such a decided taste for French wines, music, and cookery that homely old Patrick Henry is reported to have said, "Tom Jefferson has abjured his native vittles." Instead of succumbing to French influences, however, his experiences and observations in France served chiefly to strengthen him in his robust Americanism. Later in his career the Physiocrats and Ideologues, especially Destutt de Tracy, appealed to him, because some of their philosophy clarified and confirmed certain ideas he himself had evolved through his experience and observation.

Jefferson was the most effective exponent of intellectual liberty that America has produced. Uniformity of opinion or of religion, he believed, is neither possible nor desirable any more than is the standardization of face or stature. The masses of the people tend to be intolerant of critics or persons who disagree with their prejudices in vital matters. Dissent gives them a sense of insecurity. Likewise, dictatorships cannot permit an uncensored press or an untrammeled radio. The lovers of liberty, on the other hand, have always been concerned with the protection of minority rights and the preservation of freedom of expression. The preservation of the right of holding heterodox opinions is a perennial problem in a democratic government, for the tyranny of the majority is more formidable, as the great Catholic historian Lord Acton observed, than the tyranny of the minority. In our own time this fact has been demonstrated by the attempts to suppress the "subversive propaganda" of those opposed to capitalistic society, by the spy hunt of the Congressional Committee on Un-American Activities, by the doctrine of "guilt by association," and by the tactics of Senator McCarthy in terrorizing public officials with the charge of communism.

The use of the force of civil government to bring about a uniformity of opinion Jefferson regarded as a violation of the rights of personality and as producing hypocrisy. In the preamble to his famous Virginia Statute of Religious Freedom he declared that the civil government should interfere with the expression of opinions only when they "break into overt acts against peace and order." Let the government practice toleration, he urged, for truth will prevail over lies and propaganda provided free argument and debate are allowed, "errors ceasing to be dangerous when it is permitted freely to contradict them." Only by zealously guarding civil rights, especially the freedom of speech, of religion, and of assembly, he thought, could the right of dissent by individuals and minorities be maintained. Thus the minority would have the opportunity, through debate and persuasion, to become the majority controlling the government.[20]

Jefferson's record in respect to civil liberties contained some startling inconsistencies. In his support of freedom of religion, he never wavered, but in the fields of politics and university education his practical actions at times deviated from his

[20] Clement Eaton, "The Jeffersonian Tradition of Liberalism in America," *South Atlantic Quarterly*, XLIII (January, 1944), 2-5.

liberal theory. In his prosecution of Burr in 1807 and in his resolute enforcement of the Embargo Acts he ruthlessly disregarded civil liberties. Especially "un-Jeffersonian" was his attempt to guard the minds of young college students from doctrines that he regarded as pernicious. Hume's history of England he thought was an elegant account but a dangerous one because of its Tory principles and because it was "so plausible and pleasing in its style and manner, as to instill its errors and heresies insensibly into the minds of unwary readers."[21] Consequently he endeavored to put into the hands of American youth a censored version published by an Englishman named John Baxter, but he could not persuade a publisher to print such a denatured Hume in an American edition. Furthermore, he advocated that all the professors of the University of Virginia be allowed to select their own textbooks, except the professor of law and government who would be required to use texts that would properly inculcate in the students the principles of Jeffersonian democracy.

This leader of the early Republicans was too great a realist to believe that political democracy could flourish in a soil of tremendous inequalities of wealth. He concluded that, although an equal division of property was impracticable, "legislators cannot invent too many devices for subdividing property."[22] Believing that the small landholders were the most precious part of the state, he wished to see the United States remain a land of modest fortunes, in which the government should assist the weaker members of society to acquire a reasonable share of property, and reduce bloated fortunes by indirect government action. His sympathy for the poor man is revealed in a letter he wrote to Marquis de Lafayette, urging the latter to travel incognito through France to observe the living conditions of the people. "You must ferret the people out of their

[21] Leonard W. Levy, *Jefferson and Civil Liberties, the Darker Side* (Cambridge, Mass., 1963), 144.

[22] P. L. Ford (ed.), *The Writings of Thomas Jefferson* (New York, 1892-99), VII, 35.

hovels as I have done," he wrote, "look into their kettles, eat their bread, loll on their beds under pretence of resting yourself, but in fact to find if they are soft. You will feel a sublime pleasure in the course of this investigation, and a sublimer one hereafter when you shall be able to apply your knowledge to the softening of their beds or the throwing of a morsel of meat into their kettles of vegetables."[23] An example of this disinterested love for humanity was his smuggling of some Italian rice in his pockets through the customs in order to introduce a superior variety into the Southern states. His zeal for human welfare caused him to think of practical means of lessening the drudgery of life. He proposed, for example, the installation of small steam engines in the homes, run by the kitchen fire to pump water for household use and fire protection.

It is the fate of many great men, including Jefferson, to evoke an uncritical hero worship that obscures their faults and limitations. A balanced portrait of Jefferson, therefore, would have to note that at times he avoided frankness and above-board conduct, causing his enemies to accuse him of dissimulation and to nickname him "Saint Thomas of Cantingbury."[24] He also lacked a well-developed sense of humor such as distinguished President Lincoln and the late President Kennedy. Although radical in thought at times and surprisingly violent in his private correspondence, but not in public utterance, he was opportunistic like Franklin D. Roosevelt. Nor was he much of a radical in action after he came into power. Indeed, he adopted a considerable part of the Hamiltonian program that he had attacked and after he became the leader of a political party he did nothing constructive in attacking the greatest social evil of his age, Southern slavery.

Jefferson's reputation has had a curious fluctuation of popu-

[23] Bernard Mayo (ed.), *Jefferson Himself, the Personal Narrative of a Many-Sided American* (Boston, 1942), 143-144.

[24] Beveridge, *Life of John Marshall* (New York, 1916-1919), III, 362-364.

lar favor and neglect.[25] In the presidential election of 1804 his popularity was at its height, when he carried every state in the Union except Connecticut and Delaware. Jeffersonian ideas underlay the democratic movement of the Jacksonian era. When the proslavery argument reached its full bloom in the decade of the 1850's, however, the ruling class in the South scrapped his natural rights theory and dismissed the Declaration of Independence as glittering generalities. Although his native section repudiated much of his liberalism, holding to his State-rights doctrine, Jefferson attracted new followers and popularity in the North among the abolitionists and Republicans. Lincoln's speeches and writings are saturated with Jeffersonian thought. Following the Civil War the Southern people regarded Lee, not Jefferson, as their greatest man after Washington. During the Populist revolt of the 1880's and 1890's, the shirt-sleeve leaders of the farmers, such as Tom Watson of Georgia, appealed to the magic name of Jefferson as the champion of the common man.

Then the fame of the philosopher-statesman subsided, to be revived once more by historical biographers in the decade of the 1920's and later by the political needs of the party of Franklin Delano Roosevelt. Ironically, the opponents of the Roosevelt administration, especially the Liberty League, likewise claimed Jefferson to be on their side, pointing to him as the advocate of State rights and of a laissez faire government and as disapproving of a third term for President. The rise of Hitler and the Fascist ideology also led to the exaltation of Jefferson as the supreme exponent of democracy and Americanism. Since 1932 the American people have been reminded of this superb liberal leader in many ways, by a Jefferson coin, a Jefferson stamp, by the speeches of the New Dealers, by the building of a marble memorial to him on the tidal basin at Washington, and by the undertaking of publishing his entire

[25] See Merrill D. Peterson, *The Jefferson Image in the American Mind* (New York, 1960).

writings. More recently, however, in this era of strong-flowing nationalism the reputation of the great Virginian has again somewhat diminished. A recent poll of 75 prominent American historians and writers (most of whom live above the Mason and Dixon line) rated Jefferson below Lincoln, Washington, Franklin Delano Roosevelt, and Woodrow Wilson in the cadre of great presidents.[26]

The party Jefferson helped to found and that Southerners dominated for so long a period has been regarded as peculiarly the champion of State rights within the United States. The doctrine of State rights was not a monopoly of the South, however, for it was frequently used as a defense mechanism by different sections of the country to protect their interests against a hostile majority in control of the government. Suspicion is aroused concerning the sincerity of this plea of State rights by the fact that when the exponents of State rights obtained control of the government they lost their enthusiasm for their cherished doctrine. Even Jefferson and Madison, authors of the Virginia and Kentucky Resolutions, when they became President abandoned their extreme State-rights position, to which they were so devoted as leaders of a faction out of power. The acquisition of Louisiana in 1803 . . . is an example of Jefferson's flexibility or opportunism in departing from his principles of State rights and strict construction of the Constitution.

The generation to which Jefferson belonged was permeated with a strong sense of *noblesse oblige* and many of its best men were disturbed by the incongruity of the existence of slavery within a republic. Scorning demagoguery, they developed a more philosophical, a larger view of politics, than did the sectional-minded leaders of the South after 1830. Perhaps the most important influences in the rise of the "great generation" were its exposure to the Enlightenment and its participation in the birth of a new nation based on great liberal ideas.

[26] Arthur M. Schlesinger, "Our Presidents: A Rating by 75 Historians," *New York Times Magazine,* July 29, 1962.

CHAPTER TWO

KENTUCKY PLANTER

CLAY'S PARTICIPATION IN DUELS tended to identify him with the Southern gentry, but even more was he attached to the Southern way of life by the acquisition of a large plantation. Ashland was the realization of a Virginia poor boy's dream, an English estate in the New World, with a two-hundred-acre woodland park that Lord Morpeth, who visited Ashland, said was the nearest approach to an English park of any he had seen in this country. Here Clay lived, with interruptions of sojourns in Washington, for over forty-five years, and here he enjoyed dispensing the hospitality of a Southern gentleman. Ashland was an almost ideal place on which to rear his large family of children. In its seclusion he planned many of his campaigns and developed his political policies, and much of his political correspondence was dated from the plantation and signed in neat, regular script, "H. Clay." His plantation, moreover, provided solace to his wounded spirit when he was defeated for the Presidency. He enjoyed immensely its flower gardens, its delicious homegrown food, and its crops growing luxuriantly in a rich soil. He was especially proud of his fine blooded stock, fattened on the lush Kentucky bluegrass. Ashland was only a mile and a half from the center of Lexington so that he and his family could easily participate in the social pleasures of a cultivated community.

This plantation of five hundred and thirteen acres Clay acquired gradually, buying the first tract in 1805 but not recording the deeds to the major portion of the estate until

1811. The imposing mansion which he built on it was probably not constructed until later. The letter books of Benjamin Latrobe in 1813 show that he made designs for the house. It was a two-and-a-half-story building, unadorned by columns, with thick brick walls, and distinguished by a three-sided vestibule having a Palladian window above it. Numerous outbuildings provided for the comforts and necessities of the mansion, a dovecote, chickenhouse, greenhouse, barns, stable, coachhouse, and, particularly interesting, two large conical-shaped icehouses which were filled in the winter and supplied ice for the master's mint juleps and the mistress's ice-cream desserts.

The furnishings of the mansion reflected Clay's tastes and achievements. There were the gold brocaded satin draperies brought from Lyons in 1815 after the Treaty of Ghent, as well as a pair of French sofas. There was the huge canopied bed in which he slept, covered with a silk quilt made by "The Ladies of Philadelphia." There were the portraits of Clay by the Kentucky artist Matthew Jouett and by G. P. A. Healy, and the marble bust by Joel T. Hart, the Kentucky sculptor. There was china brought from France in which ice cream and strawberries and rich Ashland cream were served. Clay's chess table, gold-bronze candlesticks, marble mantel, rosewood cases, chandeliers, his deerskin trunk, a portrait of Washington and his family by Inman, and cut-glass vases filled with roses marked a style of life far different from that of his poverty-stricken youth.

Associated with this luxury was a patent bedstead manufactured by Mr. Bell of Lexington, for which the great statesman wrote a testimonial. He found it "greatly superior to those in common use. . . . They will hardly ever require any precaution to destroy bugs as they afford no place of retreat to them."

As host of Ashland Clay was extremely gracious and hospitable. Numerous famous persons as well as plain American citizens visited the "Sage of Ashland." Among those who crossed the threshold were James Monroe, Aaron Burr, Martin Van Buren, William Henry Harrison, Daniel Webster, and many European visitors such as Lafayette, Harriet Martineau, and Lord Morpeth. A traveler in 1845 described a call. His nervousness over meeting the eminent statesman disappeared at once when Clay grasped his hand and by his simple, affable manner made him feel at home. "Mr. Clay sat in his easy chair, every thing about him neat and simple as his own dress, and taking his occasional pinch of snuff from a silver box, on the lid of which I could see a log cabin engraved, he looked and seemed more like the quiet happy farmer than any thing else." Clay was proud to show to visitors his garden, his green lawn and shrubs, his blooded horses and cattle, and even his Portuguese pigs.

Major-domo of the mansion was Charles, Clay's favorite slave and his valet whenever he went to Washington. Charles was the perfect servant, "a kind of second master of household to Mr. Clay, and enjoys the greatest trust and confidence. To him can the keys of the wine-cellar be given without fear and on all occasions where help was needed, Mr. C. called for Charles. Charles brought us wine, Charles was at the door, at the carriage, at the gate, every where in fact, and as polite and civil as a man asking for office. He is a fine looking middle-sized negro, about thirty years old and I do not believe he could be drawn from Mr. Clay except by absolute animal force, so great is his devotion to him."

Mrs. Clay played a dominant role in the Ashland household. Caring little for the pleasures of fashionable society, Lucretia devoted her energies to rearing eleven children and to managing the plantation during the frequent absences of the master. She gave her attention especially to the dairy and cheese-making establishments and to the garden. Some of the eggs, chickens, butter and vegetables were sold to the Phoenix Hotel in Lexington. In January, 1843, her husband wrote Lucretia from New Orleans that he had sold the hams which she had sent down the river at 12½ cents a pound and used the proceeds to buy sugar, coffee, and rice. Clay, easy-going in money matters, paid grateful tribute to Lucretia's managerial abilities and her thrift: "Again and again has she saved our home from bankruptcy." Lucretia's practical nature is illustrated by a piquant story told of her. A New England lady said to her, "Isn't it a pity that your husband gambles so much!" "Oh, I don't know," she quickly replied, "he usually wins."

A kind and hospitable woman, Mrs. Clay was a very indulgent mother who failed to discipline her boys with a steady hand. Clay himself was a lenient and tolerant father. In 1814, while he was in Europe negotiating the Treaty of Ghent, Mrs. Clay employed the New Englander Amos Kendall as a tutor for her children at a salary of $300 a year. This young graduate of Dartmouth College found that he had no easy task, for Theodore, thirteen years old, and Thomas, twelve, were almost ungovernable. Their education had been so badly neglected that they knew nothing of Latin or of English grammar.

Kendall's journal depicts a tug of war with the Clay boys. They strenuously resisted learning Latin and they were constantly fighting each other. When the tutor tried to discipline Thomas, the boy fought his schoolmaster like a tiger, cursing him and calling him "a damned Yankee rascal." In his journal the New Englander noted the evil effects of slavery on the rearing of Southern children: May 29: "Yesterday, Mrs. Clay being absent, Thomas got into a mighty rage with some of the negroes, and threatened and exerted all his little power to kill them"; August 23: "Hearing a great noise in the kitchen, I went in and found Theodore swearing in a great rage with a knife drawn in attitude to stab one of the big negroes."

Mrs. Clay, he observed, belonged to "the polite world." She was quite unlike Rachel Jackson, the wife of her husband's great rival, who liked to smoke a pipe with her husband and who spent her Sundays going to church and her Thursdays attending prayer meetings. Mrs. Clay entertained the polished aristocracy of Lexington in her drawing room, and, like the "polite world," she did not hesitate to tell small social lies to save other people's feelings. Whenever the Yankee tutor criticized the Kentuckians, she defended them in a spirited manner. Yet Kendall always retained an affection for the mistress of Ashland, who had introduced the awkward New Englander to the young ladies of Lexington and who had warmheartedly cared for him during an illness, even cooking a beefsteak for him with her own hands. In Washington, she was so kind and discreet that she never made an enemy. "She is what you call a good woman," observed Margaret Bayard Smith, "but has no qualities of mind to attract–none of the heart to endear. She is a most devoted mother, and to sew for her children is her chief, almost exclusive occupation." The deaths of many of her children seem to have made her husband more affectionate toward her as they together grew older.

Clay was a good citizen of the Lexington community. In his young manhood he promoted the Lexington library, receiving donations for its support. Although he had little formal education he was elected one of the law professors of Transylvania University, served as a trustee for many years, and took an active interest in its affairs. In 1824 he wrote to Edward Everett asking him to recommend a Harvard man for professor of mathematics for the university, "One free from objection and from peculiarity on the score of religion." In a letter to Senator Josiah Stoddert Johnston of Louisiana in 1830 asking his support for a petition of Transylvania University for a public grant of land he said, "Transylvania was the first temple of Science erected in the wilds of the West." In 1834 he tried to secure a professorship at Transylvania for the brilliant Francis Lieber, who later joined the faculty of

South Carolina College and became an eminent writer on government, the author of *On Civil Liberty and Self-Government.*

In addition to his generous support of this Lexington institution, Clay rendered another service to the advancement of learning in the United States by his advocacy of an international copyright law. In 1837 he made a report to Congress in favor of such a law. After having presented the cause of American and British authors in the Senate on three occasions, he concluded that the prospect of getting Congress to enact an international copyright law was very bad. Such was his report to Francis Lieber, December 28, 1839, when he wrote that the principal opposition to the law came from the large book printers of the country, who had a powerful influence on members of Congress. This opposition could be overcome, he observed, only by enlightening public opinion, by sending petitions to Congress, numerously signed, by agitating through the press, and by sending a committee of authors to Washington to answer questions and combat objections to the proposed law before committees of Congress. During Clay's lifetime and for many years afterwards, however, Congress refused to pass an international copyright law.

Clay's correspondence with Lieber indicates that he seldom read a book. Lieber occasionally sent him some of his books and manuscripts on political theory, which Clay acknowledged but only rapidly skimmed through. He did not have much of a library at Ashland. His speeches contained few quotations or references to books. He did, however, refer frequently to examples of Roman and Greek history, which he probably derived from reading Plutarch's *Lives* in his youth. Although he read little himself he sought to persuade his sons to become well-educated men. On December 18, 1837, he sent a list of history books for his son James to read, including Plutarch's *Lives,* Tacitus, Gillie's *Greece,* Gibbon, Hume, Russell's *Modern Europe,* Hallam's *Middle Ages,* Robertson's *Charles V,*

Marshall's *Life of Washington,* and Botta's *History of the American Revolution.*

He advised his son that the great secret of happiness was constant employment. Clay himself practiced this precept of the strenuous life. Margaret Bayard Smith wrote in 1829, "Henry Clay was made for action—not for rest." Excitement was his natural medium, but he also needed the repose and tranquillity of his Kentucky plantation. To his son James he wrote at the end of his life: "For myself I believe that the chance of happiness is greater there [on the farm] than in public life."

After he retired from office as Secretary of State in 1829 he returned to Ashland to give his personal attention to the plantation. He had been active in farming only a year when he wrote his close friend Francis T. Brooke of Fredericksburg, Virginia, "My attachment to rural occupations every day acquires more strength; and if it continues to increase another year as it has the last, I shall be fully prepared to renounce forever the strife of public life. My farm is in fine order, and my preparations for the crop of the present year are in advance of all my neighbors. I shall make a better farmer than a statesman." Nevertheless Clay could not resist the lure of public office and was a candidate for the Presidency oftener than any other man except Eugene V. Debs and Norman Thomas. Even his letter of apparent renunciation contains an account of his elation at being so cordially received during a recent visit to Louisiana and his belief that should he run for President he could count on the vote of Louisiana, whose staple, sugar, needed tariff protection as much as the hemp interest of Kentucky.

Clay employed an overseer at Ashland, and like most Southern planters he frequently changed his overseers. The Lexington newspapers contain various notices, over a period of years, in which different overseers at Ashland advertised the services of imported bulls, jacks, and stallions. When he departed for

Washington Clay left detailed written instructions for the overseers which show his practical knowledge of farming. Letters from the Clay family indicate that the overseers treated the Negroes well and that some of the overseers, particularly Mr. Florea, were quite satisfactory. Others, however, were guilty of serious neglect of the plantation during the master's absences. In the fall of 1819 William Faux, an English farmer, visited Ashland and reported: "The windows are broken and the frames and doors are rotten for want of paint or tar; the gardens in a piggish state, full of weeds, the walks gullied by heavy rains; the grass borders and lawn wild, dirty, and unmowed and everything else inelegant; although the soil is rich to excess, and almost all kinds of vegetables spring spontaneously and grow luxuriantly, and the house is brimful of negroes who might keep all in the neatest order."

In December, 1833, Clay asked his son Henry Clay, Junior, to ride over from the latter's plantation, Maplewood, to report on conditions at Ashland. The younger Henry wrote that the overseer had neglected to keep up the plantation, the fences were falling down, and the slaves were not working properly. Furthermore, the overseer had been frequently absent from the plantation, being engaged in "petty trading and speculations." Clay ordered the overseer dismissed and his son Thomas Hart temporarily employed in his place, provided that the latter had "sufficiently renounced his old habits." Thomas Hart was a profligate but beloved son of Clay who had spent some time in a jail in Philadelphia.

The money crop of the Bluegrass in Clay's time was not burley tobacco, as it is today, but hemp. The slender stalks, eight to ten feet high, were cut with a knife in the middle of August and allowed to lie in the fields to be rotted by the dew so that the long fibers could be easily detached from the glutinous material of the stalk. Dew-rotted Kentucky hemp was inferior to Russian hemp rotted in vats and pools, and it was necessary to protect it from competition with foreign fibers, a fact that contributed to making Clay an advocate of a high protective tariff. Clay revealed his intimate knowledge of the art of growing hemp and preparing it for the market in a detailed letter to an agricultural society in Ohio which was published in the *Western Agriculturist and Practical Farmers Guide* of Cincinnati in October, 1830.

Most Kentucky farmers refused to go to the trouble of using the water-rotting process in preparing their hemp. They were prejudiced against the process partly because the pools and vats in which the hemp was rotted smelled bad and were believed to cause disease, but the main reason, Clay believed, was the want of water at the proper season. The master of Ashland tried the Russian method in the 1840's at Ashland and produced some superior hemp, but in the end he failed. The hardest work in preparing hemp for the market was "breaking," or separating, the fibers from the stalk. This task was done in the winter, usually by slaves, who employed a crude device known as a hemp brake. Clay was interested in the invention of a modern machine to take the place of the old device. On October 12, 1846, he wrote to Thomas L. Fortune, "I have seen so many hemp brakes tried and fail–yet I would pay $100 for your invention if successful."

Clay displayed imagination and freedom from tradition in farming and raising stock. Although he gave close attention to the experience of practical farmers, he was willing to adopt scientific innovations. He experimented with sugar beets, gave seed to his neighbors, and advocated government encouragement of the cultivation of this crop. He also tried different grasses for pasture, but he awarded top honors to bluegrass, which he believed was imported into Kentucky from England. A traveler who visited his farm in the 1840's noted that the fences were in fine order, the crops of wheat, corn, and rye were free of weeds, and that he had a ten-acre lot of corn upon which he bestowed especial care in order to win a premium at the agricultural fair.

As time passed, Clay devoted more and more of his attention and capital to stock raising. In 1831 he wrote that he was much engrossed in his farms, having purchased nearby Mansfield, containing three hundred acres. On these estates he employed fifteen hands, cultivated two hundred acres of corn, one hundred and twenty acres of other grains, and had approximately one hundred head of cattle and one hundred head of horses and mules. "There is a great difference, I think," he observed two years later, "between a farm employed in raising dead produce for market and one which is applied, as mine is, to the rearing of all kinds of livestock. I have the Maltese ass, the Arabian horse, the merino and saxe merino sheep, the English Hereford and Durham cattle, the goat, the mule, and the hog. The progress of these animals from their infancy to maturity presents a constantly varying subject of interest, and I never go out of my house without meeting with some of them to engage agreeably my attention. Then our fine green sward, our natural parks, our beautiful undulating country everywhere exhibiting combinations of grass and trees or luxuriant crops, all conspire to render home delightful."

Clay was a pioneer in importing Hereford cattle from England. He had been impressed with the Hereford red cattle when he attended the Smithfield Stock Show in 1815. After some correspondence with Peter Irving (brother of Washington Irving), who resided at Liverpool, he was able to purchase two bulls and two heifers which were brought to Baltimore in 1817 and thence along the National Road to Ashland. Other Kentucky stock raisers followed Clay's example, but the Herefords lost their popularity and in the 1830's Durham Shorthorns displaced them as the favorite imported cattle. When Clay's famed Durham bull Orizimbo died, he announced the event to the Senate as "a great loss public and private." Clay's importations of fine English cattle improved the stock of Kentucky and his correspondence shows that in his importations of blooded stock he was motivated not merely by the hope of private profit and satisfaction, but by a desire also to be a public benefactor.

One of the most important enterprises at Ashland was the raising of mules. The mule was the common draft animal on the Southern plantations. In 1831 Clay wrote that a vast number of these animals were raised in Kentucky for the Southern market and that so great was the demand in his neighborhood for good jacks to propagate mules that he had refused $500 for one that he owned. He imported jacks and jennets from Malta, Spain, and France, seeking animals of extraordinary height. As early as 1828 his overseer advertised in the *Lexington Reporter*, "The Jackass Ulysses," imported from Malta in the naval vessel *North Carolina*, whose services would be limited for the season to thirty mares and jennets at a fee of ten dollars. Some of Clay's famous asses were the jennet Calypso and the jacks Don Manuel and Magnum Bonum; of the two latter he employed the artist Troye to paint pictures.

The Ashland plantation raised many fine specimens of mules which were driven along the roads to the Black Belt of Alabama and through the Cumberland Gap to the Southeastern plantations. One of his customers was the Whig congressman and planter Ebenezer Pettigrew, to whose plantation in eastern North Carolina he sent in 1841 twenty-three mules of high pedigree. Some of them, he informed Pettigrew, were the get of a Poitou jack brought from France, while others were produced by a Maltese jack descended from the Knight of Malta, the property of General George Washington.

Henry Clay's interest in breeding race horses was characteristic of the gentleman farmers of the Bluegrass. In 1808 the *Lexington Reporter* advertised "the Celebrated imported turf horse Buzzard" standing at stud on Clay's farm. This racing sire, imported from England, was described by one of Clay's correspondents as "the finest horse upon the Continent."

In partnership with four other gentlemen Clay paid $5500 for this famous stallion. From Governor James Barbour of Virginia he purchased Allegrante, an imported brood mare for which he paid fifteen hundred dollars. When the Sultan Mahmud II gave four Arabian horses to the American minister at Constantinople in 1830, Congress confiscated them because the Constitution prohibits government officials from accepting gifts from foreign powers. Clay bought a one-half interest in one of these stallions, named Stamboul. For the purpose of training and exercising his race horses he built a private track at Ashland, one of the first private courses in Kentucky.

Clay wrote to Nicholas Biddle, the Philadelphia banker, in 1838 that he had thought it expedient to open a new source of revenue by the purchase of an English stallion. In a humorous and gossipy vein he remarked, "Our worthy little President has been represented as aspiring to the hand of the Queen Mother and his son ["Prince John"] to that of the Queen of England. If one-half of that be true, I shall be pardoned . . . for attempting to deal in far less noble and less aristocratic English blood." He would reverse, he quipped, the saying of the English monarch Richard, "I would not give my horse for a kingdom."

After his defeat as Whig candidate for President in 1844, admiring friends presented three fine thoroughbreds as gifts to him. Dr. W. N. Mercer of New Orleans sent up in the steamboat *Uncle Sam* the mare Magnolia, which he wrote had run in one race and had been "defeated but not dishonoured." This mare had thirteen foals, one of them Iroquois, a winner of the English Derby, and established such a famous bloodline that she has been described as the "Empress of the American Stud Book." The aristocratic South Carolina planter Wade Hampton II in June, 1845, sent to Clay the bay filly Margaret Wood as a token of his regard, and Commodore Morgan gave to him the stallion Yorkshire, a highly successful sire. "Long John" Wentworth in his reminiscences of Clay in

1850 relates Clay's great pride in announcing to a group at the National Hotel that one of the colts of his son John had recently won his first race, whereupon the Kentucky statesman discoursed expertly on the descendants of English race horses imported into America.

The master of Ashland was also active in importing fine blooded sheep and pigs to improve his stock. In 1829 he purchased in Washington County, Pennsylvania, fifty full-blooded Merino sheep, which were driven on foot to Lexington. Six years later he bought eleven Saxon sheep from Hyde Park, Dutchess County, New York, which were shipped to Baltimore and from there were brought to Kentucky. Clay won prizes on both his sheep and cattle at the stock fairs in Lexington. The proximity of his farm to Lexington made it easy for dogs to kill his sheep so that finally he got rid of his pedigreed stock. In 1850 the manuscript census returns show that Ashland did not have a single sheep. He continued to raise a large number of pigs at Ashland, experimenting with the different breeds of Berkshire, China, and Portuguese. He delighted personally in feeding the pigs. Family tradition also tells that he kept a bowl of shelled corn in the dining room with which he called up his chickens.

Harriet Martineau, the English bluestocking, visited Ashland in 1835 and described the home as a very happy one. She enjoyed the flowers, trees, and birds, the sunny woods, the glades that reminded her of *Ivanhoe,* the delicious food, especially "daily piles of strawberries and mountains of ice cream," the fine horses in the stable, and "the drolleries of the little negroes." The great charm of Ashland, however, was the conversation of Mr. Clay. Miss Martineau and the Scottish traveler Charles Augustus Murray were surprised that so impetuous a person as their host could be remarkably frank, detached, and moderate in speaking of parties and personalities that were opposed to him.

Yet life at Ashland was not always the Kentucky idyll

that it seemed to be to the traveler or casual visitor. There were troubles with overseers, with runaway Negroes, with mortgages on the plantation, with numerous deaths in the family, and with the visitation of plagues. In the summer of 1833 cholera struck the Bluegrass for the first time. Nearly five hundred citizens of Lexington died, including many of Clay's friends; but fortunately the white and black family at Ashland escaped. Clay himself apparently prescribed the remedy when some of his slaves had violent abdominal pains—twenty grains of calomel, twenty grains of rhubarb, and a mixture of salt and mustard. In letters to his friend Peter B. Porter of New York he vividly described the appearance of Lexington during the plague—stores and shops closed, and no one moving in the streets except those concerned with the sick and the dead.

Clay's free and easy ways in spending money and his generosity in endorsing notes often brought him into grave financial difficulties. He was constantly borrowing and placing mortgages on his property. Among his creditors was John Jacob Astor. In 1828 his political enemies charged him with bankruptcy. Clay protested that they had searched the records of Fayette County and had "extracted from them a formidable list of mortgages which are paraded as evidences of my bankruptcy." In rebuttal, he declared that he had never been sued for an uncontested debt, that the cause of his temporary withdrawal from public life in 1821 was because of heavy financial responsibilities caused by endorsing notes for friends, but that since then he had resolved not to endorse for others except in extraordinary cases. The mortgages against his estate, he declared, were now less than ten thousand dollars and he was in good financial condition, his estate being worth approximately one hundred thousand dollars.

But on November 15, 1842, during an agricultural depression in the South, he gave a mortgage on Ashland for $20,000 due on May 21, 1845. At least part of his mortgage was incurred in aiding his sons, particularly Thomas Hart Clay, who had failed in the hemp business. The old statesman could not meet his obligations on the due date of the mortgage, but anonymous friends raised $25,750 and paid off the mortgage so that the "Sage of Ashland" could spend his last days with a tranquil mind as to the fate of his home.

Subtly the plantation life at Ashland influenced Clay's political philosophy. Here he came into direct contact with a large number of slaves, saw slavery in its paternal aspects, and obtained an insight into race relations that no Northern statesman could have gained. Ashland was quite different from the cotton plantations. Their interests required free trade while hemp plantations like Ashland, as noted in the discussion of Clay's tariff speech of 1824, demanded protection from foreign competition. Kentucky hemp, however, was produced largely for the Southern market, its main use being for cotton bagging and plow lines. Hence a politician like Clay, who represented the hemp planters, was confronted with a painful conflict of interests. Clay responded also to the aristocratic pressures of plantation life. His manners were democratic and simple, but from his associations with the plantation gentry he tended to absorb their sense of values and conservative viewpoint. He had moved up from poverty and insignificance into the company of the Breckinridges, the Shelbys, the Combses and the Wickliffes. His stock-raising interests, moreover, brought him into the circle of the wealthy men who bred and raced blooded horses. Clay subscribed to their code of honor, their practice of lavish hospitality, and their disdain of rabble rousing.

CHAPTER THREE

THE ART OF POLITICS IN THE WEST

HENRY CLAY WAS A BLUEGRASS POLITICIAN, the representative of a relatively conservative Western community. The "Ashland District" which sent him to Congress consisted of the counties of Fayette, Jessamine, and Woodford, the area of the best agricultural land and of the greatest concentration of slaves in the state. It was essential for the success of his presidential ambitions that he should retain the complete loyalty not only of the Bluegrass but of the entire state. Consequently, he watched the annual August elections with the keenest of interest, for they were one of the barometers of his hopes for political promotion.

Clay never won the mastery over the political life of Kentucky that Calhoun exercised in South Carolina. He was not the absolute dictator that "the Great Nullifier" became, crushing all political opposition and casting such a deep shadow over the state that young and ambitious politicians were suppressed. Yet he had tremendous prestige in Kentucky so that only once did any candidate oppose him for election to Congress. This occurred in 1816 after he had supported the passage of the unpopular Compensation Act, which raised the compensation of congressmen by substituting a salary of fifteen hundred dollars for the per-diem allowance. Numerous congressmen suffered defeat because of their unlucky votes in favor of this bill and Clay had a hard contest to keep his seat. "Gallant Harry" attacked the opposing candidate, the one-armed John Pope, as a former Federalist in a spirited debate on the hustings, and promised to work for the repeal of the controversial compensation law. Thus he managed to overcome the prejudice aroused against him among the plain people by his support of the odious measure.

His most difficult problems of local control followed the severe financial panic of 1819, producing political reverberations in Kentucky that seriously menaced Clay's leadership. As a result of popular pressure the legislature enacted a number of stay laws for the relief of debtors, created the Bank of the Commonwealth for the purpose of issuing cheap paper money, and took the great humanitarian step of abolishing the law providing for imprisonment of debtors (December 17, 1821). This latter piece of liberal legislation occurred ten years before Congress finally enacted the bill of Senator Richard M. Johnson of Kentucky abolishing imprisonment for debt in federal cases.

Clay tried to avoid becoming involved in the turmoil of the relief struggle, but his private correspondence indicates that he strongly disapproved of the acts of the relief party. He was a moderate conservative who had little sympathy with the burgeoning of a rough and tumble democracy reckless of property rights and vested interests. In the fall of 1822 he wrote to his aristocratic friend Benjamin Watkins Leigh in Virginia that although the relief party had been successful generally in the late elections, many of the seats for the legislature had been closely contested and the governor had sent a strong antirelief message to the legislature, so that "we begin to see day break."

In the following year the Court of Appeals declared some of the relief laws unconstitutional. This overturning of the popular will by the judiciary threw the voters into great agitation and for approximately three years divided the state into acrimonious factions. Clay regretted that public opinion should have become so inflamed over these decisions. It would have been better for the peace of the state, he thought, if the Appellate Court could have avoided passing on the constitutionality of the relief laws. His statement on this point is so characteristic of the temper of his mind, which instinctively sought to avoid violent public controversy, that a portion of his letter is quoted below. He did not doubt that the courts possessed the right of declaring unconstitutional laws of the legislature invalid, but he thought the courts sometimes "pushed the principle too far and that, erecting themselves into a sort of tribunal to remedy . . . *all* the evils of bad legislation, they have not allowed to operate other probably more efficacious correctives." In the end, "most of the pernicious acts of legislation would be rectified by the operations of public sentiment. When so corrected there is always tranquillity and general acceptance. But if, during the existence of the excitement the Courts interpose, the consequence is, that the public disorders are prolonged instead of being healed."

The relief party was so aroused and so powerful that its victory in the August elections in 1824 alarmed Clay. He feared that they would oust the appellate judges from their office by repealing the law organizing the court. Such a procedure he condemned as violating the constitutional security intended for the judges. But he hoped the good sense of the legislature would reject it. These statements of Clay on the judiciary and trust in the people to correct the evils of government are so Jeffersonian in sentiment that they could have been written by Jefferson himself.

Clay's confidence in the wisdom of the people was unfounded, for the legislature passed on December 24, 1824, a law abolishing the old court of appeals and setting up a new court. The old court refused to abdicate, with the result that for two years there existed rival supreme courts, each claiming to be the only legal court of appeals in the state. Most of Clay's close friends supported the "Old Court." One of these, John J. Crittenden, wrote to Clay in 1825 that a state of anarchy existed in Kentucky and that he had postponed introducing resolutions in the legislature endorsing Clay and Adams because of fear that the relief party would defeat them. Nearly a year later he commented that Kentucky politics were based on feeling and resembled a mighty quicksand. But on December 30, 1826, the legislature abolished the New Court and the conservatives reasserted their dominance over the state government. Bitter feelings, however, continued for years to exist between the former Old Court and New Court factions.

Clay pursued a conscious policy of avoiding active intervention in local politics. He kept himself informed on state affairs by letters from his friends and relatives. In 1830 Crittenden appealed to Clay to intervene in state elections to get the proper men to run as candidates for the legislature. But in making this request he apologized, "I know that you have almost a fastidious disinclination to interfere in such subjects." Clay's policy of abstaining from obvious participation in state politics arose partly from an Olympian conception of the role of the national statesman. Also there was less reason for him to interfere in state politics since he did not have to struggle to retain his seat in Congress.

Clay's prestige as a national political leader, however, was at stake in the presidential election of 1828, when Adams was a candidate for re-election. The partisans of General Jackson made vigorous preparations to elect "the hero of New Orleans," who, they maintained, had been cheated out of the office by a corrupt bargain between Clay and Adams. In Congress they formed a vociferous party that, largely for political effect, attacked practically every measure and policy of the Adams administration. The President, remarkably aloof from the game of playing politics, refused to use the patronage to strengthen his position, declining to remove from the federal service even those who were actively hostile to him. Although the Secretary of State was not a spoilsman, he believed in pursuing a moderate course in regard to appointments and removals from office. Accordingly, he advocated the dismissal from the federal service of those who actively opposed the executive policies.

Clay, despite ill health, virtually took charge of Adams's campaign for re-election. In Kentucky he realized that he would have a hard fight to keep the state from going over to Jackson. The struggle over the relief laws and the Old and New Court issue had stirred the voters profoundly and had brought to the surface the radical elements and the smoldering discontent of the common people. The supporters of the New Court largely went into the Jacksonian movement. Among Clay's former friends who joined the opposition party were Colonel Richard M. Johnson, one of the most popular men of the state; Francis P. Blair and Amos Kendall—the former tutor of the Clay boys—both Kentucky editors to become powerful in the Kitchen Cabinet; and William T. Barry, Chief Justice of the New Court, whom Jackson appointed Attorney General.

Realizing the progress that the Jacksonians were making in Kentucky, Clay bestirred himself to counteract their efforts. In 1827 he wrote to his lieutenants from Washington urging a thorough organization of the Clay and Adams forces. He proposed that an elaborate system of committees should be established to win public support. These committees, he suggested, should call public meetings in every county to support Adams and should collect campaign literature to distribute among the voters. He urged that these public meetings pass resolutions approving of Adams's administration and "particularly resolutions expressive of their detestation of the calumny by which their fellow-citizen [Clay] has been assailed; of their confidence in him and of their conviction of the entire failure to establish through Mr. Buchanan anything injurious to his character." In the August elections of 1828, nevertheless, the Jackson party won control of the legislature and elected the lieutenant governor, but its candidate for governor, William T. Barry, was defeated by a narrow margin.

The Jacksonians also triumphantly carried the presidential election of that year. Even those Western states which in 1824 had voted for "Harry of the West," Kentucky, Ohio, and Missouri, deserted him to vote for "the Old Hero." Two weeks after the election Clay wrote to a correspondent, "Nothing has ever heretofore occurred to create in my mind such awful apprehensions of the permanency of our liberty."

The election of 1828 sharply revealed that the day of the old type of politician was over and that new men and a new type of politics had arrived. While James Monroe, the last of "the Virginia dynasty," was President, there still lingered the tradition of the early Republic, that a gentleman should not seek public office but that the office should seek him. The electorate was relatively small, for many of the common people did not have the vote. Moreover, the common people regarded governmental officials with respect as men whose personal opinions had great weight. The leading figures in public affairs were not forced as a rule to truckle to popular passions and whims. The best of them were philosopher-statesmen, well grounded in a knowledge of political theory, of Locke, Sidney, Harrington, and the debates of the Constitutional Convention of 1787.

Yet in Clay's lifetime, a revolution took place in the political mores of the American people. The aristocratic attitude toward politics disappeared with the spread of Jacksonian democracy. The politician then tried to identify himself with the common people, to wear old clothes, claim a log-cabin origin, and conceal his superior education and his command of the king's English. It became a common practice to treat the voters with whiskey and to speak grandiloquently of "the sovereign people." Kemp Battle, who was long the president of the University of North Carolina, described this custom in his *Memories of an Old-Time Tar Heel.* He witnessed a candidate for office in a mountain village in North Carolina who harangued the Demos, standing before a grog shop waving in his hand a tin quart pot to give point to his arguments. After his speech was finished he invited the sovereign people to follow him into the shop. He was elected.

Clay, however, retained something of the old dignity in political campaigns. He was very anxious to give the impression that he did not seek public office. He tried to conduct himself in his campaigns as a statesman of the old Virginia school. When he was invited to visit the commencement exercises of Franklin College at Athens, Georgia, in 1838, he declined, explaining that his attendance would be construed as political in intent. "My duty," he wrote, "is to remain perfectly passive and suffer the public judgment to be formed unaffected by personal efforts of my own." The Presidency, he declared, was neither to be sought nor declined. As for himself, he would use "means to attain it only reconcilable to the nicest sense of honor and the strictest propriety."

The crude democracy of Jackson's time, moreover, led to a lower quality of government. The voters, de Tocqueville observed, failed to elect their superior men to office. To obtain the suffrage of the people it was not necessary for a politician to have a superior education or a brilliant mind. Rather, he must be able to sense the common man's discontents, his economic grievances, his prejudices, and his dreams. The successful politician in the 1830's and 1840's was, as a rule, a vigorous or eloquent stump speaker, a man who could devise popular slogans and organize political workers, and who gave the common people a feeling of their own importance. As party warfare developed into violent partisanship and as sectional tensions arose, the politician who had strong convictions and had taken a courageous public stand on issues was often pushed aside in favor of a candidate of availability. This development operated as an important factor in preventing Henry Clay from ever becoming President.

Clay was well aware of the fact that elections were more often won by good organization and by emotional appeals to the voters than by intelligent issues. When he was a candidate for the Presidency in 1832 the Jacksonians in Kentucky elected their candidate for governor in the August elections. He wrote to a correspondent that he was mortified by this defeat, which he attributed to Tennessee voters crossing the state line into the border counties and illegally voting and also to the circumstance that the Whig candidate for governor was a Presbyterian and "against that sect the most deep rooted and inveterate prejudices exist" in the state, so that he estimated the Whigs lost not less than three thousand votes.

Clay recognized the value of appealing to the voters by means of eloquent speeches, barbecues, Clay clubs, Clay balls, by thorough organization in the states, by distribution of campaign literature, and by campaign biographies. With toasts at banquets he presented slogans for his party. He was accused of writing anonymously and of inspiring editorials and articles for the newspapers. In Kentucky his chief political organs were the Lexington *Observer and Reporter*, the Louisville *Journal*, and the Frankfort *Commonwealth*, while nationally he was supported by the influential *National Intelligencer* of Washington and Hezekiah Niles's *Niles' Weekly Register* of Baltimore.

The Kentucky politician often expressed a fear that his opponent would influence elections by the corrupt use of money. His own attitude toward money and politics was more ethical than that of his rival Webster, but perhaps not as admirable as that of the high-minded Calhoun. His personal borrowing from the Bank of the United States may have had some bearing on his political activity. In 1827 Clay requested Webster to collect money from the Eastern cities to subsidize the anti-Jackson newspapers of Hammond at Cincinnati and Pleasants in Richmond. The Massachusetts politician responded by collecting the desired funds. Although Clay did not have the enslaving love of money that Webster exhibited, nevertheless he sought the friendship of the same men, the Northern industrialists, who patronized Webster, because he wanted their votes.

Clay's ideals of political behavior belonged to the early Republic, when leaders like Jefferson, Madison, and Monroe scorned demagoguery. In 1827, when the party of Jackson won alarming victories in the congressional elections in Kentucky, Clay refused to resort to some of their low tactics, admonishing his supporters not to employ "means of detraction and corruption, which we would scorn to use, and with which we would not sully our cause." Only honorable and legitimate methods to win the voters should be used. Furthermore, he consistently declared in private letters that he would make no political deals or bargains, but if elected would enter office untrammeled and free of commitments.

In the election of 1840, when William Henry Harrison was the Whig candidate for President and the Whigs engaged in an undignified campaign featuring log cabins, hard cider, and coonskins, Clay was faced by a dilemma. He regretted the practice "of appealing to the feelings and passions of our Countrymen, rather than to their reasons and judgments to secure his election. The best and only justification of this course is to be found in the practise, which was resorted to in the instance of the election of General Jackson. But that does not prevent my regret that either party should have ever been induced to employ such means." He was also very much disturbed that the Whig party failed to adopt a platform for the campaign of 1840. He believed that both parties and candidates should appeal to the voters on the basis of principles. In a confidential letter to John M. Clayton in May of that year he wrote that he was thinking of promulgating a "creed" for the Whig party, for he feared that the Democrats would say that the Whigs had no principles which they dared openly to avow. He hesitated, however, to carry out his plan, for "The danger is of supplying fresh aliment for demagogues." He finally decided not to promulgate his proposed platform for the party.

One of the attributes which Clay thought was essential for the public officer was consistency. He upheld the necessity for consistency in order to maintain the confidence of the people in the judgment and sincerity of a politician. In a speech at Lexington in 1842 reviewing his political career he declared that the only inconsistency which marred his record was the reversal of his position on a national bank. Actually, after the great change following the Treaty of Ghent, Clay's career was far more consistent than the records of the major politicians of the period.

Clay's use of the patronage in advancing his political interests is commendable in comparison with the practices of his opponents. It is true that when he was Secretary of State under Adams he tried to persuade that stern Puritan to use the patronage to strengthen his administration. But Adams refused to make realistic concessions to political expediency and lost the election of 1828. Clay's party was out of power from 1829 to 1841, when Harrison was inaugurated. After the election Clay had an interview with Harrison in Lexington and made some suggestions as to cabinet appointments, especially the necessity of having Webster in the cabinet, but Harrison was noncommittal on cabinet appointments. In the following February Clay wrote to his intimate friend Peter B. Porter in New York that he had adopted the rule of noninterference in official appointments except on rare occasions in order to prevent very bad selections. To another friend he declared that he had not recommended a person for any position in the federal government for a period of twelve years. The victory of the Whigs in 1840 brought no patronage to the great Whig leader. In a letter to President Harrison of March 15 he said that "A thousand times have my feelings been wounded" in replying to office seekers that he was "obliged to abstain from interference in all appointments."

When the Whigs were victorious in 1848, Clay wrote to the President asking for the appointment of his son James Brown Clay to a diplomatic post. He said that he had never during the course of his life used his political influence to secure the appointment of a relative. He was departing from his rule in seeking the appointment of his son to a diplomatic mission. He described his son as thirty-two years old, free from dissipation, industrious, and an able lawyer. Taylor appointed James to the post at Lisbon.

The death of Taylor in the summer of 1850 placed Millard Fillmore, a friend of Clay's, in power. Shortly afterwards Clay wrote the new President that he made no demands as to the patronage in Kentucky, but that he hoped his son would be retained in charge of the Portuguese mission. He also made some suggestions as to the appointments of Whigs outside of Kentucky. Surveying the appointments in the different states, he observed that Georgia, whose congressmen had been "far from supporting your administration," had received more patronage than any other state. He protested against the appointment of Henry Hilliard of Alabama, who had opposed Whig measures as regards the tariff, the organization of the House of Representatives, and the River and Harbor bill. "To see foes promoted and friends overlooked," he warned, "has a discouraging effect. Should you not exercise more control in the patronage of the several Departments? An intimation of your wish to any of them ought to be decisive."

Clay was not an original political thinker and he did not make any notable contribution to political theory, as did Calhoun. Clay had a more optimistic view of human nature than that which the stern Calvinistic senator from South Carolina expressed in his political writings. When his friend

Francis Brooke wrote to him on November 3, 1838, that the Bluegrass politician entertained too high a view of human nature he replied, "I confess that I have throughout life striven to think well of them [people], but the last thirteen years have shaken my faith very much. I yet, however, believe the mass to be honest, although very liable to deception." Clay had much reason to lower his opinion of human nature, for as he told Alexander H. H. Stuart when the latter visited Ashland in 1839, he had been the subject of more obloquy than any man living. He consoled himself by observing that such abuse was the price that every man who becomes prominent in public affairs must pay. Washington, Jefferson, and Madison, he pointed out, were represented in their day and generation as being among the vilest of the vile.

Clay was a Madisonian in political theory. On one occasion he said that Madison was the greatest statesman whom the United States had produced, with the exception of Washington. Although he believed that Jefferson had more genius than the younger statesman, he thought that at the same time he was visionary and lacking the common sense which was characteristic of Madison. In 1831 he wrote that his constitutional doctrines were those of the epoch of 1798. "I am against all power not delegated, or not necessary and proper to execute what is delegated," he wrote. "I am against all nullification, all new lights in politics, if not in religion. . . . Applying the very principles of Mr. Madison's famous interpretation of the Constitution, in the Virginia address, I find in the Constitution the power to protect our industry, and to improve our country by objects of a national character."

He was thus a moderate conservative in his political views. His conservatism was based on his belief that change in society should be accomplished by political means in a gradual fashion so that all interests would be protected. This point of view was best expressed in a letter to Francis Lieber of January 18, 1838, praising the latter's *Political Hermeneutics,* particularly the section on "Precedents." The legislature of a free country was obligated, he wrote, "to conform to those expositions of its constitution, which may have been often and deliberately made. If considerations of security and stability to private rights require that judicial precedents should not be lightly departed from, the same considerations of stability and security in respect to the rights of the whole nation enjoin that fundamental principles, which have been deliberately settled in the administration of the government should not be too easily departed from."

Clay's conservatism was not expressed in a desire to curb political democracy. He encouraged a practice of expressing the popular will in memorials to Congress and by putting pressure on congressmen by the writing of letters to them. He believed also in the exercise of the right of legislative instruction of the senators, despite the fact that it was used as a weapon by the Jacksonians against his party. Although a majority of the congressmen from the slave states were opposed to the abolitionists' exercising their constitutional right of freedom of petition, he upheld that right.

Circumstance rather than reasoned conviction, probably, led him to become a strong champion of the prerogative of the Senate against the power of the President. The expansion of the executive powers during Jackson's administrations, he thought, distorted the Constitution. "The election of Gen. Jackson," he wrote to an English traveler, "ought to be regarded as an exception from the general good sense with which the American people have conducted their affairs." Jackson's vetoes he regarded with extreme aversion and disgust. He therefore strongly favored limiting the veto power of the President as well as amending the Constitution to limit the President to a single term.

"Harry of the West" was a strong nationalist, but, like Madison, he believed firmly in preserving a proper balance between the federal and state power. His belief in a truly federal government underlay his strong opposition to any interference with slavery within the states by the federal government. Its powers were strictly limited to national affairs, he maintained, and did not extend to the domestic institutions or the police powers of the state.

Henry Clay was a skilled practitioner in the art of politics as that art was developed within the conditions of the United States of the 1830's and 1840's. His first rule was the principle of empiricism. "It is a rule with me, when acting either in a public or a private character," he wrote, "to attempt nothing more than what there exists a prospect of accomplishment." He thought that he acted from fixed political principles, but actually he moved largely by intuition, playing by ear, very much as another master politician of the era, Andrew Jackson, did. Jackson called Clay "that Demogogue," but "Harry of the West" thought that Jackson was the crafty demagogue who under the mask of being an exponent of democracy was destroying "pure republican government." Actually, neither was a demagogue in the ordinary connotation of that term; both were practicing a new type of politics that was conditioned by the rise of the common man into political power in America.

The true story of politics in America is often to be found not in the formal actions of politicians, but in their informal contacts with each other. In the boardinghouses of Washington, in the congressional "messes," at the whist table, and in the committee rooms congressman initiated bills and made deals and formed alliances that determined the course of legislation. Clay was undoubtedly highly effective in these informal and mostly unrecorded contacts. An example of his skill in practical politics, revealing his native shrewdness, occurred in 1833, when he suppressed a rebellion in the ranks of the anti-Jackson coalition. Webster temporarily deserted his allies during and immediately after the nullification crisis by joining Jackson and seeking to form a new nationalistic party on the basis of the preservation of the Union. Clay won him back to his old allegiance by cleverly securing his selection as chairman of the strategic Senate Committee on Finance, where he would be forced to oppose Jackson's bank policy. Clay was a practical politician in the sense that a statesman must use the art of politics to accomplish desirable social and political reforms.

Abraham Lincoln called Henry Clay "my beau ideal of a statesman, the man for whom I fought all my humble life." Dennis Hanks, his cousin, in attempting to account for the fact that Lincoln became a Whig when his family and relations were Jacksonians, said he "always Loved Hen Clays Speaches I think was the Cause Mostly." Lincoln campaigned for the election of Clay as President, ardently supporting his platform of the American System. Yet the Illinois politician described the methods of Clay in terms that do not befit the beau ideal of a statesman. When Clay wished to carry an important measure, he took care that its language was not offensive to those whose support was indispensable. "He then presented it to the strong men whose help he must have or whose opposition he must stifle, and who were of strong wills, and either argued them into support or made modifications as they insisted on, or added palatable features to suit them, and thus got a powerful force enlisted in behalf of his measure; —then he visited the members of feeble wills and simply bullied them into its support without yielding one iota to them."

Clay was particularly effective in the party caucus, a relatively new device for determining party strategy. William Gilmore Simms, the Southern novelist, in a letter to Senator James H. Hammond in 1858 described such a caucus held by the Whigs during Harrison's brief administration. Simms's account belongs to the realm of oral history, for it was based on a description given him probably by a South Carolina congressman. The question before the caucus was whether to recommend to the President the summoning of an extra session of Congress, a proposal strongly favored by Clay. At this caucus, according to Simms, all the members except two were opposed to the calling of an extra session. But Clay "entered the assembly, passed down its lines, speaking as he went, in triumphant manner, with bold fearless eloquence, breast open, and, at length, confronting Webster, he seemed to concentrate the whole weight of what he had to say upon him. And so powerful was his eloquence, so keen his shafts, so personal their aim, that Webster actually crouched under him, and slid down in his seat, so that his head was almost on a level with his belly. And Clay triumphed. There were but *two* after he was done, who voted in opposition to the measure."

Yet Clay had one serious defect that disqualified him from being a consummate master of the political art: he talked too much and wrote too many letters. His devoted follower, Congressman Robert Letcher, who indiscriminately referred to the great man as "the old Prince" or "the old horse," realized this defect and tried to restrain him. Clay's friends were afraid that he would express himself too freely during the preconvention campaign of 1844. Accordingly, Letcher wrote to Crittenden: "The old Prince must hereafter remain a little quiet and *hold his jaw*. In fact he must be *caged*—thats the point—*cage him*. But he swears by all the Gods, he will keep cool and stay at home. I rather think he will be entirely prudent, tho' I have some occasional fears that he may write too many letters." It was impossible, however, for Clay to be a sphinxlike politician or to follow the noncommittal course that later brought success to Calvin Coolidge, who won the sobriquet of "Silent Cal."

A comparison of Clay with his rival Andrew Jackson reveals another deficiency of the Kentuckian as a politician. American politics has demonstrated again and again that the surest way for a politician to win votes is by identifying himself with the average man through folksiness, especially by shaking hands, remembering the first names of plain citizens, and by a warm sincerity of manner. These are more important than orations or platforms. Clay was affable and simple in manner, but his success and associations had made him a dignified gentleman rather removed from the level of thought of the common people. Jackson was closer to them because he was earthier and more coarse-grained and shared their prejudices. He was a man whom they could trust, a good hater and a violent denouncer. Although Clay had numerous friends they were not the little people. In his speeches and letters he does not say much about the working man; his main concern was for the manufacturer and the wealthy planter.

CHAPTER FOUR

THE SOUTHERN YEOMAN: THE HUMORISTS' VIEW

THE MASS OF SOUTHERN PEOPLE did not share Clay's view of the wisdom of preserving freedom of speech and of the press. In any society the mass of the people are intolerant of ideas repugnant to them; nor are they creative thinkers but take their ideas mainly from the preachers, teachers, editors, and politicians. This does not mean, however, that in the Old South the great majority of slaveless farmers had no weight in determining the direction of the Southern mind. Indeed, after the 1820's the politicians usually moved in the direction of what they thought was the popular will. Often the weight of this pressure was exerted through partisan channels, particularly by legislative instruction of the federal senators.

The modern historian finds it difficult to fathom the mind of the Southern yeomen, who constituted the great majority of the people, because they were not vocal; they kept almost no diaries that have been preserved, and their personal papers, except for Confederate letters, are almost nonexistent. A few manuscript travel accounts written by yeomen (notably Micajah Clark's diary of a sentimental journey from Mississippi to his old home in South Carolina in 1857) and some observations by travelers such as Frederick Law Olmsted, who had a special interest in the lower classes, cast a feeble light on their lives. Moreover, the election returns cannot be trusted as reliable indexes of the consensus of popular thought, partly because a large proportion of the lower classes did not vote. Some clues as to what the people thought and felt can be obtained from editorials, from the sermons of evangelical ministers, and from the appeals that politicians made to the electorate. In county courthouses and at state capitals are to be found legal documents such as wills, laws, and records of cases which throw light upon the activities of the common people, especially when they got into trouble. There are also various types of informal evidence—folklore, isolated newspaper items, occasional bits of memorabilia (such as the manuscript memoir of Newton Knight by his son), and the semirealistic writings of the Southern humorists with a rich vein of social history running through them.

This latter type of evidence—usually neglected in formal histories—is prejudiced, but valuable truth can be sifted from its distortions and bias. In studying the writings of the Southern humorists of the ante bellum period the social historian has a different purpose from that of the folklorist, the student of American literature, or the investigators of the Southern vernacular. He is interested in the by-products of this type of literature—authentic details of manners, customs, amusements, and social institutions such as the militia muster, the religious revival, and the law courts. The historian must be able to distinguish between the bias of the humorists and the facts about their subjects, for these writers were not primarily reporters but creators of literature. Nevertheless, they present through their imagination and firsthand knowledge of the plain people a kind of truth that eludes the researchers in documents.

Some of the most important humorists sought faithfully to record the mores and manners of the common people by their descriptions of frontier life, courthouse scenes, militia musters, and the uninhibited amusements of the yeomen and poor whites. After Augustus Baldwin Longstreet, the author of *Georgia Scenes,* had become a preacher and a college president, he was disturbed at times by the frivolity and indelicacy of his humorous writing, but he justified his work on the ground that it was authentic social history which a later age would value. In his preface to *Major Jones's Chronicles of Pineville,* William Tappan Thompson also affirmed a historical purpose—to preserve a record of the "cracker" before education had changed him "by polishing away those peculiarities which now mark his manners and language, reduc[ing] him to the common level of commonplace people, and mak[ing] him a less curious 'specimen' for the study of the naturalist. As he now is, however, I have endeavored to catch his 'manners living as they rise.'" Likewise, Thomas Bangs Thorpe and Joseph M. Field seem to have purposely recorded characteristic features of frontier life and quaint customs in out-of-the-way places which were rapidly disappearing. In reporting Southern conditions the humorists had an advantage over most travelers, for they observed Southern life from within. The keen observations which they made were the fruit of a lifetime of association and understanding rather than the product of a hasty visit.

A recent student of Southwestern humor, Kenneth Lynn, has presented a thesis (which he rides hard), that these humorists were principally Whigs, who wrote with a strong aristocratic bias. He maintains that they used their humorous writings as a weapon to combat and discredit the Jacksonian movement. Some evidence can be found, especially in the writings of Johnson J. Hooper and Joseph G. Baldwin, to support this tenuous thesis. But many of the writers wrote merely to entertain, to tell a good story, without political intent. Some of them—notably John Basil Lamar—had a genuine appreciation for the sterling virtues of the yeoman and the frontiersman—his independence, democracy, naturalness, courage, hospitality, and patriotism.

The attitude of Southern humorists toward the relatively small class of "poor whites" may have had something of aristocratic hauteur in it, but on the whole it represented the general attitude of Southern society to this debased class of people. To modern eyes the lowest class of whites of the Old South (often called "poor white trash" by the slaves) appear to be tragic figures, but to the planters and the residents of the towns they were a comic element. The upper plantation group as a class felt little sense of responsibility for the poverty, the illiteracy, the peculiar diseases of hookworm and malaria, and the drunkenness which beset the lower classes. What could be more laughable to these aristocrats than the quaint vernacular and the crude manners and dress of the "tackies" and "sand-hillers"? Even the slaves of the big house made fun of "poor white trash." In his *History of the Dividing Line* Colonel William Byrd set an example of snobbish aristocratic wit by his satire on the lubbers or backwoods people of North Carolina.

One of these aristocrats who was amused by the poor whites and collected their colloquialisms—"the piney-woods parlance" —was the Georgia doctor and poet Francis Orray Ticknor. Though Ticknor is known for his romantic poems, notably "Virginians of the Valley," his correspondence reveals that he had an earthy sense of humor. He lived on his plantation Torch Hill near Columbus, from which he made trips on his horse Kitty into the pine woods to minister to poor people. He described a learned reply that he gave to the question of a piney-woods mother: "What's the matter with my child's nose, he keeps a-picking of it?" His patients usually paid him with an X mark, but sometimes he got a cash case, "a temptation thrown in my way to reconcile me to my lot." He attended a sheriff's sale of the property of a poor white who had decamped owing him a bill. The property consisted of a cow and calf, a table, two chairs, a coffee mill without a handle, a tin pan with two holes in the bottom, and a pig of soft soap: all brought less than five dollars.

The customs and manners of the poor whites as well as of the yeomen of the South presented a rich tapestry of local material for the literary artist. This material, unsuited for use by the dominant romantic school of Southern writers, was exploited by the humorists who flourished in the period from 1830 to 1860. Unhampered by European traditions, except for the slight influence of Addison, these writers freshly observed the life about them and reported their findings without much effort at literary finish. They found around them the racy and individualized characters of the crackers and the yeomen, whose uncouth language and provinciality afforded substance for mirth. They could therefore create a native American humor based on realistic observation and illuminated by many sidelights of local color.

The Negro, on the other hand, was seldom or only incidentally used (as in Simms's novel *Woodcraft*), as a subject for comedy by ante bellum Southern writers. Not until the time of Joel Chandler Harris did the "darky" assume a prominent place in Southern humor. Perhaps the detachment essential for seeing the ludicrous side of the poor white man was lacking in the case of the Negro, who was a form of property bitterly assailed by the abolitionists. Besides, the black slave was a congruous element in the plantation regime, whereas the cracker was not.

The origin of this semirealistic literature dealing with the common man can be explained partly by the Democratic upsurge of the Jacksonian movement. The rise of the Nullification movement also stirred up an intense feeling of Southernism and an interest in Southern themes. In addition, economic and social conditions were ripe for the development of a school of broad humor below the Mason-Dixon Line. Georgia was the cradle of Southern humor. In this state a remarkable contrast developed between the yeomen of the red hills and the planters of the long-settled tidewater region. Indeed, the frontier had only recently been erased in the 1830's with the removal of the Cherokees. This juxtaposition of seasoned culture and the rude frontier produced incongruities and comic situations that evoked laughter.

The school of Southern humor was founded in Georgia by Augustus Baldwin Longstreet, a graduate of Yale and of Judge Tappan Reeve's law school at Litchfield, Connecticut, and editor of the Augusta *State Rights' Sentinel.* In his *Georgia Scenes,* published in book form at Augusta in 1835, Longstreet first set forth the ludicrous aspects of the life of Southern yeomen, crackers, and poor whites. He was soon followed by others, notably William Tappan Thompson, his protegé on the *State Rights' Sentinel;* Johnson J. Hooper, who had emigrated from North Carolina to Alabama where he became an editor and politician; John Basil Lamar, a Georgia planter; Henry Clay Lewis, the "Madison Tensas" of *Odd Leaves from the Life of a Louisiana Swamp Doctor;* Joseph M. Field, editor of the St. Louis *Reveille;* and Albert Pike and Colonel C. F. M. Noland of Arkansas.

Prominent among the humorous writers from the upper South were Joseph G. Baldwin, who emigrated from Virginia to the lower South during the flush times of the 1830's; George W. Bagby, editor of the *Southern Literary Messenger* at Richmond; Hamilton C. Jones and Harden E. Taliaferro of North Carolina; and George Washington Harris, whose bold and earthy descriptions of the mountain whites of east Tennessee remind one of the pictures of Thomas Hart Benton such as "I got a Gal on Sourwood Mountain" and "In the Ozarks." The humor of the Old South found its most powerful expression in Harris's *Sut Lovingood's Yarns.* Unfortunately, the difficult dialect and the extreme realism of his work have hampered its popularity.

The creator of Sut Lovingood, after having long been neglected, has come in recent years to be regarded as the most original and imaginative of the Southern humorists. Born in Allegheny City, Pennsylvania, in 1814, he spent the formative years of his life in Knoxville and east Tennessee. Here he became a Jack-of-all-trades, never able to make much money from a succession of jobs; he was apprentice to a jeweler, farmer in the foothills of the Great Smokies, steamboat captain, railroad man, sawmill manager, and postmaster of Knoxville. Though many of the humorists were Whigs, he was a Democrat, an ardent secessionist, and a sympathizer with the common people. His writings are full of vivid pictures of the common folk—an old mountain lady with a pipe in her mouth standing by her ash hopper, a poor white riding on a bull with a saddle made with forks of dogwood, a hypocritical circuit rider who guzzled bald-face liquor, a Yankee razor-grinder cheating the gullible country folk, and mountain people dancing at a Tennessee frolic. His rich imagery is homely almost Chaucerian in freshness, and redolent of the Southern countryside.

Some of these writers, by virtue of their background, held a position of detachment from the plantation culture. Dr. Henry Clay Lewis, who wrote *Odd Leaves from the Life of a Louisiana Swamp Doctor* under the name "Madison Tensas," was of part Jewish origin and though born in South Carolina, described himself as "a Southerner by adoption." He could make fun of the pretensions of the plantation aristocracy in such delineations as the "Man of Aristocratic Diseases." Writers such as Lewis, being outside of the aristocratic culture, could appreciate the antithesis between the folk culture and the culture of the colonnaded mansion.

A considerable number of writers who described the humorous aspects of Southern yeomen were Northerners who resided in the South. William Tappan Thompson, the creator of "Major Jones," was born in Ravenna, Ohio, and worked on Northern newspapers until he came to Georgia, where he was given a job by Longstreet on his *State Rights' Sentinel,* and later he founded the Savannah *Morning News.* Thomas Bangs Thorpe emigrated from Massachusetts in 1836 to Louisiana, where he worked as a portrait painter and journalist. John S. Robb, a journalist on the staff of the St. Louis *Reveille* who wrote *Streaks of Squatter Life,* was born in Philadelphia.

Albert Pike was a native of Boston and attended Harvard College before he settled in Arkansas in 1832 to become an editor, lawyer, diplomat, and commander of an Indian brigade in the Confederate Army. William T. Porter of Vermont, who founded *The Spirit of the Times,* a sporting and humorous magazine of New York City, was the great encourager of the Southern humorists by publishing their stories in his periodical. In the 1850's the connection of the Southern humorists with Porter's magazine was one of the few friendly links between North and South.

The writers who exploited the vein of Southern humor were chiefly journalists seeking to enliven the pages of their newspapers by local anecdotes, or lawyers who entertained each other on the circuit by swapping stories. They collected tales and gave them literary form, and they described comic happenings of the yeomen and crackers. These anecdotes originated in village taverns, livery stables, barrooms, or at the campfires of wagoners and hunters; they represented a different standard of stories, as Shields McIlwaine has pointed out, from the type of polite and witty anecdotes told in the parlors and on the verandahs of the planters' homes. The former brand of humor bore the unmistakable stamp of the common man, having frequently evolved from the practical joking of the frontier. It had an earthy tang and was characterized by broad farce—a bull playing havoc with a quilting party, the antics of a preacher when some lizards were placed in his trousers, or the comedy arising from a horse swap in Georgia.

Despite the place of honor which romantic literature held in the estimation of Southerners, these amusing stories of low life were keenly relished. This Rabelaisian taste was indicated by the fact that ten editions of *Georgia Scenes* were printed before 1860, and *Major Jones's Courtship* appealed to such a wide circle of readers that it ran through eleven editions. Furthermore, some of the most droll personalities of the Old

South—notably the plebeian Governor "Zeb" Vance of North Carolina, Judge Dooley of Georgia, and "Lean Jimmy" Jones, who defeated James K. Polk for governor in 1841—remained storytellers and wits who never committed their humor to the printed page.

From the pages of the Southern humorists we gain our most vivid descriptions of the appearance of the poor whites and of the crackers—a term often used to describe the upland farmers of Georgia as well as the poor whites. On court days they would come into the somnolent villages of the South, driving two-wheeled carts pulled by mules, bony horses, or oxen which they guided by a rope around their horns, and cracking their long whips. In the morning they seemed to be the most harmless individuals on earth; "their bilious-looking eyes, and tanney, shrivelled faces . . . wore a meek and pensive expression," according to *Major Jones's Chronicles of Pineville*. But towards noon, after they had imbibed heavily of bald-face corn liquor, a transformation occurred. "Then might be seen the cadaverous looking wiregrass boy in his glory, as he leaped out into the sand before the door, and tossing his linsey jacket into the air, proclaimed himself the best man in the country. Then, too, might be seen the torpid clay-eater, his bloated, watery countenance illuminated by the exhilarating qualities of Mr. Harley's rum, as he closed in with his antagonist," cursing, biting, and gouging.

The gregarious nature of the yeomen found an outlet in numerous social gatherings in which they combined work with pleasure. Their sports and amusements were an especially rich field for comic delineation. These diversions were mainly an outgrowth of frontier conditions. In the less developed sections of the South, as well as north of the Ohio River, wrestling matches and rude fights took place that were completely devoid of chivalry. The victor would jump up on a stump and crow like a cock, flapping his arms. Or he would boast: "I'm the yallow blossom of the forest; I'm kin to a rattlesnake on the mother's side; I'm the stepfather of the yearth; I'm a lion with a mangy tail, a bear with a sore head, a flying whale." A distinctive sport of the Southern backwoods was gander pulling, in which the contestant galloping on horseback, sought to pull off the head and neck of a well-greased gander hung high on a pole. The yeomen of Georgia indulged in a drinking game called "Bingo," in which gallons of liquor were consumed to the accompaniment of a song that began, "A farmer's dog sat on the barn-door and Bingo was his name, O!"

The tremendous vitality and optimism of Southern yeomen often found expression in tall stories with a Baron Munchausen flavor. Franklin J. Meine has collected some of these extravagant stories in his *Tall Tales of the Southwest.* This type of humor was especially prevalent on the frontier where the mysteries of an undiscovered country and the bigness of the mountains and the prairies excited the imagination. But the tall tale also flourished in the interior regions of the South. Harden E. Taliaferro has related some of these impossible stories which he heard in the back country of North Carolina in *Fisher's River Scenes and Characters.* There were stories of marvelous snakes that took their tails in their mouths and rolled along like a hoop, of people who ate impossible quantities of peaches or watermelons, of magical trees that grew so fast that a horse who was hitched to a branch was hoisted high into the sky, of incredible fights with catamounts, and of bears that displayed human sauciness and sagacity. Finally, there were ghost stories such as those which the superstitious old hatter told Joel Chandler Harris when he was a small boy on the Joseph Turner plantation near Eatonton, Georgia.

A peculiar quality of Southern yeomen humor was its emphasis on what Professor Alphonso Smith called "the humor of discomfiture." This laughter at the painful or embarrassing predicaments of others probably arose out of the practical joking of the frontier. Good examples of such roistering humor are to be found in the Sut Lovingood tales, such as "Bart Davis's Dance" and "Sicily Burns's Wedding," or the drover's tale related by Olmsted in his travel account *A Journey Through Texas.*

From the reports of travelers in the ante bellum South we gain the impression that the poor whites, unlike the yeomen, were lacking in humor. The conditions of life were so hard for them, especially in the mountain regions, that they developed a fatalistic melancholy. James Lane Allen has described the unchanged mountaineers of Kentucky: "eyes with a slow long look of mild enquiry, or of general listlessness, or of unconscious and unaccountable melancholy; the key of life a low minor strain, losing itself in reverie, voices monotonous in intonation; movements uniformed by nervousness."

The ignorance and provincialism of these secluded people were a frequent theme of the humorist. "McAlpin's Trip to Charleston" by Hamilton C. Jones, for example contrasts the openmouthed naiveté of the country greenhorn with the sophisticated culture of the city. The countryman who had seen the wonders of "Augusty," Georgia, was looked upon as a man of the world, and a plausible Yankee with a common school education like the politician Franklin Plummer was regarded in the backwoods of Mississippi as a walking encyclopedia. The suspicion about city people entertained by the yeomen was portrayed in numerous stories, such as T. S. Lane's "The Thimble Game," and Thompson's *Major Jones's Sketches of Travel.*

One of the most valuable pictures of the rusticity of the natives is given by Johnson J. Hooper in "Taking the Census," a story based on his experience as a census enumerator in 1840. The old ladies in the rural districts of Alabama confronted the enumerators with grim countenances and with the threat of "setting the dogs on ye" for prying into such personal affairs as, "How many chickens have you?" and "How much cloth have you woven?" The government of Washington was regarded by the country people in these isolated sections of the South almost as an alien enemy.

Southern humorists presented the daughters and wives of the farmers and the poor whites in a realistic light, quite different from the romantic halo cast over the ladies of the gentry by the novelists. The humorists portrayed cracker women engaged in quite unladylike practices like fighting; they pulled out hair and scratched faces, dipped snuff, chewed tobacco, and smoked corncob pipes. The young doctor Henry Clay Lewis ("Madison Tensas") found on his first visit into the swamp country of Louisiana to attend a farmer's wife that the neighbors believed the hoot of an owl to be an omen of death. A favorite theme of the humorists was the embarrassment of travelers who spent the night in a yeoman's crowded log cabin and had to go to bed in the presence of the female members of the family. The daughters of the farmers were usually modest girls, who became speechless before strangers and blushed deeply. The farmers' womenfolk were gullible patrons of Yankee peddlers, who sold them ribbons, pins, needles, nutmegs, clocks, and bustles. "Mike Hooter's" daughter in the backwoods of Mississippi did not have the money to buy a bustle—the latest in fashions—so she improvised one by tying a thick sausage under her dress. At a camp meeting when the end of the sausage came loose, she thought that the dangling object was a snake climbing up her leg; accordingly, she writhed with fear instead of with religious ecstasy.

The religion of the cracker was dramatized in the camp meeting, a method of soul-saving that gave spice to an otherwise monotonous rural life. Consequently the camp meeting holds a prominent place in Southern humor. A most realistic description of the emotional extravagance that often accompanied these religious gatherings is given in Hooper's *Some Adventures of Captain Simon Suggs, Late Captain of the Tallapoosa Volunteers.* The Captain stood on the outskirts of a great crowd of people at the Sandy Creek camp meeting in Alabama and coolly observed this mass of humanity in the throes of religious excitement. A half dozen preachers, serving in relays, were exhorting their audience, terrifying them with their somber theology and loud raucous voices. On the outer circle Negroes were singing, screaming, and praying with primitive African vehemence. Delicate women had become hysterical, so that their nerves played strange tricks known as "the jerks" or "the holy laugh"—a phenomenon that was terrifying because it resembled a maniac's chuckle. Some of the men wore a hideous grin; others were barking like dogs; while still others were shouting "Gl-o-ree!" In front of the mourner's bench the ground was covered with straw, upon which the converts were rolling in religious ecstasy or lay swooning upon each other in promiscuous heaps.

In sketching the political mores of the yeomen and crackers, the humorists emphasized their violent partisanship and their susceptibility to the arts of the demagogue. The autobiography of David Crockett tells how he won his elections by treating the voters liberally to liquor and amusing them with his folksy humor. On one occasion he defeated an opponent with a devastating smile by comparing him to a grinning coon. Crockett then boasted of his own prowess in killing coons by outgrinning them. Any sign of aristocracy exhibited by a candidate was a distinct handicap in winning the votes of the "sovereigns." John S. Robb's story of "The Standing Candidate" presents an old Missouri squatter named "Sugar" who appeared at all elections to the legislature as the standing candidate to represent Nianga County. He always came equipped with a jug of homemade whiskey and a bag of brown sugar. After one of the opposing candidates had paid him generously for his liquor supply, he would then make a speech yielding his claim to office to his patron until the next election. When a fastidious candidate refused to drink his mixture of whiskey and brown sugar (a rustic old-fashioned), he held up the unfortunate man to ridicule: "He's got an *a*-ristocracy stomach, and can't go the *native-licker.*"

The Southern yeomen and poor whites, indeed, were strong advocates of democracy—a white democracy. They immediately resented any assumption of superiority of one class over another. An amusing story illustrating this trait is told in Thomas D. Clark's *The Rampaging Frontier.* John C. Breckinridge and Robert Letcher were traveling together through eastern Kentucky in 1852, stump speaking as candidates for Congress. Letcher would make a short speech to "the sovereigns," and then while his rival spoke would play his fiddle nearby. The lively music invariably drained off the auditors of Breckinridge until only a handful of followers resisted the lure. Finally the wily Breckinridge concocted a scheme that ruined his musical opponent. At the next meeting, when Letcher began to play, a lank fellow wearing a coonskin cap, yelled out, "Why don't you fiddle with that t'other hand o'yourn?"

"T'other hand!" shouted the hillbillies.

Letcher, who was left-handed, became deeply embarrassed. The man with the coonskin cap continued to roar: "T'other hand! We've heard about you! You fiddle down thar in that d——n Bluegrass country, 'mong rich folks, with your right hand and think when you git up in the hills 'mong pore folks, left-hand fiddlin's good enuf for us; you've cussedly missed it. Left-hand doin's won't run up hyar."

Indeed, the most notable trait that distinguished the Southern yeomen from European peasants was a conviction of the equality of all white men. This frontier attitude never disappeared from the great middle class of the South, a virtue that was perpetuated by the rise of Jacksonian democracy. John Basil Lamar's humorous story "Polly Peablossom's Wedding" caught the authentic spirit of this movement. At the wedding when the preacher failed to appear and a squire was asked to perform the ceremony, Mrs. Peablossom objected that "the quality" in her day in Duplin County, North Carolina, had a prejudice against being married by a magistrate. But old Mr. Peablossom remonstrated: "None of your Duplin County aristocracy about here, now. . . . North Ca'lina ain't the best state in the Union nohow. . . . *Quality,* eh! Who the devil's better than we are? An't we honest? An't we raised our children decent, and learned them how to read, write, and cipher? An't I *fout* under Newman and Floyd for the country? Why, darn it! We are the *very best* sort of people."

Southern yeomen had many virtues to balance against some of the ludicrous aspects of their rural lives. William Tappan Thompson paid a high tribute to their sterling qualities when he wrote in the preface to his *Chronicles of Pineville:* "As a class they are brave, generous, honest, and withal possessed by a sturdy patriotism. The vagabond and the dissolute among them are only the exceptions to the rule, and in a few generations more, education will have made the mass a great people." This prophecy was realized within two generations. During the building of the New South, the leadership in politics, in education, and in business was often taken over by the sons and the grandsons of yeomen.

The resemblances between the Southern yeomanry and the small farmers and villagers of the North were much greater than their differences. Major Jack Downing of Maine, whom Seba Smith created for his newspaper in 1830, has much in common with Major Jones of Pineville, Georgia. They belonged approximately to the same economic level, and they had that sturdy independence and fine disregard for class distinctions that were natively American. The Yankee farmer, however, was more likely to be thrifty and enterprising, with a down-East shrewdness that was caricatured in the stock figure of Sam Slick the clockmaker, whom Haliburton popularized. The Northern humorists of the ante bellum period dealt more extensively with politics than did the Southern humorists, and they drew realistic pen pictures of female comic characters. There is no character in ante bellum Southern humor to correspond to Mrs. Partington or to the Widow Bedott, those garrulous old New England ladies whom Shillaber and Whitcher portrayed so skillfully.

How far does the picture of poor whites and yeomen drawn by Southern humorists correspond to reality? With respect to the relative numbers of the poor whites, they did not exaggerate, as did the abolitionists. Contrary to the abolitionist stereotype, the poor whites formed only the shabby fringe of Southern society—not the mass of whites. When Governor Henry A. Wise of Virginia addressed the legislature in 1856, he estimated that 10 per cent of the children of the state belonged to families too poor to pay for elementary schooling. In South Carolina Governor Hammond estimated that the poor whites composed 20 per cent of the whole white population.

The humorists did not realize, however, that the degraded condition of the poor whites was largely owing to their environment and the enervating diseases which beset them. Living in the isolated and infertile areas of the South—the sand hills of Carolina and Georgia, the piney woods of the coastal plain, and the mountainous areas—the poor whites were primarily hunters and fishermen; many of them were squatters like Sam Bostwick in Simms's novel *Woodcraft.* Despite their poverty, the "crackers" and the "piney woods folk" had a striking personal pride. As the Northern traveler Frederick Law Olmsted observed in 1853, they would not deign to engage themselves to the planters to do menial work—wait on tables, carry water, bring wood, black boots, cut hair, drive a coach. Such was "nigger's work," as they phrased it.

The yeomen were often confused with the poor whites by contemporary travelers and even by native writers. They judged from appearances, for many of the independent farmers lived in log cabins that were no better than the dwellings of the poor whites. The yeomen dressed in homespun or blue jeans, and their cattle and hogs were frequently hidden in the woods where they grazed. Yet there was a real difference —not merely in material possessions, but in spirit—between the yeomen and the poor whites. The true poor white was a creature like Ransy Sniffle in Longstreet's story "The Fight" in *Georgia Scenes* or the clay eater in Hooper's *The Widow Rugby's Husband.* Such a type was comparable to the slum element in the Northern states. Besides these people, who were often scattered in the interstices of the plantations, there were the mountain whites. These secluded people preserved the ways of their ancestors, the pioneers, without the spirit and hope of the pioneers. As Rupert Vance has observed, they represented the ebb of the frontier.

In their writings the humorists described both the yeomen and the poor whites and occasionally the tradesmen in small villages. It is sometimes difficult to distinguish in their work between the yeomen, frontiersmen, and poor whites, for the classes shaded into each other. The small farmers and the villagers, in contradistinction to the poor whites, were respectable citizens forming the bulk of the population of the South. Thomas Bangs Thorpe has drawn an attractive portrait of a member of this class in "The Big Bear of Arkansas." This mighty teller of tall tales was a man in the prime of his life, enjoying perfect health and contentment: "his eyes were as sparkling as diamonds, and good-natured to simplicity. Then his perfect confidence in himself was irresistibly droll." Representative specimens of the yeomen class were sympathetically portrayed by Lamar in "Polly Peablossom's Wedding" and by Thompson in *Major Jones's Courtship.*

The humorists do not appear to have realized the importance of the middle class of small farmers. Daniel R. Hundley of Alabama, who studied at Harvard and the University of Virginia, was one of the first writers to recognize the significance of the yeoman class in the social structure of the Old

South. In 1860 he published a pioneer study of Southern society entitled *Social Relations in Our Southern States,* in which he combated the abolitionist stereotype of Southern society as consisting of only three classes—planters, poor whites, and slaves. On the contrary, he maintained, its society was composed of five classes, of which the yeoman farmer constituted a large and important element.

Hundley noted some of the distinguishing characteristics of this class—their independent and democratic spirit, their industriousness, and their warmhearted hospitality. He observed that yeomen who owned slaves worked side by side with them in the fields, treating them with great kindness, almost as equals; these slaves were often allowed to call their masters by their first or Christian names and both ate the same fare.

The yeomen of the South, Hundley maintained, were much like Northern middle-class farmers, fully as intelligent though not as sophisticated as the tradesmen and mechanics in the cities. They were superior to their counterparts in the North in handling the rifle, judging the quality of liquor and brandy (for they brewed or distilled their own), and in a grasp of politics, which they acquired not from newspapers but from public speakings, barbecues, and the talk of county courthouse gatherings. In confutation of Frederick Law Olmsted's criticism of Southern hospitality, Hundley cited the testimony of a Connecticut mechanic whom he had met. This man, thrown out of work by the panic of 1857, had traveled penniless through the South seeking employment and had found a warm welcome in the homes of the farmers along his route.

The yeomen who moved into the villages and became artisans or tradesmen retained the characteristics of their former rural life with its democratic spirit and sense of equality. The Scottish wool carder William Thompson who traveled in the Southern states in 1840-1842 seeking employment reported that the mechanics and tradesmen in the South, unlike their class in Great Britain, considered themselves as "men of honour"; they resented any indignity that might be shown them "even at the expense of their life, or that of those who venture to insult them."

The humorists' view of the yeomen gives no indication of the most important economic fact about them—namely, that a very large proportion of them owned their farms. According to studies made by Professor Frank L. Owsley and his students at Vanderbilt in the 1940's, approximately 80 per cent of the farmers of the South in the decade 1850-60 owned the lands they tilled. This economic stake in society, as well as the wide participation of the people in their government after the emergence of the Jacksonian movement, made the Southern yeomen one of the freest and most independent groups in the world.

Nor does the literature of the humorists really mirror the relatively unstratified and fluid society of the South in the ante bellum period. This condition was partly owing to the constant emigration of the slaveless farmers, especially to western lands. There were some exceptions to the generally democratic organization of Southern society in the ante bellum period, particularly in the low country of South Carolina, among the "cotton snobs" of the black belt of Alabama and Mississippi, in the delta country of the Mississippi Valley, and in several enclaves of aristocracy in Virginia and Maryland.

Numerous examples could be cited of how easy it was for an energetic and intelligent yeoman to rise high in Southern society, but one of the most interesting was the career of David L. Swain of North Carolina. This son of a hatter, small farmer, and postmaster of Asheville had a precocious and phenomenal success. He was an unusually tall, ugly, and bumbling youth when he attended the academy in Asheville. Benjamin F. Perry, who was his classmate, has left this description of him: "He was six feet two inches in height, slender and ill-shaped, with a long pale face, thick lips, sharp nose, and dull expression of the eyes. The boys all loved him most affectionately. He was an accomplished Latin and Greek scholar, and took great pleasure in reading for the younger students any hard sentence which they came across in their lessons. I remember with what pleasure I listened to his reading of Homer, with a sort of musical drawl, that to me, was sweet and charming."

Young Swain either did not have the money to attend the University of North Carolina longer than four months or he was too eager to enter a career in law and politics to stay for a degree. After being admitted to the bar in 1822 he represented Buncombe County in the legislature. Within a few years he was appointed a superior court judge and at the age of thirty-one was elected governor of the state. He proved to be a great liberal and constructive leader. A powerful figure in the constitutional convention of 1835, he advocated complete religious toleration in respect to the holding of state office, popular election of the governor, and a fair apportionment of representation in the legislature to heal the bitter sectional controversy between the western and eastern sections of the state. Also he opposed the disfranchisement of free Negroes.

In 1835 he was chosen by the trustees to become the second president of the University of North Carolina, a position that he held until his death in 1868. He taught law, history, and moral science in the university and did much to make that institution popular throughout the state. His manuscript diary in the Southern Collection at Chapel Hill reveals that he was a very religious man who constantly sought to educate himself by reading and observation. Particularly did he have a strong interest in the colonial history of North Carolina, which led him to do research in the manuscript papers of the colonial governors. Though he owned slaves, he seems to have emancipated himself from many of the illiberal prejudices of his society, and in 1860-61 he was one of the strong Union leaders of the state. David L. Swain was a living demonstration of the open society of the Old South. It was open to the movement of poor boys upward to wealth and leadership of the state, but it was closed to any criticism of its fundamental way of life, as the career of Hinton Rowan Helper demonstrates.

CHAPTER FIVE

THE CREOLE CIVILIZATION

ONE HAS ONLY TO READ the diaries of two young Creoles of fashion, Lestant Prudhomme and Placide Bossier, to realize that the world of the Creoles in Louisiana was quite different from that of the Anglo-Americans. It was not simply because the Creoles spoke French and were Catholics, but the two groups were separated by different traditions and by a different sense of values. Although some Anglo-Americans, such as the Whig Senator Alexander Porter, Edward Livingston the great merchant, Maunsel White, and Judah P. Benjamin, married Creole women, the Creoles and the Anglo-Americans lived to themselves. The Prudhomme and Bossier diaries mirror a gay life of parties, hunting, fishing, dancing, serenades, and constant visiting. But seldom does an English name intrude in the pages of these Creole diaries; they tell of the belles of *la côte joyeuse* in the Red River Valley, of Odalie, Desirée, Julie, Celestine, Nizilda, and Attala, and of their carefree companions Achille, Narcisse, Felix, Hippolyte, Antoine, and Serdot.[1]

The Creoles occupied the lower part of Louisiana from Baton Rouge to the Gulf Coast; there were also oases of French-speaking natives in eastern Missouri and in the area around Mobile, Alabama. The languorous climate of their home and the known willingness of Latin colonists to mingle their blood with other races might provide some basis for a popular picture of the Creoles as a mixture of French and Negro blood. Such a conception, however, was manifestly incorrect and was greatly resented by them. According to

George Washington Cable, the New Orleans novelist, the term Creole applied only to the descendants of French and Spanish colonial stock of Louisiana who had no Negro blood in their veins.[2] A modern student, on the other hand, has concluded that the word was used in the early decades of the nineteenth century to designate a native of Louisiana regardless whether he was black or white or of mixed blood or of Spanish, French, or English stock.[3] In the later ante bellum period, and in common usage, the term was applied chiefly to the French-speaking natives of Louisiana, Alabama, and Missouri.

Despite its outward charm, Louisiana was a land of many drawbacks and contrasts. The climate was exceedingly hot and humid; the average rainfall during the year was sixty inches as compared to forty-five or forty-six in the upper South. The lagoons and bayous produced a plague of mosquitoes. A French traveler to Louisiana in the summer of 1831, invited to dinner in a Creole home, was disturbed by movements and noises under the table. Thinking that they came from a dog prowling under the table, he kicked the moving object and discovered that he had hurt a little black boy who had been stationed under the table to chase away "mosquitoes from under the marbled petticoats of our hostess."[4] Moreover, the prevalence of malaria and the recurrent epidemics of yellow fever, cholera, and smallpox sapped the energy of the

[1] P. Lestant Prudhomme Diary, January 29, 1850–November 24, 1852, 3 vols., courtesy of the owner, Mrs. Irma Sompayrac Willard, and of Eugene P. Watson, Librarian of Northwestern State College of Louisiana, Natchitoches; Placide Bossier Diary, January 1 and February, 1861, owner, Miss Carmen Breazeale of Natchitoches, microfilms loaned by Northwestern State College of Louisiana.

[2] George Washington Cable, *The Creoles of Louisiana* (New York, 1884). In his novels, particularly *Old Creole Days* (1879), Cable romanticized Creole civilization, yet he was bitterly attacked by Creole aristocrats for falsely portraying the Creoles by representing them as poor and ignorant.

[3] Joseph Tregle, Jr., "Early New Orleans Society: a Reappraisal," *Journal of Southern History*, XVIII (1952), 20-36.

[4] George J. Joyaux (ed.), "Forest's Voyage aux États-Unis de l'Amérique en 1831," *Louisiana Historical Quarterly*, XXXIX (1904), 465.

people and made life precarious. Tremendous effort, also, had to be exerted to keep the levees and dikes of the treacherous Mississippi standing firmly; even then, crevasses and floods during many months of the year imperiled the property and lives of the Creole country.

On the other hand, there were many advantages to living in this opulent land. The visitor in early spring was charmed by the bright flowers and semitropical vegetation; the orange, lemon, and banana trees; exotic birds, such as the parakeet and hummingbird; and the romantic vistas of lagoons and bayous bordered by magnificent live-oak and cypress trees. Gray Spanish moss hung in long festoons from the trees. For some visitors, such as actress Fanny Kemble, the sight of it produced feelings of melancholy and aversion, but to others the graceful drooping strands appeared romantic; to Thomas Rodney of Delaware they looked like a "Dunker's beard and makes the wood look very Venerable."[5] Certainly the Spanish moss softened the sleep of many a slave who used its pliant fibers for mattresses and to sell for pin money.

Travelers admired the vast fields of waving sugar cane which they saw from the Mississippi steamboats growing on plantations "level as a billiard table." Especially pleasing were the gardens of the sugar planters with their Cherokee rose hedges and flowers that did not grow in the North, such as oleanders, camellias, purple bougainvillea, tuberoses, the sweet-smelling cape jasmine, and pink crepe myrtle. After the heat of a summer day it was pleasant for a traveler to sit on the veranda of a planter's house and sip mint juleps (which were often served before breakfast) and engage in quiet conversation, watching the innumerable fireflies glow in the darkness and breathing the magnolia-scented air. William H. Russell, the London *Times* correspondent in America in 1861, enjoyed the utter silence and peacefulness of the planters' homes,

[5] Arthur P. Hudson, *Humor of the Old Deep South* (New York, 1936), p. 57.

interrupted only by the song of the mockingbird and the tolling of the plantation bell at noon and at sunset.

Indeed, Louisiana was a colorful part of the South, not only because of its sugar plantations and beautiful perfumed gardens, but because of the variety of its population. Dominant were the descendants of the early French settlers who founded New Orleans in 1718 and of the Spaniards who ruled Louisiana from 1766 to 1803. There were also descendants of the Germans who had settled on the "German Coast" of the Mississippi above New Orleans in the time of John Law. To the original French settlers, mostly humble people, including some prostitutes like "Manon Lescaut" and some virtuous "casket girls," there had been added several later infusions of French blood. In 1764, ten years after the expulsion of the Acadians from Canada, the first group of these French-speaking exiles arrived in Louisiana. They settled in the southwestern part of the colony around St. Martinville, along Bayou Teche and Lafourche. Mostly poor peasants, they were far different from the sentimental picture of them in Longfellow's *Evangeline.* Although some of them became substantial yeoman farmers, and one of their number, Alexander Mouton, became governor, these so-called Cajuns were looked down upon by the old French population. Preserving the dialect of Normandy, modified by the incorporation of English and Creole words, they formed as a whole an illiterate and unprosperous people comparable to the poor whites of the sandhills.[6] The Cajuns of southern Alabama continued in the twentieth century to be a backward people, characterized by xenophobia, resentful of any imputation that they had Negro blood in their veins, but admitting some admixture of Indian blood.[7]

Another important French element which joined the old population was the Santo Domingo planters. In 1791 the

[6] See Arthur G. Doughty, *The Acadian Exiles . . .* (Toronto, 1916).
[7] Carl Carmer, *Stars Fell on Alabama* (New York, 1934), pp. 255-269.

mulattoes of this island, influenced by the French Revolutionary movement, arose in revolt, stirred up the black slaves, and established a reign of terror in the island, during which many of the planters who survived fled to Charleston, Norfolk, and Louisiana, bringing their slaves with them. It is estimated that over ten thousand of these refugees entered the United States. Some of them were people of cultivation; they were responsible for starting the French theater in New Orleans. They also had an important part in establishing the sugar industry in Louisiana. Among the Santo Domingans were teachers of the French language, musicians, pastry makers, fencing masters, and wigmakers who contributed to the art of pleasant living in the South.[8] At the same time it is probably true that they increased the fear of servile insurrection wherever they settled.

The Revolutionary movement in France and the disturbances of the Napoleonic period resulted in a number of political exiles settling in Louisiana. These émigrés were usually much better educated and more sophisticated than the native population, and they regarded themselves as superior to the provincial Creole; one of these immigrant Frenchmen, Étienne Mazureau, was called " the eagle of the Louisiana bar." After the purchase of Louisiana by the United States these émigrés became formidable contenders for the political leadership of the territory and state.[9]

Besides the French element, there was a considerable contingent of the offspring of the Spanish settlers and the Islenos from the Canary Islands. A large number of Cubans and natives of the West Indies emigrated to Louisiana, particularly

[8] Howard Mumford Jones, *America and French Culture* (New York, 1927), p. 134.

[9] Dunbar Rowland (ed.), *Official Letter Books of W. C. C. Claiborne* (Jackson, Miss., 1917), 6 vols.; Henry M. Brackenridge, *Views of Louisiana* (Baltimore, 1817); Vincent Nolte, *The Memoirs of Vincent Nolte, or Fifty Years in Both Hemispheres* (New York, 1934).

around the year 1810. Always the port of New Orleans was receiving numerous European immigrants, some of whom continued their journey up the Mississippi River, but others who remained to become citizens of the state. Cheap passage to New Orleans could be obtained on the cotton ships returning from Liverpool and Le Havre, which usually were in ballast. The census of 1860 reported 80,975 foreign-born persons in the state, constituting 22.6 per cent of the white population. Of this group the Irish ranked first in numbers, the Germans second, and the English third.

Nowhere in the world, perhaps, was there such a mixture of Negroes with other races and nationalities. On the streets of New Orleans one could see fair-skinned, blue-eyed octoroons, griffes, mulattoes, and particularly quadroons (three-fourths white). On Congo Square on Sundays some of the Negroes danced voodoo dances. The "Red Bones" of the Natchitoches area were a mixture of French, Indian, and Negro.

The Creole myth has exalted the French-speaking inhabitants of Louisiana as superior in culture to the Anglo-Americans, as aristocrats above the undignified pursuit of money. The Creole historian Charles Gayarré, Grace King, Lafcadio Hearn, and, in more recent times, Lyle Saxon, have portrayed the Creoles as a people who had learned the art of gracious living. The elite of their society had courtly manners and an Old World charm, but they were not the great patrons of art and culture which the Creole myth makes them out. Joseph Tregle, Jr., has removed much of the reputed glamour from this picturesque minority in the lower South. He has shown that it was the Anglo-American element that supported the theater, education, newspapers, and libraries. The Creole women, on the other hand, had undoubted charm that impressed the travelers; Louis Tasistro, the actor, for example, commented that the perfection of female beauty and dress was to be seen oftener among the Creole circles of New

Orleans than anywhere else in America. To see these captivating ladies with lustrous dark eyes and hair, he wrote, one should go to the French theater on opera nights.[10]

The Creoles, to a greater degree than the Anglo-Americans, lived a life of sensation and careless enjoyment. They loved to dance, gamble, fish, attend feasts, play on the fiddle and to live without much thought of the morrow. Often beautiful and vivacious when they were young, the Creole women became fat and domesticated early; most of them were completely lacking in intellectual qualities. The men, dressed in crude, ill-fitting pantaloons of blue cottonade, whiled away the hours smoking cigars, playing dominoes, and gossiping long over a glass of wine. The Creoles seldom joined the westward movement to better their condition or prospects in life. Consequently, as their sons grew up, they subdivided their farms into small acreages to accommodate the expansion of their families. On these diminutive farms they raised perique tobacco, rice, and small quantities of sugar cane for juice, using antique and inefficient plows. Their homes were cottages made of cypress logs, with steep roofs and galleries or verandas around them.[11]

These generalizations apply only to the lower and middle classes, for there were many refined and aristocratic Creole planters and professional men, such as Pierre Beauregard, Governor Roman, and the planter Valcour Aimé. A representative of the New Orleans *Crescent* wrote, in an account of his visit in 1860 to the sugar parish of St. James, that the planters almost to a man belonged to "the old Creole-gentleman type, who were hospitable, chivalrous, and high-spirited."[12]

[10] Louis F. Tasistro, *Random Shots and Southern Breezes* (New York, 1929), Chap. VII.

[11] H. I. Priestly, *The Coming of the White Man, 1492-1848* (New York, 1929), Chap. VII.

[12] Pritchard (ed.), "A Tourist's Description of Louisiana in 1860," p. 1119; see also Grace King, *Creole Families of New Orleans* (New York, 1921).

After the United States' purchase of the colony in 1803, Americans flocked to this land of new opportunity. Previously, the French population had formed an unfavorable opinion of the Americans because they had seen chiefly the crude boatmen, "the half-horse, half-alligator" type, who had brought the produce of Kentucky, Tennessee, and the Ohio Valley to New Orleans in flatboats. After the purchase, a new American type appeared, planters seeking rich land; lawyers, doctors, professional men, and businessmen seeking money. These Americans were in general better educated than the French colonials, more enterprising, energetic, and resourceful.

Many of the newcomers were New Yorkers, businessmen and professional men. In 1860 5,538 New Yorkers lived in the state, while there were only 2,986 natives of Virginia. Among the Anglo-Americans who came to New Orleans with an urge to make profits was Simon Cameron, later to become a political boss in Pennsylvania and Lincoln's first Secretary of War. Cameron arrived in New Orleans in 1831 and was delighted with its balmy climate and hospitable people. He was quick to note that although New Orleans had an immense business of shipping and commerce, it was sadly lacking in manufacturing enterprises. To Governor J. A. Schalze of Pennsylvania, he wrote, "Everybody here makes money, at every business. . . . It would be a great place for a brewery—not one within 1,500 miles. A tallow chandler could make a fortune soon. Tallow 3½¢ a pound—candles 20¢. Everything is the same way. Raw materials very cheap—manufactures very high. The reason is that nobody likes to work. All depend upon the negroes."[13] Many lawyers emigrated to New Orleans, the most notable being Edward Livingston, the recently resigned mayor of New York, who arrived in 1804, and James Brown of Kentucky, Henry Clay's brother-in-law, who became attorney general of Louisiana and in 1812 United States senator.

[13] Simon Cameron to Governor J. A. Schalze, November 28, 1831, Simon Cameron Papers, Historical Society of Pennsylvania.

With their close-knit family feeling and Catholic affiliation, the Creoles tended for many years to keep apart from the Americans. They spoke a different language, had a different religion, different customs, and a different philosophy of life. In contrast to the Anglo-Americans they had little conception of the value of time. In New Orleans they lived in a separate section called the Vieux Carré, which seemed to visitors like a foreign city. At the beginning of the War of 1812 the Creoles displayed complete indifference to the American cause; it was difficult to raise troops among them. A young Harvard graduate, John Winship, who had come to New Orleans to practice law, observed that the Creoles were discontented with American rule and wished to be reunited with France. The French-speaking inhabitants voted as a national group, and even on jury service they displayed their national prejudice in favor of men of French descent. But in 1814 Governor Claiborne reported that public sentiment had changed in favor of loyalty to the United States, and many of the French inhabitants, including a Creole battalion of free Negroes, fought with Jackson to repel the English invasion.[14]

The legal system of the Creoles was another point of difference between the Anglo-Americans and the old inhabitants. It was based on the Roman law as codified by Napoleon—the Code Napoléon. In 1822, the legislature appointed three jurisconsults, headed by Edward Livingston, who had married a Creole and become one of the principal leaders of the Creole faction against the Americans, led by Governor Claiborne. The work of the jurisconsults resulted in the adoption in 1825 of the Civil Code and the Code of Practice in Civil Cases, as well as a commercial code. Approximately 80 per cent of their provisions were taken from the Code Napoléon and most of the remainder from commentaries of French

[14] Rowland, *Letter Books of Claiborne,* VI, 285-289; Everett S. Brown (ed.), "Letters from Louisiana, 1813-1814," *Mississippi Valley Historical Review,* XI (1925), 560-579.

jurists. The law of Louisiana, therefore, was different from that of any other state, representing as it did an amalgam of Roman and French and Spanish elements with the common law of England. In the courts and in the legislature, both French and English were used as official languages.[15]

The conflict between the Creoles and the Anglo-Americans was settled in favor of the Americans by the rapid spread of cotton and sugar culture. Until 1830, observers believed that the Creoles constituted the majority of the population. Between 1810 and 1820, the greatest increase of the population of Louisiana occurred, over 100 per cent. There was a let-up in immigration in the decade of the 1820's, but from 1830 to 1840 population increased again, over 63 per cent. The proportion of French-speaking Creoles to the other elements of the population can be roughly measured by the proportion of Catholics in the state, for the Creoles were stanchly Catholic. It is likely that the majority of the immigrants from Europe, notably the Irish, were Catholic too, but the French-speaking Creoles formed the bulk of the membership of the Catholic Church. The Census of 1850 reported that the Roman Catholic churches had accommodations for 37,780 persons out of a total of 109,615 accommodations for all denominations; that is, a little over one-third of the people presumably were Catholics. In 1860 the proportion estimated to be Catholic had declined to approximately one-fourth of the population.[16]

The distinctive crop of the Creole country in the nineteenth century was sugar cane. Small quantities of cane had been cultivated for syrup in the middle of the eighteenth century, but the money crop at that time was indigo. In the early 1790's, however, the ravages of insects and declining prices threatened to ruin the Creole indigo planters. Then, after the

[15] William B. Hatcher, *Edward Livingston, Jeffersonian Republican and Jacksonian Democrat* (University, La., 1940), Chap. XI.

[16] J. D. B. De Bow, *The Seventh Census of the United States: 1850* (Washington, 1853), pp. 490-491.

slave uprising in Santo Domingo in 1791, sugar planters from that island fled to Louisiana, stimulating an interest in the cultivation of sugar cane. In 1795 Étienne de Boré, a Creole planter who had been educated in France, experimented with raising sugar cane and granulating its syrup into sugar. He succeeded brilliantly in his pioneering attempt and sold his first crop for $12,000. In thus leading the way to economic revival he has rightly been called "the savior of Louisiana."

Growing sugar cane in Louisiana was somewhat hazardous; an early frost could ruin the crop. Consequently the parishes of the Sugar Bowl extended no farther north than Baton Rouge, a hundred miles from New Orleans. The planters waited to the last practicable moment in October before cutting the cane, so that it would be as fully matured as possible. In the West Indies, where there was no danger of frost, the cane did not require replanting for a dozen years, so it had time to mature fully. In Louisiana, on the other hand, for lucrative returns the cane had to be replanted every three years. Louisiana sugar could compete with the West Indies product only because of the protection of the American tariff and the remarkably fertile soil of the delta region. The introduction in 1817 of ribbon cane, which had a stronger resistance to cold weather, gave greater security to the Louisiana planters and enlarged the area of the sugar country.[17]

Sugar cane was ordinarily planted, not from seed, but by laying the stalks in furrows, six feet apart, and covering them with soil. From the joints of these stalks the new cane sprouted in early spring. By late summer the stalks had grown higher than a man's head. After the cane was cut in October it was transported to the sugar mill, where the juice was pressed out by machinery operated by steam engines or on small plantations by horse power. The grinding season, two months long, was a period of intense activity; the slaves often

[17] See J. Carlyle Sitterson, *Sugar Country, the Cane Sugar Industry in the South, 1753-1950* (Lexington, 1953), Chaps. II, VI.

worked eighteen hours a day. During the early period of cane culture the syrup, tempered with lime to purify it, was boiled in open kettles. This inefficient method made the cost of fuel one of the large expenses on sugar plantations. Accordingly, during slack seasons, the Negroes were frequently employed in retrieving driftwood from the Mississippi River. In 1843 a brilliant Creole Negro, Norbert Rillieux, who had been educated in France, developed a process of boiling the cane juice in vacuum pans and using the vapor from one pan to heat another. Judah P. Benjamin was one of the earliest planters to introduce this process; by the eve of the Civil War it was being widely adopted. After the juice of the cane had been reduced to a thick syrup, it was poured into hogsheads of 1,100 pounds capacity, where it granulated; the part that did not granulate drained from the hogshead through cane stalks placed in holes in the bottom; this by-product formed molasses, and amounted to 600 gallons per hogshead of sugar.

Running a sugar plantation required much capital. Land for sugar raising cost twice as much as cotton land, partly because of the need of numerous ditches to drain the soil. A sugar mill with its steam engine was costly, too, involving a capital investment of $40,000 or more. Usually, planters had to employ a sugar maker, a skilled white man, to supervise the making of sugar during the grinding and boiling season. The planter often had to buy coal or cordwood to supplement his fuel supply of bagasse, that is, the dry pressed-out stalks of cane. His labor force had to be strong adult Negroes, who usually cost more than the land. Because of the need of capital and the limitations of the climate, the number of sugar plantations was small, the highest being 1,536 in 1850; this number declined to 1,308 in 1860, partly because the small plantations using horse-power mills had been absorbed by the more efficient larger units. Because of the need for extensive capital to operate sugar plantations, 28 per cent in 1859 were owned by partnerships. Besides the production of the

Louisiana plantations, an average of 300,000 hogsheads of sugar annually during the decade of the 1850's, Texas produced approximately 8,000 and Georgia around 1,000 hogsheads a year. Nevertheless, the Southern states provided less than half of the sugar consumed in the United States. Louisiana sugar was sold largely in the Western states. Only 20 to 25 per cent was disposed of in the East.

Solon Robinson has left in his journal accurate descriptions of some of the great sugar plantations that he visited during an agricultural tour in 1849. One of the largest was the Houmas estate, which had originally been purchased by Wade Hampton of South Carolina in 1811, but at the time of Robinson's visit was managed by John S. Preston, son-in-law of Wade Hampton II.[18] It consisted of 2,000 arpents of land (an arpent being one-seventh less than an acre). The labor force on the three plantations into which it was divided was 750 slaves, of whom over half were field hands. Each adult slave normally cultivated nine or ten acres of sugar cane, which yielded usually a hogshead or a hogshead and a half per acre.

Houmas Plantation was sold in 1857 to John Burnside, an immigrant from North Ireland who had made a fortune as a merchant in New Orleans. He acquired five plantations, valued at $1,750,000, and 937 slaves, valued at $500,000; these constituted the largest holding in sugar land in the South. His sugar production annually exceeded 3,000 hogsheads, together with a vast quantity of molasses. Sugar sold for five or six cents a pound during the last decades of the ante bellum period. The Negroes on the Burnside plantations received five pounds of pork a week, as much Indian cornbread as they could eat, with a portion of molasses, and occasionally fish for breakfast, and were allowed to raise poultry and cultivate garden patches. The children seemed to be happy and healthy; they increased by about 5 per cent each year.[19]

[18] Kellar, *Solon Robinson*, II, 166, 179.
[19] Russell, *My Diary North and South*, pp. 257-259.

Robinson also described in detail Madewood, near Napoleonville, the plantation of Thomas Pugh, one of the most successful of the sugar planters. The Pugh brothers moved in 1820 from North Carolina, where the soil of their plantations was exhausted, to southern Louisiana. Here they continually bought land and Negroes by borrowing money. By 1849 Thomas Pugh had accumulated 3,000 arpents of rich land and over 250 slaves. Each of his field hands produced about seven hogsheads of sugar. To his adult slaves he issued five and one-fourth pounds of pork a week and one and a half pecks of cornmeal as well as fresh vegetables. He raised a sufficient supply of corn for the plantation needs, but he bought his meat supplies. To take care of the health of the slaves, he paid a physician a fixed sum of $1.75 per slave for the year. His overseer, who was a Yankee, received a salary of $1,200 a year and living expenses. He also hired an engineer to operate his sugar house and a sawmill. His taxes were $2,000 a year on an assessed value of land and slaves of $206,265. His profits were considerable, for his sugar crop sold for $30,000 to $40,000.

Although there were great fluctuations in the price of sugar and numerous hazards, the cultivation of sugar cane was a profitable enterprise for many planters. One of the unsuccessful planters, however, was Bishop Leonidas Polk of the Episcopal Church. A native of North Carolina and a graduate of West Point, Polk had first settled in Maury County, Tennessee, where he managed a cotton plantation and served as a clergyman. After being appointed bishop of Louisiana, in 1841 he purchased a plantation on the Bayou La Fourche, to which he transported the 400 slaves which he and his wife owned. His plantation, Leighton, represented a large investment. He had superior sugar-making equipment, valued at $75,000, housed in a building 290 feet long. In good years his plantation produced five hundred hogsheads of sugar, bringing in an income of $27,500; his expenses amounted to approximately $10,000. Of the 2,500 arpents of land in his plantation, about a thousand were in cultivation. Polk was described by Solon Robinson as an "improving planter" who believed in good tillage and in manuring his fields. Although he bought his meat supplies for his slaves, he raised all the corn and hay needed for the plantation.[20]

Polk treated his slaves with paternal kindness. He fed them well, giving each adult slave a ration of four pounds of meat a day. Every family had a chicken house and a garden. There was a nursery for the children and a hospital for the sick; Mrs. Polk personally attended to the welfare of sick slaves. In addition to the long Christmas holiday the master gave others to the slaves on church festivals. He paid a clergyman $300 annually to preach to them, and himself often read the Bible to them and prayed with them.

At Leighton the Polk family lived an idyllic life for a few years. A visitor in 1850, Mrs. Hilliard of Arkansas, was greatly impressed with the refinement and comfort in the life of the family. Mrs. Polk, she wrote, had a faithful Negro nurse, "to whose care she abandons her babes entirely. Only when she has a fancy to caress them does she see them. Eight children and cannot lay to their charge the loss of a single night's sleep." Also she had a housekeeper, "who gives out, regulates, and is everything she ought to be." An Irish woman trained in music served as a governess for the older daughters. Mrs. Hilliard was charmed by the Bishop's extensive and rare library. "I could linger forever," she wrote, "over the Books of prints collected in Italy." The garden also was charming with its orange trees, "pyramids of picayune roses," and other fragrant flowers.[21]

Yet this Southern idyll came to an end in 1854 when the Bishop was forced to surrender Leighton and its slaves to his creditors. Possibly he had been too indulgent a master. He

[20] Kellar, *Solon Robinson*, II, 201-204.

[21] Mrs. Isaac H. Hilliard Diary, 1849-1850, typed copy, Department of Archives, Louisiana State University.

would allow no work on the plantation on Sundays even during the critical grinding season. Sugar planting, especially at the time of sugar making, required the presence of the master, but Polk was frequently absent on his episcopal duties. He was a generous and noble man who gave freely of his time to serve humanity and refused to take a salary for his work as bishop. But he had bad luck, for in 1849 he lost seventy of his valuable slaves during a cholera epidemic. In the following year a severe storm damaged his plantation to the amount of $100,000 loss. Confronted by these misfortunes, he had to sell the plantation and move to New Orleans.[22]

The story of the expansion of sugar and cotton culture in Louisiana after the coming of the Americans is largely the story of enterprising men, who had moved in from other states and had made fortunes in planting. Such was the career of Claudius Le Grand, who sold his plantation in Maryland in 1836 and emigrated to the delta country of Louisiana, where he established a cotton plantation. Although there were some fine houses in this region, he noted that it was no uncommon thing to see a planter who raised from 600 to 1,000 bales of cotton live in a house so open that he could not keep a dog out by shutting the door. "They laugh if you say anything about the uncomfortable way in which they live," he wrote, "and point with pride to the fields which bring them in this yearly fortune." He reported that one of his crops of cotton was worth the entire sum he had received from the sale of Portland Manor in Maryland. He treated his slaves well and observed that they were hearty and much pleased with their situation. He gave them the privilege of chopping wood from the plantation and selling it to the passing steamboats (for $3 a cord). He permitted his body servant, John, to follow

[22] William M. Polk, *Leonidas Polk, Bishop and General* (New York, 1915); Vera L. Dugas, "The Ante-Bellum Career of Leonidas Polk," M.A. Thesis, Louisiana State University, 1943, Chapter V.

his inclination and work at a hotel in Vicksburg, refunding to his owner $25 a month and receiving a considerable sum for his own use.

At this time credit was easy in the Southwest. Colonel Le Grand observed that it was easier to get a loan of $20,000 to $30,000 without any security but one's word than to borrow $5,000 on a mortgage on the best property in Maryland from the "cold-hearted" Marylanders. The Le Grands lived with considerable luxury and refinement. Their daughter, Julia, became one of the South's most charming ladies, a writer and intellectual. But after the death of the master the Le Grand fortune was lost, and Julia and her sister supported themselves by establishing a "select school" for young ladies in New Orleans.[23]

The Creoles and American farmers in the prairie region of Attakapas and Opelousas raised cotton and entertained themselves by all-night dancing at weekly balls. The Creole girls would arrive at the small villages in *calèches* made entirely of wood, the wheels having no tires. The young men, instead of working, hunted and frequented taverns where they dissipated their lives in drinking and gambling. Judge Thomas C. Nicholls, whose family was among the earlier American settlers in this region, described how he was led into habits of intemperance as a young lawyer at Opelousas because of a lack of employment and "the taunts, gibes and entreaties of my dissolute companions."[24]

The diary of a young Creole of fashion who lived on a cotton plantation in the Cane River Valley, fifteen miles from Natchitoches, reveals how enervating life on a slave plantation could be to the sons of the planter. Lestant Prudhomme was twenty-two years old in 1850; he had finished his career at college in New Orleans and had come home to live on his

[23] Lyle Saxon, *Old Louisiana* (New York, 1929), Chap. XII.
[24] *Ibid.*, p. 119.

father's plantation and study law. His record of his daily routine shows that he spent his time largely in a round of pleasures—simple pleasures as a whole—visiting his numerous relatives; playing cards; hunting snipe, bullfrogs, and deer; fishing; feasting on good food. The chief excitement of the day came when the steamship stopped at the landing, or when he went to Natchitoches to attend a dance or Mass, to visit his cousins in the convent school, or to see a circus. Occasionally, there were minor misfortunes, such as when the cotton crop had to be replanted, or when he was sick with breakbone fever, or when he bruised his hand and sprained a thumb in whipping a slave.

He seems to have had little ambition or to have been much concerned with the affairs of the outside world. He began his diary on January 29, 1850, on the day that he commenced to read Blackstone. He had intended to begin his study of the law the day before, but was diverted by vast flocks of wild pigeons passing over, and he must go out to shoot them. Later, beautiful and demonstrative girls, billiards, cards, dances, and dinners lured him constantly from his studies. Nevertheless, he rode at intervals into Natchitoches and took an oral examination on what he had read.

He had a body servant whom he scarcely mentions; indeed, his diary contains few references to slavery. One April morning he visited his old nurse, who had been freed by his grandfather, and later he sent her some delicacies. When the overseer became sick, he gave out rations to the slaves and weighed the cotton of each picker at the end of the day. He seems to have had no class feeling in regard to overseers, for his journal mentions supping with the overseer, going fishing with him, and even attending a wedding in the company of the two overseers; the guests danced all night to a fiddle played by a Negro boy.

His diary reveals the indifference of the Creoles to public

education. Lestant records that Mr. Harris, the common schoolteacher of the neighborhood, had received no pay for his trouble, and that he had become a victim of malaria and was so destitute that he was a subject for charity. Yet aristocrats like the Prudhommes did not neglect the education of their children; a brother of Lestant was sent to the Western Military Institute in Kentucky and an English governess was employed for the younger children, while his cousins attended the convent school in Natchitoches. Lestant and some of the younger Creoles thought that the American system of raising children was better than the Creole way, for he commented that sending young girls to the convent school was a cruel and unnatural separation of children from their families.

Lestant seems to have been morally an exemplary young man, dutiful to his parents, often assisting at Mass. His mind was almost completely orthodox; he was a strong believer in property and the natural inequality of man; an admirer of Clay and Webster, he rejoiced when the Compromise of 1850 was adopted. Despite his gay flirtations and his many praises of the Creole maidens, he never married; and his study of Blackstone seems to have been fruitless, for he never practiced law. Outstanding in his diary, however, are the revelations of warm family feeling among the Prudhommes and their numerous kin.

Ten years after Lestant began the study of law while the wild pigeons were flying, another young law student of the Natchitoches area, Placide Bossier, kept a brief diary. Like Lestant he found the study of Blackstone so tedious that he would doze away in a rocking chair. His mind was centered upon gay parties, playing billiards and euchre, enjoying oyster suppers, and hunting ducks on the lake. Though he delighted in visiting many young ladies and singing with them, he was madly in love with one. His young manhood was spent in a different period from that of Lestant; the shadows of the approaching war fell upon him, for he drilled with a cavalry company. Lestant had been a Unionist, but on January 7, 1861, Placide voted for the independence of Louisiana.[25]

The Louisiana planters varied widely in culture and background. There were, for example, a number of free Negro planters like Alexander Durnford, who owned the plantation Sainte Rosalie in Plaquemines Parish. Durnford formed a strong friendship with the New Orleans merchant John McDonogh, whose plantation apparently adjoined his. In the McDonogh correspondence are letters from Durnford which show that the possession of economic power by Negroes tended to break down some of the race barriers between colored and white men. The colored planter and the white capitalist exchanged gifts and rendered mutual services. McDonogh gave the Negro planter a gold watch, and the latter endorsed notes for McDonogh to the amount of $26,666. On one occasion in 1844, Durnford sent fifty-two of his slaves to McDonogh's plantation to plant five and a half acres of cane.[26] Durnford was only an outstanding example of the Negro Creole planters, many of whom lived on Cane River, a tributary of the Red River. Some were well educated, lived in handsome houses, employed tutors, spoke both French and English, and were respected for paying their debts and living sober and respectable lives. They were reserved in demeanor, and seldom associated with the whites.[27]

One of the highly cultivated Anglo-American planters was Samuel Walker, who named his plantation Elia because of his fondness for the writings of Charles Lamb. Here he lived in style, sending his children off to good schools rather than employing a tutor. In his diary he wrote that he had an ideal

[25] Both the Prudhomme and Bossier diaries were written in English; the Prudhomme diary, according to its present owner, was corrected by the governess of the younger children of the family.

[26] Alexander Durnford to John McDonogh, letters, 1842-44, John McDonogh Papers, Tulane University Library.

[27] Olmsted, *Seaboard Slave States*, pp. 633-634.

Negro woman to preside over the plantation nursery, which contained twenty little blacks. She had a mild, gentle voice and was never out of humor. Walker's benevolent attitude toward his slaves was expressed in a notation in his diary, "Let the Southern gentleman stay at home and treat his slaves well."[28] Walker read widely in the British reviews and in such works as those of John Selden and Jeremy Taylor. He had a critical attitude toward religion, a low opinion of Southern politicians, and a strong prejudice against Yankees. His wealth and assured social position as a large planter tended to deprive him of driving energy and ambition. In 1856 he was engaged in writing a novelette, but there was little likelihood of his enduring the drudgery of finishing and revising it, for he confessed that his besetting sin was "literary idleness"—he was a dreamer—he did not complete literary projects, because there was no necessity for it.

The sugar planters, whose sugar houses appeared almost like factories, were engaged in a capitalistic enterprise. Consequently they were inclined to be conservative men, members of the Whig party and supporters of a protective tariff and federal aid for internal improvements. Despite their wealth many of the sugar planters lived in unpretentious frame houses. Charles Daubeny of Oxford University, who visited Judge Alexander Porter on his plantation on Bayou Teche in 1838, wrote that it was rare "for the planters to aspire to anything beyond a cottage on their country estates."[29] He frequently saw "mean dwelling houses" on the borders of the Mississippi River connected with large Negro quarters and expensive sugar houses. Judge Porter had left northern Ireland as a penniless young man and had acquired a plantation of over 2,000 acres, 160 slaves, and a fine library. Like Judge Porter,

[28] Samuel Walker, "Diary of a Louisiana Planter—Elia Plantation," Feb. 10-March 11, 1856, Tulane University Library.

[29] Wendell H. Stephenson, *Alexander Porter, Whig Planter of the Old Louisiana* (Baton Rouge, 1934), p. 121.

the McCollam brothers, who had emigrated from New York to Louisiana, were relatively poor men who became large planters. They borrowed money to buy slaves and land, frequently at 8 per cent interest, and became rich.[30] Indeed, mortgages and loans were common in the lives of the sugar planters, for the risks were great; several bad crops, cholera among the slaves, floods and crevasses, fluctuations in the price of sugar, would bring bankruptcy.[31]

The stereotype of ante bellum Louisiana portrays it as a land predominantly of large landowners, but this image is far from the truth. In 1860 approximately two-thirds of the agricultural property in the state were farms containing less than one hundred acres. In the Sugar Bowl three-fourths of the agriculturalists were small farmers. Louisiana contained a vast amount of unimproved land; out of a total acreage of 26,461,440, only 2,707,108 were cultivated, but most of the arable land in the delta was cultivated and purchased at a high price. The value of land in the sugar parishes increased 93 per cent during the last decade of the ante bellum period, while the production of sugar increased only about 21 per cent. Louisiana had a relatively large proportion of land devoted to livestock grazing, chiefly the prairie country of the southwest and the pine-belt district, where the owners of slaves were few in numbers. Between 1850 and 1860 the relative number of landowners increased in Louisiana, as in the other Southern states, so that in the latter year over 80 per cent of the agricultural operators in the southern alluvial district of Louisiana,

[30] J. Carlyle Sitterson, "The McCollams: a Planter Family of the Old South," *Journal of Southern History,* VI (1940), 347-367.

[31] J. Carlyle Sitterson, "The William J. Minor Plantations: a Study in Ante-Bellum Absentee Ownership," *ibid.,* IX (1943), 59-74; "Magnolia Plantation 1852-1862; a Decade of a Louisiana Sugar Estate," *Mississippi Valley Historical Review,* XXV (1939), 197-211; "Lewis Thompson, a Carolinian and his Louisiana Plantation 1848-1888, a Study in Absentee Ownership," in Fletcher M. Green (ed.), *Essays in Southern History* (Chapel Hill, 1949), pp. 16-27; P. S. Postell, "John Hampden Randolph, a Louisiana Planter," *Louisiana Historical Quarterly,* XXV (1942), 140-223.

the sugar parishes, owned their lands; while in sample counties of the northern alluvial districts, the cotton-producing area, 92 per cent owned their lands. In the oak uplands of Louisiana only 68 per cent of the agricultural operators owned their farms in 1850, but ten years later between 70 and 80 per cent had become landowners.[32]

Of the white population of Louisiana, 357,629 people in 1860, approximately 45 per cent lived in New Orleans and its suburb across the river, Algiers. The city was divided into three municipalities, the First, where the French-speaking Creoles lived; the Second, which was divided from the French quarter by Canal Street, where the Anglo-Americans dwelt; and the Third, inhabited by the Spanish and West Indian group. The divisions had been made in 1836 because the Creoles usually elected a majority of the council and the English-speaking group resented this control.[33] By this arrangement there was a common mayor, but each of the municipalities elected its own council and controlled its own affairs. Since this system resulted in extravagance and corruption, it was abolished in 1852 and a central government was adopted. New Orleans was the capital of the state until 1844, when the state government was moved to Baton Rouge.

New Orleans impressed travelers as a French city in America. Its architecture, however, was Spanish, for disastrous fires in 1788 and 1794 had swept a large part of the old French city away. Some of the public buildings, notably the Cabildo (the municipal building), and St. Louis Cathedral on the Place d'Armes (now Jackson Square), were rebuilt through the generosity of Don Andreas Almonaster y Roxas, a wealthy Spanish citizen. The shops and houses, with their stucco walls

[32] See H. L. Coles, "Some Notes on Slave Ownership and Land Ownership in Louisiana, 1850-1860," *Journal of Southern History*, IX (1943), 380-394, and F. L. Owsley, *Plain Folk of the Old South* (Baton Rouge, 1949), pp. 549-561, 167-170, 205-209.

[33] William W. Howe, "Municipal History of New Orleans," in *Johns Hopkins Studies in Historical and Political Science* (Baltimore, 1889), VII.

painted every pastel shade, patios, and the lacelike iron grillework of their porticoes and balustrades, preserved an Old World flavor. Patios, gay with semitropical flowers and plants, provided a touch of nature in the crowded city.

The great sight in New Orleans was the levee, a broad dike of earth along the Mississippi River where the ships docked. Here at the river bank were moored hundreds of flatboats, bringing the produce of the upper Mississippi and Ohio valleys —hams, whisky, flour, tobacco, butter, skins, hemp, etc. For four miles along the levee ships of all kinds were docked, often in five or six tiers. The number of steamboats that arrived in New Orleans in 1860 was 3,566. Because of the lack of proper warehouses, the levees for many years were crowded with the miscellaneous produce of the upper Mississippi Valley and with thousands of hogsheads of sugar and bales of cotton. At the close of the ante bellum period, however, cotton bales overwhelmingly dominated the scene. The city's commerce grew astonishingly despite the serious drawbacks of its port. The city lay seventy-five miles from the multiple mouth of the Mississippi. The great river washed tons of soil into the Gulf, making a formidable bar across the principal channel, so that by 1830 the largest cargo ships could not reach the city. Moreover, after the completion of the Erie Canal in 1825, much of the produce of the Middle West was diverted from the Southern port.[34]

New Orleans was regarded by many of the visitors as "the Southern Babylon." One of the reasons for this reputation was the Creoles' conception of Sunday. After attending Mass in the morning they regarded the rest of the day as a holiday. When young Henry Benjamin Whipple, the future bishop of Minnesota, visited New Orleans in the spring of 1844, he was shocked by the worldly manner in which the Sabbath was kept. His catalogue of the violations of the sacred day on

[34] Harold Sinclair, *The Port of New Orleans* (Garden City, 1942), Chaps. 11, 13; Wendell H. Stephenson, "Ante-Bellum New Orleans as an Agricultural Focus," *Agricultural History*, XV (1941), 161.

Sunday, March 24, will serve as a list of amusements enjoyed by the citizens:

> 1st, three companies of military were out parading the streets and destroying the solemnity of the day by their music and show. 2nd, Horse race of seven horses and this attracted many. 3rd, a duel with small swords between a Mr. Richardson & Dubeyes. 4th, a match fist fight for a $300 bet between two boxers. 5th, A cock fight opposite the St. Louis. 6th, Masquerade ball at the Orleans ball room. 7th, Two theatres open. 8th, French opera ballet dancers. 9th, two circuses. 10th, Exhibition of wax works, etc. 11th, German magician. 12th, Organ grinders playing in the corners of the streets. 13th, Stores, grog shops open. 14th, Ten pin alleys, billiard rooms, & other gambling amusements. 15th, Several parties of pleasure to the lake, Carrollton, etc. 16th, Italian Fantoccini. 17th, Kentucky minstrels. 18th, Ordinary ball. 19th, Dinner parties. 20th, Ride on horseback, in carriages, etc., besides one or two lectures on subjects of such a nature as would be only made on a week day at the North.[35]

The highest point in revelry in New Orleans was reached in March just before Lent began, when the Mardi Gras festival with its street processions and masquerade balls was held, but this did not begin as an organized institution until about 1837.

Another feature of New Orleans life that served to blacken its reputation was the institution of quadroon mistresses. Harriet Martineau showed great curiosity in ferreting out and exposing this institution, which was chiefly confined to the French-speaking population. A businesslike arrangement would be made between the mother of the quadroon girl and the white suitor. The mother would inquire into his financial resources; if they were sufficient, provision would be made for supporting the quadroon mistress in proper style and, if the liaison should be broken, for providing a proper sum for support of the mistress and the children. James Davidson, a

[35] L. B. Shippee (ed.), *Bishop Whipple's Southern Diary 1843-1844* (Minneapolis, 1937), p. 119.

young Virginia traveler, reported that to maintain such a mistress cost from $1,500 to $2,000 a year, a sum that only the wealthy could afford.[36] Olmsted described the quadroons as practically a separate class of people, "far above the negroes and will not associate with them."[37]

The quadroon balls were also a New Orleans feature, and much glamour has been falsely attributed to these masquerades. No Negro men were allowed to enter the ballroom, and the white men were searched for weapons before being admitted. Although some of the quadroon girls were refined and dressed with taste, and a few were educated in France, many were crude and promiscuously licentious. Davidson in 1836 saw two females promenading in their nightclothes at one of the balls. An Ohio merchant who visited New Orleans four years later noted that the most beautiful of the quadroon girls did not wear masks, for their charms were for sale, and that there were no virtuous women at these balls.[38]

The two centers of Creole social life in the gay metropolis were the French Opera and the St. Louis Hotel. The French Opera was built in 1816, an elaborate structure in classic style with parquet, two tiers of boxes, a gallery, and even grilled loges on the side for those in mourning. It was looked upon as the center of Creole social life, not to have a subscription being tantamont to being outside the pale of society. Patrons wore full formal evening dress. So popular were operas such as Meyerbeer's *Les Huguenots* and *Robert le Diable* that it was virtually impossible to buy seats.[39] In 1823 James H. Caldwell, an English actor, built the New American Theater in the American quarter of the city, which became a great

[36] Kellar, "Diary of James Davidson," pp. 358, 361.

[37] Olmsted, *Seaboard Slave States*, II, 243-248.

[38] William Reynolds, Journal of a Trip from Steubenville Ohio to New Orleans by Flatboat, September 5, 1839–March 4, 1840.

[39] [William H. Coleman], *Historical Sketch Book and Guide to New Orleans and Environs* (New York, 1885), pp. 136-138, 71-78, and Saxon, *Fabulous New Orleans*, pp. 280-281.

success and a rival of the French Opera. The rivalry of the Creole and the English-speaking population was exhibited also in the hotel life of the city. The Creole St. Louis Hotel was a huge, ornate structure, where elaborate society balls were held; it contained gambling rooms and the finest bar in the city. In its rotunda slaves were auctioned and business was transacted. The chief hotel patronized by the English-speaking people, on the other hand, was the St. Charles, a building in the classic revival style, where the wives and daughters of the planters displayed the elaborate dresses and jewelry that advertised the wealth of their husbands.[40]

New Orleans had a kaleidoscopic population, with more transients than any other city, at least one-third of the people leaving the city during the summer. Being an immigrant port, the city had a plentiful supply of cheap white labor. Irishmen and Germans took the place of the Negroes in many occupations. Most of the cabmen were Irishmen and the best hotels both in New Orleans and in Mobile used mainly Irish labor. Indeed, New Orleans lost a considerable proportion of its slaves during the decade 1850-60, a loss of 3,626, or over one-fifth of its number. Also a large proportion of the Negroes in the city were free, approximately 45 per cent. In New Orleans both the slaves and the free Negroes seemed to have enjoyed a freer life than elsewhere in the South.[41]

The Creole civilization was not confined to Louisiana; sporadic islands of French influence existed in the Mobile area and in Missouri. Whipple described Mobile in 1844 as a town of "about 15,000 inhabitants in the winter and 2,500 in the summer." A large part of its population was of French and Spanish descent, many of its streets had French names, and the architecture of its houses was influenced by French

[40] See Matilda C. F. Houston, *Texas and the Gulf of Mexico, or Yachting in the New World* (Philadelphia, 1845), pp. 63-64, 83-84.

[41] A. L. W. Stahl, "The Free Negro in Ante-Bellum Louisiana," *Louisiana Historical Quarterly,* XXV (1942), 301-396.

and Spanish styles. Gamblers infested Mobile as well as the Mississippi River towns, and lotteries were a characteristic passion of the Creole inhabitants. The Sabbath was observed as a day of pleasure. "The tone of society in Mobile," Whipple wrote, "is very gay and to a certain extent dissipated, although there are many here who prefer literature and its rational enjoyments to the theatre and gay revels."[42] Mobile grew rapidly as the cultivation of cotton expanded in Alabama, and at the close of the ante bellum period it was the second greatest cotton-exporting port in the Southern states.

In Missouri, the Creole influence in the Mississippi River towns contended with the rough elements of the Anglo-American frontier. There were four principal settlements of the French in the Missouri country, St. Genevieve, founded in 1735; St. Louis, founded in 1764; and the lesser towns of St. Charles and Cape Giradeau. The American settlement began with the founding of New Madrid on the Mississippi River by George Morgan in 1789. Henry Marie Brackenridge visited the Missouri country in 1811 and reported favorably on the genial and gay character of the "ancien habitants." They lived mostly in one-story log cottages built perpendicularly rather than in the horizontal style of the American frontiersmen. The roofs extended over the galleries, giving shade to the houses. He observed there a village culture without much education or material wealth. St. Genevieve was the shipping port of a lead-mining district which employed primitive methods in mining and smelting the lead.[43] When Thomas Hart Benton emigrated in 1815 to St. Louis, a town of 2,000 white inhabitants and 300 slaves, he found that political affairs were still dominated by a small class of French aristocrats possessing good libraries and reading the works of the French freethinkers, in fact being better educated than the Americans.

[42] Shippee, *Whipple's Southern Diary,* pp. 85-86, 90.

[43] H. M. Brackenridge, *Views of Louisiana* (Baltimore, 1817), Chap. VI.

"The Junto," composed chiefly of the leading French merchants and fur traders, particularly the Chouteau family, controlled the city.[44]

The coming of the Americans after the Louisiana Purchase wrought a revolution in the civilization of old Missouri. The 6,000 Creoles and Negroes reported by the Spanish census of 1799 were overwhelmed by the rush of American settlers, which by 1820 increased the population of the territory to 66,586, of whom 10,200 were slaves. French geographical names were corrupted or displaced; the Gallic Sunday with its gaiety was frowned upon by the intolerant Anglo-Americans; the American spirit of enterprise seized the territory and there were many lawsuits over Spanish grants and titles to land.[45] In 1808 the *Missouri Gazette,* the first newspaper of the region, was published in English. Ten years later Benton became editor of a rival paper, the St. Louis *Enquirer,* which vigorously supported the old French leaders and advocated the interests of the small farmers, a hard-money currency, and the admission of Missouri into the Union without slavery restrictions. By the time Missouri became a state, much of the old French culture had been erased and the Creoles were rapidly being assimilated by the American civilization.[46] When William Kingsford visited St. Louis in 1857, he saw only a few traces of its former French culture, particularly green jalousies, and the city gave little indication that it supported slavery.[47]

The Creoles made important contributions to Southern civilization and American life. Many useful words from the Creole language have enriched the American vocabulary, such as bayou, levee, crevasse, chute, bureau, depot, picayune, and

[44] See William N. Chambers, *Old Bullion Benton, Senator from the New West* (Boston, 1956), Chaps. IV, V.

[45] Harvey Wish, "The French of Old Missouri, 1804-1821; a Study in Assimilation," *Mid-America,* XXIII (1941), 167-189.

[46] J. F. McDermott (ed.), "Diary of Charles De Hautt De Lassus from New Orleans to St. Louis 1836," *Louisiana Historical Quarterly,* XXX (1947), 359-438.

[47] Kingsford, *Impressions of the West and South,* p. 34.

lagniappe, the latter referring to the pleasant custom of tradesmen giving their customers something extra beyond their purchases—an additional yam or fig or flower—as a sign of good will. The French of the Missouri country were noted fur traders; they, as well as French settlers from the North, gave us such words as prairie, bateau, pirogue, rapids, portage, voyageur, cache, gopher, and brave for Indian warrior. The Roman law instead of the common law of England, owing to Creole influence, became the basis of the law of Louisiana.

They developed a type of architecture that spread up the Mississippi River and affected the style of domestic architecture in towns hundreds of miles away from New Orleans. They made valuable contributions to the development of lead mining and the fur trade. Creole cuisine—such foods as gumbo, bouillabaisse, frog legs cooked in wine, *poulet Creole,* orange wine, and pralines—added variety to American cookery. The Creole celebration of Sunday, the French opera, the Creole folksongs, also added gaiety to the life of the lower South. Finally, the Creoles of Louisiana, although they themselves contributed little toward creating a Southern literature, provided rich material for the school of local color that arose after the Civil War. Writers such as George Washington Cable, Kate Chopin, Grace King, and Lafcadio Hearn have re-created in their novels and short stories the life of the Creoles in the picturesque Latin quarter of New Orleans and in the dreamy bayou country.

CHAPTER SIX

POLITICS AND HUMAN SLAVERY

In 1839 James Silk Buckingham, an English traveler, recorded a typical Southern scene which he saw near Fredericksburg, Virginia. He met a slave gang being driven by Negro traders from the upper to the lower South. The men were chained together in pairs to prevent their escape while the women walked with their children in the melancholy procession carrying their possessions in large bundles. The slave dealers rode on horseback, armed with long whips.[1]

This scene was symbolic of the revival of slavery, which resulted from the invention of the cotton gin and the rise of the Cotton Kingdom. The rejuvenation of slavery is strikingly illustrated by a chart of slave prices made by Ulrich B. Phillips, the historian of American Negro slavery. In 1795 a prime field hand (a young man eighteen to twenty-five years old) was worth less than $300 in Virginia or South Carolina. In 1860 such a hand was worth $1,250 in Virginia and $1,800 in New Orleans.[2] During that span of time there were fluctuations in the price of slaves, depending on boom times or depressions, but the general trend of prices was upward.

The slave trade was the darkest side of the peculiar institution. Always there had been a certain amount of buying and selling of slaves within local communities; but after the legal closing of the African slave trade in 1808 and the opening of rich cotton lands in the West, a thriving trade developed in buying the surplus stock of slaves in the upper South and transferring them to the lower South. Slave traders made individual deals with planters or attended auctions of estates and sales by the sheriff of the slaves of bankrupts. Moreover, masters sometimes disposed of slaves because they were incorrigible runaways or drunkards or had vicious dispositions. Dr. John J. Cabell, a salt producer in western Virginia, sold a boy for the New Orleans trade because he kept running away and redeeming him had recently cost $84, plus jail fees.[3] When the state condemned a slave to death or transportation for a crime, it had to pay the owner his appraised value. Some states reimbursed themselves for such loss by selling criminal slaves in the lower South. Virginia, for example, sold more than 600 criminal slaves between 1800 and 1850. The practice of selling bad or criminal slaves became so notorious that states of the lower South, Mississippi in particular, required a certificate of good character for all slaves sold in the state, signed by two freeholders of the county from which the slave came.

Slave auctions were usually held in front of the county courthouse on sale days or on days of county court meetings, but some were held in the auction rooms of slave dealers and even, in New Orleans, in the lobby of the St. Louis Hotel. Buyers of slaves on the auction block carefully examined them, looking at their teeth, fingers, and especially at their backs to see that they were not scarred by whip marks, indicating an unruly character. Slaves were often spruced up for the occasion with new clothes, their skins oiled, and gray hairs blackened.

Many slaves were apparently not moved by the ordeal of being sold and were proud of the high prices that they brought. On occasion, however, harrowing and tragic scenes occurred involving the separation of families. William Reynolds, the

[1] James Silk Buckingham, *The Slave States of America* (London, 1842), II, 552-553.

[2] Ulrich B. Phillips, *American Negro Slavery* (New York, 1929), p. 370.

[3] John J. Cabell to Richard K. Crallé, July 2, 1832, John J. Cabell Papers, Brock Collection, Huntington Library.

itinerant merchant, witnessed in Memphis the sale of twenty-three slaves at auction, which he described in his journal: "One yellow woman was sold who had two children. She begged and implored her new master on her nees to buy her children also, but it had no effect, he would not do it. She then begged him to buy her little girl (about 5 years old) but all to no purpose, it was truly heart rending to hear her cries when they were taking her away."[4] Only Louisiana, and Alabama after 1852, prohibited the sale of a child under ten years of age from its mother.

Among the various causes for the sale of slaves were the settlement of estates after the death of the owner and the foreclosure of mortgages on slave property. Thomas B. Chaplin, a planter on St. Helena Island, South Carolina, wrote in his journal on May 3, 1845, that hospitality had caused him to live beyond his means and he was forced to sell ten of his slaves. "Nothing can be more mortifying and grieving to a man," he commented, "than to select out some of his negroes to be sold—you know not to whom, or how they will be treated by their new owners, and negroes that you find no fault with —to separate families, Mothers & Daughters, Brothers & Sisters —all to pay for your own Extravagance."[5]

Nevertheless, there were many efforts to ameliorate the cruelty of the slave trade. Owners frequently stipulated in wills that their slaves should be sold only in family groups or should not be sold out of the county in which they were born. Some, when they felt the necessity of selling a slave, sought to find a humane master for him, and there were innumerable cases of masters who endeavored to unite husband and wife living on different plantations by offering to sell or buy one of the couple. Some masters who sold their slaves did so reluctantly and with the reservation in their minds to repur-

[4] Journal of William Reynolds, MS. in private possession, p. 96.

[5] Journal of Thomas B. Chaplin, January 12, 1845–September 14, 1860, Archives of South Carolina Historical Society.

chase them as soon as they could. Such a one was the Transylvania student William Little Brown, who sold his slave Abram in order to finance his education. In his diary he recorded: "Necessity compels me to sell Abram. I have told him so and he acquiesces. Justice forbids slavery and traffic in human flesh. The money, therefore, which I may receive for him I shall esteem so much borrowed from Abram. In consideration of which, I do promise should heaven prosper me at some future date to redeem him and give him his liberty."[6]

On the other hand, there were slaveowners who in their dealings with their bondsmen consulted their own interests to the limit that the law permitted. A poignant episode of the slave traffic is revealed in the diary of the Baptist minister William Moody Pratt of Lexington, Kentucky, in 1860. On County Court Day two sisters, seventeen and nineteen years old, were sold at auction by court order to satisfy creditors. Their father had formerly bought their emancipation, but their freedom papers had been obtained from their mother under false pretenses and they had nothing to show that they were free. Because of the pleas of their grandmother, Pratt bid for them. They were "handsome and active girls," and the bidding was spirited. After the minister had bid up to $1,500 for one of the girls, he felt that he could go no further, and a slave trader bought her for $1,700 and took her to his slave jail. Pratt commented in his diary: "Such scenes are shocking to our moral nature. Negro traders are the greatest curse of our society—should be driven out of Kentucky by prohibitive taxes."[7]

The slave-trading firm of Isaac Franklin and John Armfield, with headquarters at Alexandria (then in the District of Columbia), was the leading slave-trading business of the South in the decade of the 1830's. This firm had a model jail there

[6] William Little Brown Diary, June 1, 1812, typescript in New York City Public Library.

[7] William Moody Pratt Diary, II, February 12, 1860, University of Kentucky Library.

which was displayed to visitors with pride. Its depot in the lower South for the sale of Virginia and Maryland slaves was located at the "Forks of the Road" near Natchez, Mississippi. Annually 1,000 to 1,200 slaves were sent there. Three ocean-going ships were used to transport their human merchandise; slaves were also driven overland in coffles.[8] That risk existed in the former method of transportation was demonstrated by the incident of the *Creole* in 1841, when the slaves seized control of the ship and took it to Nassau, where the British authorities liberated them.

Slave traders varied widely in character and reputation. Some of them, such as Lewis Robards of Lexington, Kentucky, who was involved in constant litigation, were as cruel, coarse, and dishonest as the stereotype pictured them. The better dealers, however, were honest and courteous. They shunned the name of slave traders or of "nigger traders," and advertised themselves as "agents," "brokers," "auctioners," or "commission merchants." Because of hostile public sentiment, the slave dealers in Lexington refrained from advertising in the newspapers until after 1848. One highly successful slave dealer, Isaac Franklin, a man of little education, made three-quarters of a million dollars from slave trading and planting, married a Presbyterian minister's daughter, and built one of the most beautiful estates of the South, Fairvue, near Nashville. Nathan Bedford Forrest of Memphis, son of a blacksmith, also made a fortune in slave trading; nevertheless he was highly respected by his fellow citizens, elected mayor of Memphis, and became a feared Confederate military figure. In Charleston the two leading slave traders, Thomas Gadsden and Louis de Saussure came from aristocratic families and lived in beautiful homes on the Battery, the fashionable residential section of the city.[9]

[8] Wendell H. Stephenson, *Isaac Franklin; Slave Trader and Planter of the Old South* (University, La., 1938).

[9] Frederic Bancroft, *Slave-Trading in the Old South* (Baltimore, 1931), and J. Winston Coleman, Jr., *Slavery Times in Kentucky* (Chapel Hill, 1940), Chaps. VI, VII.

Despite the bad reputation of the slave trade, a considerable number of Southerners pursued it because of its high profits.[10] The *Directory* of Richmond in 1860 listed eighteen Negro traders, eighteen agents, and thirty-three auctioneers. In the 1850's Charleston surpassed Richmond as a slave market and had some fifty slave dealers. New Orleans was the greatest slave mart of the lower South and was known as "the Modern Delos"; it supported 200 Negro traders. In Montgomery during the period 1839-60, 164 dealers paid the license tax for engaging in selling slaves.[11] Many slaves were sold for credit, usually at 10 per cent interest. Although some slave traders made fortunes, the majority operated in a small way. The correspondence of a Virginia slave trader in 1834 indicates a practice of forming partnerships between dealers and Virginia planters for the venturing of joint capital in the business—buying slaves in Virginia, taking them to the lower South in the fall after the planters had sold their crops and had money, selling them as quickly as possible, and hiring out those that could not readily be sold until a favorable market occurred.[12]

Frederic Bancroft has estimated that Virginia exported annually an average of 9,371 and Kentucky 3,400 slaves. The receiving state of Mississippi imported approximately 10,000 annually. In the decades of early settlement of the Southwest the majority of the slaves transported there were taken by emigrating masters; but in the 1850's, Bancroft estimated, 70 per cent of those exported to the lower South were taken there by slave traders.

Prices of slaves were long closely geared to the selling price of cotton. In the last decade of the ante bellum period,

[10] Daniel R. Hundley, *Social Relations of Our Southern States* (New York, 1860), Chap. III.

[11] James B. Sellers, *Slavery in Alabama* (University, Ala., 1950), pp. 155-156.

[12] A. H. Ryland, Mobile, to William S. Field of Culpeper Court House, Va., October 30, December 11, 1834; February 1, 10, 1835, William S. Field Papers, Huntington Library.

however, a veritable "Negro fever" carried the price of bondsmen above the old values based on the profits to be expected from cotton. Men speculated on the rising market for slaves, as they do in stocks today, and prices became artificially high, partly because of the prestige value of holding slaves. A considerable difference existed between the price of servants in the lower and the upper South, slaves selling for at least $300 to $400 more in Louisiana than in Virginia. Women sold usually at one-fourth less than the value of men, but "fancy girls" sold for $2,500 or more.

The demand for slaves in the expanding Southwest and the high prices paid for them led to a movement in the decade of the 1850's to reopen the African slave trade legally. In 1853, Leonidas W. Spratt, editor of the Charleston *Daily Standard,* began an agitation to repeal the constitutional amendment and laws prohibiting the African slave trade. Three years later Governor James H. Adams of South Carolina espoused the cause in a message to the legislature. The advocates of this measure proclaimed that it would enable the poor nonslaveholder to acquire slaves and thus be attracted more strongly to the proslavery cause; not only would it prevent Virginia and Maryland from becoming free-labor states, but it would enable slavery to expand into the West. The movement was supported by *De Bow's Review* in New Orleans and by a few extremists in the upper South, such as George Fitzhugh, author of *Sociology for the South* and *Cannibals All,* who reversed his former opposition to the revival of the traffic. The Southern commercial conventions voted the proposition down until 1859, when the states of the upper South were unrepresented. Even in South Carolina, Robert Barnwell Rhett and the *Mercury* and the ardent proslavery leader James H. Hammond opposed agitating the subject on the ground that it would divide the South. So strong was the opposition that Governor Adams himself became silent and was defeated for the U.S. Senate in 1858. Most of the advocates of the reopening of the slave trade seem to have been fire-eaters, motivated by a desire to agitate for the formation of a Southern confederacy.[13]

Smuggling of slaves into the lower South increased notably during the decade of the 1850's. A slaver with a large cargo of African slaves was captured in 1858, and the Africans were imprisoned in Fort Sumter until they could be sent back to their native land. D. H. Hamilton, the officer in charge of them at Fort Sumter, wrote Senator Hammond that twenty-five had died while in his custody and that he anticipated one hundred more would die because of the cruelties to which they had been subjected in the slave ship.[14] The British consul reported to his government on May 26, 1857, that some fifteen vessels had been dispatched from New Orleans on slave-trading expeditions within the past two months. Baltimore as well as New York ships were sold to slavers plying between the Congo and Cuba. In 1857 a trial in the federal court in Maryland of persons involved in fitting out and sending slave ships to Africa resulted in acquittal of the defendants. In 1858 Charles Lamar, member of an aristocratic Georgia family, imported 420 slaves from Africa into Brunswick, Georgia. Travelers, and advertisements for runaways, mentioned the presence of African slaves in the South with tattooed skin, marks of lion claws, and filed teeth.

With the increasing demand for labor, it is striking to note that on many plantations less than half of the slaves worked in the fields. On old plantations in the upper South and even in the Southwest, often only a third of the labor force were field hands. Captain Basil Hall in 1828 visited a sea-island plantation in Georgia containing 122 slaves, of whom forty-eight were children under fourteen years of age and four

[13] Harvey Wish, "The Revival of the African Slave Trade in the United States," *Mississippi Valley Historical Review*, XXVII (1941), 569-588; W. J. Carnathan, "The Proposal to Reopen the African Slave Trade in the South," *South Atlantic Quarterly*, XXV (1926), 410-429.

[14] D. H. Hamilton to James H. Hammond, September 1858, James H. Hammond Papers.

superannuates. The working hands, men and women, were classified as follows: thirty-nine full hands, sixteen three-quarter hands, eleven half hands, and four quarter hands.[15] On Bishop Leonidas Polk's plantation in Louisiana, only a third of his force of 396 slaves were effective field hands, thirty were entirely superannuated, and nearly twenty were children under ten years of age. The new plantations of the lower South, however, bought a large proportion of prime field hands. Solon Robinson described in his journal a sugar plantation in Louisiana on which 80 of the 139 slaves were field hands. But on the other hand, Thomas Pugh, one of the great sugar planters, had 251 slaves on his plantation Madewood, of whom only one-third were effective field hands; there were 98 children and 17 over fifty years of age; 20 per cent of the men had partial or total disabilities.[16] In that day of shortened lives there were relatively few aged "aunties" and "uncles" whom the plantations had to support, since only 1.2 per cent of the slaves lived to be over seventy years of age.[17]

A great distinction was made between the house servants and the field hands. The former were much better treated than the common field hands; ate better food, usually from the master's kitchen; wore the castoff finery of the master and the mistress; and became more refined and intelligent as a result of close association with white families. Frequently house slaves slept on a blanket on the floor at the foot of the bed of the master and mistress. In the plantation hierarchy, the driver, the house servants, and the skilled craftsmen ranked at the top; also there was some feeling of superiority among the lighter-colored Negroes over their darker brethren. The "mammy" Negro nurse ranked highest among the female

[15] Basil Hall, *Travels in North America,* I, 218.

[16] Barnes Lathrop, "The Pugh Plantations, 1860-1865; a Study of Life in Lower Louisiana," Ph.D. Dissertation, University of Texas, 1945, p. 50.

[17] Kenneth M. Stampp, *The Peculiar Institution: Slavery in the Ante-Bellum South* (New York, 1956), p. 319.

servants. Many of the house servants showed deep affection for the white family in the "big house"; when the master returned from trips, they welcomed him with demonstrations of joy. The master would shake hands with the Negroes; this sign of respect on both sides vanished later. The idealized legend of the plantation is based largely on the relations between the planters and their house servants rather than their field slaves.[18]

Nevertheless, a much closer integration of blacks and whites occurred during slavery days than has existed in this century; indeed, strict segregation was largely a product of the 1890's and the early twentieth century.[19] In the ante bellum period Negro and white children played happily together. Slave women often nursed the master's children at the breast. Negroes belonged to the same churches as the whites, and joined with their masters in singing hymns. Only after the Civil War did they withdraw, of their own volition, from the white churches. Travelers recorded numerous instances of Negroes riding in stagecoaches and railroad cars with whites. E. S. Abdy, the Cambridge don, traveling in a stagecoach between Lexington and Frankfort in 1834, found that two of his fellow passengers were Negroes. The driver refused to eject them to make places for two white ladies.[20] The Englishman Richard Cobden noted in 1835 that a Southern planter brought his slave, riding on top of the coach, inside the vehicle when it began to rain and squeezed him between the white passengers, and that the Negro ate in the tavern in the same room but at a different table as the master.[21] On some of the small farms the slave ate at the same table as the yeoman farmer.

[18] Bell I. Wiley, *Southern Negroes 1861-1865* (New Haven, 1939), pp. 19, 20, 21.

[19] C. Vann Woodward, *The Strange Career of Jim Crow* (New York, 1955), Chap. I.

[20] E. S. Abdy, *Journal of a Residence and Tour of the United States* (London, 1835), II, 354.

[21] Elizabeth H. Cawley (ed.), *The American Diaries of Richard Cobden* (Princeton, 1952), p. 95.

The field slaves worked according to two main labor organizations, the gang system and the task allotment, or a combination of the two. The task allotment, by which a slave was assigned a definite amount of work to do by the overseer or Negro driver, was employed chiefly in the rice, sea-island cotton, and hemp regions. When a slave finished his task, he could go to his cabin and the remainder of the day was his own; since the tasks were adjusted to the slower slaves, an energetic worker often finished at three or four o'clock in the afternoon. The gang system was used in the cultivation of tobacco, sugar cane, and cotton fields. This system in the lower South employed a slave driver, usually one of the largest and strongest of the Negroes, who supervised the work of the slaves under the direction of the overseer, and acted as a policeman in the slave quarters. The slaves were awakened at sunrise by the blowing of a horn or the ringing of the plantation bell; then they worked until sunset. In the summer they were usually given a two-hour rest period at lunchtime. They usually received a week's vacation at Christmas, and they got Saturday afternoons off.

These gang slaves lightened their labor with music. William Cullen Bryant visited a tobacco factory in Richmond, where the foreman told him that sometimes the Negro hands sang all day with great spirit, but that on other days they were silent. Their tunes, he said, were all psalm tunes and the words were from the hymnbooks.[22] Bryant recorded a song that he heard at a corn shucking by a lightwood fire, in which jollity was mingled with a sad note:

De cooter is de boatman
Johnny come down de hollow
Oh hollow
De mocking-bird is de lawyer
Johnny come down de hollow
Oh hollow

[22] Parke Godwin (ed.), *Prose Writings of William Cullen Bryant* (New York, 1884), II, 25.

The nigger trader got me
Oh hollow
I'm going away to Georgia
Oh hollow
Boys good-bye forever
Oh hollow

The Negro boatmen and firemen frequently sang in rhythm with their work, the leader improvising and the chorus repeating a phrase. Fanny Kemble noted the natural musical ability of the Negroes who rowed her boat between the rice islands and the mainland of Georgia, but she rebuked them for singing that "Twenty-six black girls not make mulatto yellow girl."[23] The spirituals had the same sadness and solemnity of the white spirituals sung by the mountaineers. They came largely from the same source, camp-meeting songs and hymns, and they spoke of the joys of Heaven, of escapes from Satan, of the troubles of this world, and of Judgment Day. The slave songs which William Francis Allen and Charles P. Ware collected among the Negroes of South Carolina at the end of the Civil War were with few exceptions religious songs such as "Roll, Jordan, Roll," "Blow your Trumpet, Gabriel," and "Jacob's Ladder."[24] Long after freedom came to the Negroes their songs generally had a high, plaintive air—even today such tunes are characteristic of Negro singing in rural South Carolina.

Perhaps the sadness in their music arose not only from mankind's common lot of trouble but also from the ever-present threat of the separation of families, rather than from any physical abuse. The food of the slaves, for example, was usually plentiful and nourishing, but monotonous. It varied little from the diet of poor white farmers, and it was better than the diet of the Russian serfs, who subsisted on black

[23] Frances A. Kemble, *Journal of a Residence on a Georgian Plantation in 1838-1839* (New York, 1863), pp. 218-219.

[24] W. F. Allen *et al.* (eds.), *Slave Songs of the United States* (New York, 1867).

bread and cabbage and seldom enjoyed meat or milk products. On Sunday the overseer apportioned the week's rations to the slaves, consisting of a peck of cornmeal and three or four pounds of fat bacon to each. In the rice country they sometimes received broken rice as a substitute for cornmeal, and in the sugar country a quart of molasses and sweet potatoes. A large number of the slaves supplemented their standard rations by raising vegetables in garden plots assigned to them, chickens and hogs, and, on some plantations, nankeen cotton. "Bull Run" Russell noted that the Negroes of a South Carolina plantation mutilated their chickens by cutting the comb, removing one claw, or pulling out feathers to distinguish their property and prevent other slaves from stealing it. They also trapped rabbits, treed opossums, and fished. It was a common practice for them to sell their eggs and chickens to the master or to trade them in town with his permission and thus obtain money to buy little luxuries. Only one state, Louisiana, required masters to feed meat to their slaves.

The clothing of the field slaves and their living quarters represented minimum comfort. Little Negroes wore a shirt and nothing else. Men were issued two shirts of cotton and two pairs of cotton pants in summer, and in the fall a pair of woolen pants, a jacket, a hat, a pair of rough brogans, and every second or third year a blanket. The women received cloth to make long dresses and a kerchief or sunbonnet. The slaves were required to take a bath once a week and to appear in clean clothes on Sunday. Much of the Negro cloth was spun and woven by the slave women. On many farms and plantations the slaves presented a ragged and dirty appearance; but on Governor A. B. Roman's plantation in Louisiana, Russell reported, the Negroes danced every Sunday in the sugar house, and the Negro girls wore crinoline dresses and pink sashes.

Behind the big house lay the cluster of log cabins occupied by the slaves. On the large plantations these were frequently arranged along a street with the overseer's house at the end. Some planters, such as Henry Clay, built brick cottages for their slaves, but most of the cabins were made of logs or frame timber, whitewashed once a year. The cabins seldom had glass windows, but they were equipped with shutters. Inside, the furniture consisted of homemade chairs, beds, a chest, a table, and wooden pegs upon which to hang clothes.

The slaves could not enjoy much privacy. Jefferson Davis and his wealthy brother Joseph were model planters in their care of their slaves; there were 28 cabins for the 113 slaves at Brierfield, Jefferson's plantation, and 76 houses for the 355 slaves of his brother.[25] In Arkansas the average slave cabin contained only one room, which housed between five and six persons. However, many white families in this semifrontier state lived in the same crowded conditions.

Discipline on the plantations was maintained by the overseer, the driver, and the master himself. Some masters did without overseers and managed the Negroes and the plantations themselves. On Forest Rill, a Virginia plantation where Catherine Hopley, an Englishwoman, taught, there was no overseer. The master was a mild, courteous gentleman, who did not whip his slaves. She noted, ironically, that the happy slaves did about one-third the work of English or Irish laborers.[26] Edwin Hall, a tutor on the plantation of Dr. Mann Page near Charlottesville, Virginia, in 1837, wrote that the slaves were seldom flogged; the most effective punishment was to deprive a delinquent slave of his meat ration. He also observed that a slave on this Virginia plantation did less than a third of the work performed by a Northern laborer.[27] Miss

[25] Charles S. Sydnor, *Slavery in Mississippi* (New York, 1933), p. 43.

[26] [Catherine C. Hopley], *Life in the South: from the Commencement of the War. By a Blockaded British Subject* (London, 1863), I, 44-45; II, 248.

[27] Katherine M. Jones (ed.), *The Plantation South* (Indianapolis, 1957), p. 41. Olmsted, *Seaboard Slave States,* II, 65-66, estimated that the slaves did less than half of the work of a Northern laborer.

Hopley later taught in the family of Governor Milton at Sylvania near Tallahassee, Florida, and here she observed that there were few whippings of the slaves but that the white children were flogged often in accordance with the mores of the period.

Most planters felt that flogging was absolutely necessary to maintain discipline on the plantation. Bennet Barrow, who served as his own overseer on his plantation in West Feliciana Parish, Louisiana, obtained excellent service from his slaves; he was young and vigorous and whipped them often, especially when they picked "trashy" cotton. He also punished them by various humiliating devices that made the culprit look ridiculous to his fellow slaves, such as exhibiting him on a scaffold with a red cap on his head or making rascally buck Negroes wear dresses or wash clothes. On the other hand, he rewarded his slaves for faithful service by giving them frequent holidays throughout the year, treating them to a special dinner, giving outstanding workers an extra suit of store-bought clothes, providing them with whisky for a dance, and donating a money gift before Christmas.[28] Maunsel White on his Deer Range Plantation in Louisiana put Negroes who feigned sickness in the stocks, and when the gang did bad work deprived them of meat, giving them only dry bread. Many well-regulated plantations had a strict code governing the administration of the punishment of slaves. Whipping was never to be done in anger or to exceed twenty lashes. Usually the corporal punishment on large plantations was done by the Negro driver or headman under the supervision of the overseer.

Overseers were inclined to rely more heavily on the efficacy of whipping than did masters. Consequently, slaves on absentee plantations were more liable to harsh treatment than those living on plantations under the master's eye. George Noble

[28] Edwin A. Davis (ed.), *Plantation Life in the Florida Parishes of Louisiana, 1836-1846, as Reflected in the Diary of Bennet H. Barrow* (New York, 1943).

Jones, who spent much of his time traveling in Europe or in the North, left the care of his plantations El Destino and Chemonie to overseers. John Evans, overseer at the latter, wrote to his employer in 1854 concerning the derelictions of the overseer of El Destino: "When he flogs, he puts it on in two Large doses. I think moderate Flogings the best . . . I always punish according to the crime, if it is a Large one I give him a genteel floging with a strop, about 75 Lashes I think is a good whipping. When picking cotton [failure to pick a sufficient amount] I never put on more than 20 stripes and verry frequently not more than 10 or 15. I find I git along with this as well as if I was to give Larger Whippings."[29] James Tait had a rule on his Alabama plantation that the last slave to rise in the morning for work after the horn was blown should be whipped.[30]

Many masters had a high sense of responsibility toward their slaves, as the diary of Richard Eppes, owner of three plantations in eastern Virginia, shows. On June 9, 1858, he recorded that he gave a slave a few licks with a switch for disobeying orders of the overseer, in order to maintain the latter's authority. He "explained to the overseer that there were certain negroes of the estate that I never whipped for light offenses, preferring to punish them in some other ways as whipping did them more harm than good." He told the overseer that since he had had no experience in managing Negroes, he should report to him and he "would do the necessary punishment." When the dairymaid displeased him on one occasion, he "boxed Susan's jaws" and, another time, gave Jane "a few blows over her clothes."[31]

The preservation of the health of the slaves was a major concern of the plantation economy, especially after prices of

[29] U. B. Phillips and J. D. Glunt (eds.), *Florida Plantation Records* (St. Louis, 1927), I, 111.

[30] Davis, *Cotton Kingdom in Alabama,* p. 54.

[31] Richard Eppes, Plantation Journal, January 1, June 9, 1858, University of Virginia Library.

prime slaves had arisen to $1,500 and $1,800. As compared to modern days, there was a fearsome amount of infant mortality among both whites and blacks. In the lower South, at the end of the ante bellum period there were approximately 150 deaths to every 1,000 live births, or 15 per cent mortality; Negro infant mortality was twice that of the whites.[32] A pregnant slave woman worked, usually at light tasks, until the birth of her child, but it was standard practice to allow her a month of rest after the delivery of the child. When she returned to field labor, the baby was cared for on large plantations in a nursery, and the mother left her job in the field to nurse her child four times a day. Thomas Jefferson was greatly concerned by the infant mortality among the slaves on his Poplar Forest plantation in southwestern Virginia. He wrote to the overseer in 1819: "The loss of 5 little ones in 4 years induces me to fear that the overseers do not permit the women to devote as much time as is necessary to the care of their children; that they view their labor as the 1st object and the raising of their child but as secondary. I consider the labor of a breeding woman as no object, and that a child raised every 2 years is of more profit than the crop of the best laboring man. In this, as in all other cases, providence has made our interest and our duties coincide perfectly."[33]

When slaves became sick the overseer or master, or the master's wife, usually prescribed remedies. Many of the plantations were equipped with manuals of treatment for disease, such as Gunn's *Domestic Medicine, Poor Man's Friend,* Ewell's *Medical Companion,* or Sime's *Guide to Health.* In the 1850's, when the theory was promulgated that Negroes were of a different species from white persons, there was a demand for a manual devoted exclusively to Negro medicine, but the Civil War prevented publication of such a book. Some of the

[32] William D. Postell, *The Health of Slaves on Southern Plantations* (Baton Rouge, 1951), p. 158; see also Stampp, *The Peculiar Institution,* p. 320.

[33] Betts (ed.), *Thomas Jefferson's Farm Book,* pp. 42-43.

larger plantations paid a fixed sum to a physician for medical care of the slaves, and virtually all of them had a slave hospital and a nursery. Overseers on most of the plantations did not call in a doctor until the case had become serious. The overseer of El Destino in Florida described, in a letter to the absentee master, his treatment of slaves who had pneumonia: "My treatment has bin Calomill, Dove powders, Laudenum, Tartar Emetick and sault peter and flaxseed and also the blistering ointment." He was proud of his remedy for curing mules of colic, boasting that he had never lost a mule treated with his remedy, which consisted of two and one-half inches of plug chewing tobacco mixed with a gallon of water and "4 or 5 shovels of Hot Oak Ashes." He also exercised his medical skill in treating a slave, who had "come very near killing himself eating dirt," with "a preparation of Steeal dust, copras, Pruvian Barks and Salt peater and Whiskey."[34]

The most common of the ailments that affected slaves were various types of fevers, dysentery, pneumonia, hernia, and lockjaw. They appeared to be more susceptible to cholera than whites, but less so to malaria, yellow fever, and hookworm. But they were not altogether immune to these diseases, for plantation records show that many Negroes, particularly the young ones, suffered from malaria or ague. Venereal diseases were occasionally mentioned in reports of Negro sicknesses. Insanity seems to have been rare among the slaves.[35] The life span of slaves and of whites, according to Charles S. Sydnor, was approximately the same. The life expectancy of a twenty-year-old white in 1850 was 23.72 years; of a Negro, 22.30 years.[36] Southern Negroes, despite a slightly higher mortality than that of whites, increased at a rate of about 23 per cent each decade between 1830 and 1860.

[34] Phillips and Glunt, *Florida Plantation Records,* p. 163.

[35] Albert Deutsch, "The First U.S. Census of the Insane and Its Use as Pro-Slavery Propaganda," *Bulletin of the History of Medicine,* XV (1944), 469-482.

[36] Charles S. Sydnor, "Life Span of Mississippi Slaves," *American Historical Review,* XXV (1930), 566-574.

Except for the havoc wrought among slaves by epidemics of cholera, the planters were not unduly harassed by the loss of labor on account of sickness. Chemonic Plantation in Florida had thirty-three field hands, of whom thirty lost time from working because of sickness in 1857, averaging for each slave an absence of twenty-four days from work. This record was unusual. Postell examined the sick records of fourteen plantations of the lower South during the 1840's and 1850's, and found that the average loss of time from work per slave was only eleven or twelve days a year, a lesser disability rate than among Negroes a hundred years later.[37] The health records, indeed, indicate that the physical abuse of slaves was not common.

Slave labor was usually protected from dangerous occupations. Irishmen were employed in posts of danger, such as handling the bounding cotton bales on steamboats as they descended the chutes from river bluffs. Masters hired out some slaves in the 1850's to help dig the Blue Ridge Railroad tunnel in Virginia, but refused to allow them to work near blasting. Most of this perilous work was done by a gang of Irish laborers. Planters often contracted with labor bosses of the Irish to dig ditches for drainage of the sugar lands. The overseer of the Louisiana plantation of Governor Manning of South Carolina told William H. Russell that the planters usually employed Irishmen to clear swampy land, for such hard work was "death on niggers and mules."[38] Planters reasoned that it was wiser to hire Irishmen than risk their own slaves in dangerous and unhealthy jobs, for the loss of an $1,800 slave was serious indeed, while the death of an Irishman was a small matter.

Negro slaves were frequently hired out in occupations in which there were only normal risks. The building of railroads and public works was a field peculiarly suited to the employ-

[37] Postell, *Health of Slaves*, pp. 164, 148-149.

[38] William H. Russell, *My Diary North and South* (Boston, 1863), p. 282.

ment of hired slaves. They were also used extensively in the saltworks of western Virginia, the ropewalks and cotton bagging factories of Kentucky, the turpentine forests of North Carolina, the coal and iron mines, on steamboats, in hotels, and in domestic service. In the tobacco factories of Virginia in 1860, hired slaves constituted 52 per cent of the hands. So careless, ignorant, and inefficient was slave labor in general—although it could be made efficient under the right incentives and direction—that Southerners regarded the slaves as unsuited to the operation of machinery. The hundreds of slaves employed in the Richmond tobacco factories as well as in the hemp factories of Kentucky did mostly handwork that did not involve operating machines.

In agriculture the most frequent use of hired slave labor arose from the practice of trustees of estates hiring out the slaves of a plantation until a settlement was made. The unpublished census returns of 1860 indicate that the hiring of slaves was less prevalent in agriculture than in industrial enterprises and in domestic service in the cities. In Virginia, where the hiring of agricultural labor was more extensive than in other Southern states, some eastern counties, such as Accomac, reported that approximately 10 per cent of slaves were hired, but the more usual ratio was 5 or 6 per cent. On the other hand, Southern towns such as Louisville, Nashville, and Lynchburg had percentages of hired slaves of approximately 16, 25, and 50.

Slaves were hired through newspaper advertisement, auction at the courthouse on January 1, and through slave-hiring brokers or commission men. The hirer gave his bond to pay the sum of the hire at the end of the year, to feed and clothe the slave adequately, and to furnish medical services if needed. The courts decided that if a slave ran away during his period of service, the hirer, not the master, suffered the loss of time, but the death of a slave released the hirer from paying for the unfulfilled part of the contract. So remarkable an increase in hiring rates occurred during the latter part of the ante bellum period that the annual rent for the labor of a hired slave was 10 to 15 per cent of his value.[39]

How efficient was the Negro worker under the conditions of slavery? Northern and European travelers, as has been pointed out, were in agreement that the Negro did about one-third or one-half of the labor of a Northern worker. Some observers, such as Catherine Hopley, said that they had never seen a Southern Negro in a hurry. Left to themselves, the majority of slaves did as little work as possible, and the free Negroes as a group followed the same course. Nevertheless, under the right incentives, the slaves on a plantation often became efficient workers. The slaves of Bennet Barrow in Louisiana, for example, often did what he called "a Brag day's work." Two men on his plantation in November 1837 picked 511 pounds of cotton each; eight of his hands averaged 431 pounds each. One of his slaves, Demps, picked 570 pounds in 1830, setting the plantation record. The average picking of all Barrow's hands on August 31, 1836, was 167 pounds and on October 1, 1842, it was 193 pounds. Barrow stimulated his slaves to this high record by offering rewards and by developing pride of work as well as a wholesome respect for his ready right arm.[40] The excellence of these Negroes' achievement should be compared with the average of 150 pounds of cotton picked per day by slaves as a whole during the ante bellum days. Sydnor points out that in Mississippi this average was approximately the same as that of free Negro workers in the South in 1933, thus indicating that there was no overworking of the slaves there.

Obviously there was a great difference in the efficiency of slaves on different plantations. Likewise the profitability of slavery varied from plantation to plantation and fluctuated

39 Clement Eaton, "Slave-Hiring in the Upper South—a Step toward Freedom," *Mississippi Valley Historical Review,* XLVI (1960), 663-678.

40 Davis, *Plantation Life in the Florida Parishes,* pp. 78-102.

according to market conditions. Earlier writers, such as U. B. Phillips (1918), Charles S. Sydnor (1933), and Charles S. Davis (1939), have held that slavery was an uneconomical system of labor and that only planters of exceptional managerial ability occupying fertile land with good transportation facilities made much profit from plantation slavery. A considerable proportion of the planters were in debt, and Davis has pointed out that "Even the planters themselves were in agreement that a large part of the food supply had to be raised at home in order to preserve the slender margin of profit which inevitably resulted because of certain fixed charges which had to be met."[41]

Furthermore, Southerners as a whole believed that the Negro slave was unsuited to the use of agricultural machinery and labor-saving tools. Olmsted was told by a Louisiana planter in 1854: "Such hoes as you use at the North would not last a negro a day."[42] An enterprising salesman for a Northern ax company wrote to his employer that in the back country, where the population was chiefly white, superior axes were appreciated, but in the slaveholding districts "the Slave holders accustomed themselves to considering any tool good enough for a Negro to use and spoil."[43] Consequently slavery hindered the South from exploiting its man power to the best advantage through the wide use of machinery and labor-saving tools.

On the other hand, recent writers have challenged the view of the general unprofitability of Southern slavery. Lewis C. Gray maintained that slave labor was efficient, even expert, on the well-managed plantations. (But how many were well managed?) Slave labor, under the system of incentive and punishments practiced on these plantations, he argued, was probably more productive than free Negro labor in the modern South. Competent observers in the ante bellum South ex-

[41] Davis, *Cotton Kingdom in Alabama*, p. 189.

[42] Olmsted, *Seaboard Slave States*, p. 666.

[43] Clement Eaton, *A History of the Old South* (New York, 1949), p. 129.

pressed the opinion that slave labor was more capable than free Irish labor or that of the available native whites. Slavery, moreover, had an advantage over free labor in that it provided a stable supply of workers, incapable of striking. Under competent plantation management, Gray contended, slave labor had an "irresistible ability to displace free labor" in competition for rich soils accessible to markets.[44] This competitive advantage of slave labor arose primarily from the low subsistence level of the slave—a melancholy evidence of human exploitation.

A recent study estimates a life expectancy of thirty years for a twenty-year-old male field hand. The total cost for his clothing, food, medical care, taxes (only 39 cents to $1.20), and supervision was estimated to have been only $20 to $21 a year. The conclusion is that slave labor engaged in raising cotton earned about 5 per cent on average lands, 12 per cent on rich lands, and 4 per cent on poor lands. Capital invested in New England cotton mills paid dividends of 16.76 per cent in the period 1844-48 and 5.75 per cent in the period 1848-53; railroad bonds and New England municipal bonds paid a return of 7 to 8 per cent and 5 per cent respectively. Southern slavery "was apparently about as remunerative as alternative employments to which slave capital might have been put."[45]

The variables in computing the profitability of Southern slavery are extraordinarily difficult to assess. Planters' diaries and letters are full of complaints: only half or one-fourth of a crop raised because of adverse weather and pests; good crops produced, but the price of their staple too low to allow any profit. Moreover, a large part of a planter's labor force might suddenly be carried off by a cholera epidemic. Frequently

[44] Gray, *History of Agriculture*, I, 474.

[45] Alfred H. Conrad and John R. Meyer, "The Economics of Slavery in the Ante-Bellum South," *Journal of Political Economy*, LXVI (1958), 95-130; see also T. P. Govan, "Was Plantation Slavery Profitable?" *Journal of Southern History*, VIII (1942), 513-535; R. W. Smith, "Was Slavery Unprofitable in the Ante-Bellum South?" *Agricultural History*, XX (1946), 62-64.

he had to pay high interest rates on mortgages. He had to support his slaves during periods of no profit or even of loss, while a manufacturer could turn his employees off; he had also to take care of disabled and old slaves and children. Plantation slavery was affected by business cycles, the constant danger of overproduction, and the variability of world markets. The decade of the 1840's, when cotton sold at a very low price, was not a time of profit for the slave system. Southern people at that time began to turn to plans of manufacturing, or even to thinking of other crops. The decade 1850-60, when export markets were good, was a time when slavery seemed to be profitable, but it would be shortsighted to base an evaluation of the institution on this decade alone.

A comparison of the standard of living in the South with that in the North should throw some light on the question of the profitability of slavery. Slavery gave the Southern states a valuable exportable surplus, for the great bulk of the cotton, rice, sugar, and tobacco crops was produced by slave labor. It is improbable that free white labor would have produced the staple crops in the quantity that the gang system of slave labor did. Despite these rich exports only a small proportion of the Southern people lived with any degree of luxury. Travelers' writings agree that after they crossed the Mason-Dixon Line and the Ohio River from the North, they found a striking contrast between the neat, prosperous farmers of the Northern states and the thriftless, unprogressive ones of the slave-tilled country. Slavery was only partly responsible for the backward condition of large areas of the South; soil exhaustion and erosion were a more important cause, to which slaveless farmers as well as planters had contributed.[46] In 1850 the average value per acre of agricultural land in the Southern states was less than half that of the Northern states. Furthermore, the average slaveholding farmer possessed little ready cash in comparison with the Northern agriculturist.

[46] See Robert R. Russel, "The General Effects of Slavery upon Southern Economic Progress," *Journal of Southern History,* IV (1938).

In the decade of the 1850's many of the slaveholding farmers had standards of living only slightly better than their grandfathers had had. They still lived in rough log houses, with few modern conveniences, and ate the same unvaried diet in the winter months. Frederick Law Olmsted, after extensive traveling in the South, wrote: "From the banks of the Mississippi to the banks of the James, I did not (that I remember) see, except perhaps in one or two towns, a thermometer, nor a book of Shakespeare, nor a pianoforte or sheet of music; nor the light of a carcel or other good centre-table or reading-lamp, nor an engraving or copy of any kind, or a work of art of the slightest merit. I am not speaking of what are commonly called 'poor whites'; a large majority of all these houses were the residences of slaveholders, a considerable proportion cotton-planters."[47]

One of the principal reasons for raising the question of the profitability of Southern slavery is its political bearing. Some students have maintained that slavery in the South, because of its inefficiency and unprofitableness to the majority of slaveholders, would have fallen of its own weight without the intervention of the Civil War. This view of the natural demise of slavery was propounded as early as 1837 by George Tucker, who predicted that slavery must expire when the lower South had used up its best lands, an eventuality, however, which would probably not take place for forty or fifty years.[48] It is perhaps ironic that recent exponents of the profitability thesis agree with Tucker that the maintenance of profits in the slave system depended upon the continued expansion of staple agriculture into the Southwest. To support slavery's slender margin of profit it was necessary for productive slave labor to be continually transferred from lands of

[47] Arthur M. Schlesinger (ed.), *The Cotton Kingdom by Frederick Law Olmsted* (New York, 1953), 520.

[48] George Tucker, *The Laws of Wages, Profits and Rents* (Philadelphia, 1837), Chap. III; *The Progress of Population in the United States* (New York, 1855), p. 17; see also Leonard C. Helderman, "A Social Scientist of the Old South," *Journal of Southern History*, II (1936), 158-174.

declining or low productivity (such as those of the slave-breeding states) to the richer soils of the Southwest.

Ramsdell has maintained that by 1860 slavery in the United States had reached its natural limits. Since this form of labor could not exist with any vitality or significance except on rich soils accessible to market, it was unsuited to the semiarid country of Utah and New Mexico, which were opened to the theoretical extension of slavery by the Compromise of 1850.[49] Here it could not compete successfully with cheap Mexican labor. On the other hand, Gray has held that there was no prospect of slavery being curbed at this time by a lack of fresh, fertile lands. Railroads were opening up new areas of rich soil suitable for exploitation by slave labor. Slaves may have been overcapitalized in 1860, he admits, but this was only a temporary phenomenon that would have adjusted itself just as stocks and bonds that are overvalued do today.[50]

The Ramsdell thesis of the natural limits of slavery expansion seems today to be on the whole a sounder view than the Gray thesis. According to the Census of 1860, despite the ten-year-old opportunity for slavery to advance into New Mexico, there was not a single slave in the territory. Only two slaves resided in Kansas and fifteen in Nebraska territory, which had been opened to the expansion of slavery by the Kansas-Nebraska Act of 1854. In Texas alone was slavery advancing appreciably in the West, and here it was held back from occupying the "black waxy" lands of the central part of the state by lack of wood for fencing materials (barbed wire was not introduced into Texas until 1878 or 1879), the fear of droughts, and the lack of railroads. It was possible for slavery to exist in southern California, but the question of its expansion into that area had been decided by the people of California in their constitution of 1850. Moreover, the

[49] Charles W. Ramsdell, "The Natural Limits of Slavery Expansion," *Mississippi Valley Historical Review,* XVI (1929), 151.

[50] Gray, *History of Agriculture,* I, 476.

northern boundary of the Cotton Kingdom remained virtually the same in 1890 as in 1860, slightly above the Arkansas line, and had not advanced westward in Texas beyond the 98th meridian.

Walter Prescott Webb has pointed out in *The Great Plains* that although the South won political victories in Washington that permitted them to carry their slaves into the western territories, they were debarred by nature from doing so beyond the 98th meridian. That the Southern people recognized this natural prohibition of slavery in the West was shown by their opposition after 1850 to the enactment of a homestead law that would facilitate the expansion of the free-labor farm but could not be utilized by the slave plantation. Nevertheless, Southern politicians and editors made a great political and emotional issue of winning the right to extend slavery into territory which they knew was not suited to its expansion.

After a hundred years it seems clear that the Southerners were shortsighted in permitting the Republican party to define the issue between the two sections as slavery extension and thus win for itself a moral advantage. It is understandable that they should have fought strenuously against the Northern attempt to exclude their human property from federal territories by political measures. The success of such an attempt would have placed a stigma on the holding of slaves and indirectly on the Southern people, who had a supersensitive spirit of honor and pride. It meant denial of the equal protection of the laws. Regardless of the question of legal right, their insistence on protecting their "peculiar institution" by seeking to extend it into a region where it did not fit the needs of the people was unrealistic statesmanship. Yet few of the Southern leaders (notable exceptions being John Bell, Thomas Hart Benton, and Sam Houston) saw that.

As to Northerners, probably the majority of them did not understand the economics of slavery and the unlikelihood of slavery expanding into the West. Furthermore, to Lincoln and to thousands of Northerners who were conservative constitutionalists and therefore willing to acquiesce in the existence of slavery in the states where it was protected by the Constitution, its expansion into the territories was not a pragmatic question but a great moral issue. Slavery was a national evil, and wherever the people through their government could strike a blow against it, it was their duty to do so.

CHAPTER SEVEN

CALHOUN AND STATE RIGHTS

THE GROWTH OF SECTIONALISM in the nation from 1820 to 1861 is the dominant political theme of the period. Increasingly the South began to realize the implications of its minority status in the nation and to rely on State rights as a means of protection. The South as "a conscious minority" could follow several paths of development, one which led to Southern nationalism, another to find allies in the North within the national parties, and a third to seek defense for its way of life by constitutional amendments. All these methods were advocated by different groups below the Mason and Dixon line. Senator John C. Calhoun sought to defend Southern interests by strengthening the federal character of the central government, by forming an alliance with the West, and finally in desperation, by forming a Southern bloc and seeking constitutional amendments protecting the South.

Calhoun was a complex personality, not "the cast-iron man" whom Harriet Martineau described, but a flexible person who adjusted himself to the changing economic interests of the South while he thought he was moved only by a devotion to "principle."[1] Indeed, the key to Calhoun's life is to be found in understanding these remarkable changes. The supreme tragedy of his life was not the wreck of his political ambitions through the intrigue of Van Buren, but the fact that despite his genuine love for the Union he was led to advocate measures that tended to destroy it. The circumstance that prevented Calhoun from being a truly national statesman was the existence of slavery in the South. After the close of the nullification struggle he devoted his life to the preservation of this archaic institution. But into this cause that seems so ignoble to us today Calhoun carried a paradoxical love of liberty—a belief in the freedom of the Southern people to determine their way of life within a decentralized government. He was not primarily a champion of property interests; actually, he never aspired to make money as an end of life, and he decried the money-making passion prevalent in the North; to him honor was far more important, and in this aspect of his personality he was very Southern.[2]

Calhoun was the intellectual leader of the proslavery South, formulating the political theories that rationalized its economic interests. He did not originate, however, the doctrines he so ably advocated, for they were implicit in the political, social, and economic trends of the beleaguered South. Not only was he a one-man "brain trust" for the solution of the problems of his section but he also became the South's greatest agitator and propagandist for southern unity against the antislavery forces of the North. Yet a modern reader may wonder whether the oratory and the great forensic battles in the Senate that Calhoun waged against Clay and Webster in behalf of States rights were really significant. When Congressmen voted, they usually voted for their interests regardless of the scintillating sword play of words.

The young Calhoun is an attractive figure in the portrait gallery of the South's heroes. Born in the back country of South Carolina, near Abbeville, in 1782, he developed into an angular young man, six feet two inches in height, with a superabundant mane of dark hair, deep-set hazel eyes, high cheek bones, strong jutting chin, and a wide mouth. His family belonged to the Scotch-Irish yeomanry who had emigrated

[1] Harriet Martineau, *Retrospect of Western Travel,* quoted by Eaton, *The Leaven of Democracy,* 78.

[2] Francis J. Grund, *Aristocracy in America* [1839] (New York, 1959), 279-280.

from Pennsylvanian into the frontier country of the Carolinas. From his Scotch-Irish forebears he had inherited some dominant traits that clearly marked his career as a statesman. He was serious in temperament, lacking in humor, and an aggressive fighter in the political arena, but never descending to fight a duel. Chaste in private life—he never sowed wild oats—he was incorruptible in public life.[3]

Calhoun matured late. Until he was nearly 19 years old he worked on his father's farm side by side with his slave companion, Sawney. He then decided to get an education, and with all the deep seriousness of his nature he studied two years in the log cabin academy of Moses Waddel at Appling, Georgia, entered the Junior Class at Yale College, was graduated with highest honors from this New England institution in 1804, and prepared for a law career by studying in the famous school of Judge Tapping Reeve at Litchfield, Connecticut. In 1811 he married an heiress of the lowland aristocracy of South Carolina and in that year entered Congress, joining the ranks of the War Hawks.

In the early part of his career Calhoun deserved great praise. "Calhoun," John Quincy Adams wrote on October 15, 1821, "is a man of fair and candid mind, of honorable principles, of clear and quick understanding, of cool self-possession, of enlarged philosophical views, and of ardent patriotism. He is above all sectional and factious prejudices more than any other statesman of this Union with whom I have ever acted."[4] In his speeches before Congress he refused to follow the custom of his period of indulging in florid oratory and artificial gesticulation. He relied upon close reasoning, logical argument, lucid statement, and sincerity to convince his

[3] For a critical estimate of Calhoun's personality, see W. H. Meigs, *Life of John C. Calhoun* (New York, 1917), II, chap. 3; Margaret L. Coit, *John C. Calhoun, American Portrait* (Boston, 1950); and Gerald M. Capers, *John C. Calhoun, Opportunist; a Reappraisal* (Gainesville, 1960).

[4] Allan Nevins (ed.), *Diary of John Quincy Adams, 1779-1845* (New York, 1928), 265.

audience. Monroe appointed him Secretary of War, in which position he demonstrated fine ability as an administrator. He reorganized the department to a high degree of efficiency, eliminated corruption, fought earnestly for an adequate system of fortifications and a strong army.[5] One of his most admirable policies was his humanitarian Indian policy, by which he sought to civilize the dependent tribes and protect them from exploitation by the powerful fur interests.

The point to be emphasized about the young Calhoun was his ardent nationalism.[6] His career as a War Hawk has already been discussed. During the period following the War of 1812 he voted for the nationalistic program of a protective tariff, the establishment of the Second National Bank, and the Bonus Bill for internal improvements. In speaking on the Bonus Bill, February 4, 1817, he declared that he was "no advocate for refined arguments on the constitution. The instrument was not intended as a thesis for the logician to exercise his ingenuity on. It ought to be construed with plain, good sense. . . ."[7] Later, Calhoun sought to attract the West into an alliance with the South by favoring a land policy that would appeal to the West, even to the extent of granting the public lands to the states to be used for internal improvements.

One of the weaknesses of Calhoun was his intense craving to become President, but he was a man of high principles who would not stoop to unscrupulous means to attain his end. At the height of his career he received a disastrous political blow from which he never recovered. He incurred the bitter enmity of Jackson, an unrelenting hostility that blasted his favorable prospects of attaining his heart's desire. The master architects in defeating Calhoun's ambition were a cabal of Van Buren's

[5] See W. Edwin Hemphill (ed.), *The Papers of John C. Calhoun,* Vol. II [1817-1818] (Columbia, 1963).

[6] Calhoun's early career has been admirably described by C. M. Wiltse, *John C. Calhoun, Nationalist, 1782-1828* (Indianapolis, 1944), Vol. I of a three-volume biography.

[7] R. K. Crallé (ed.), *The Works of John C. Calhoun* (New York, 1853), II, 192.

friends, intent on making "the Little Magician" the successor of Jackson. The Peggy O'Neale affair had done much to elevate Van Buren in the good graces of the President and to sow distrust of Calhoun in his mind. The breaking point, however, did not occur until May, 1830, when Jackson received proof that the South Carolina statesman had favored a court martial in 1818 to try him for his Florida invasion.

For years Jackson had believed that Calhoun had defended him on that occasion in Monroe's cabinet. Calhoun had allowed the vindictive general to hold this illusion.[8] At a strategic moment in the developing rivalry between Van Buren and Calhoun to succeed to the presidency a group of Van Buren's friends devised a plot to alienate Jackson completely in his support of the formidable South Carolinian. It was a complicated intrigue, engineered by friends of both Jackson and Van Buren, especially Major William B. Lewis and James A. Hamilton, son of the famous Alexander. The ultimate stage of the plot was reached when Jackson was shown a letter from William H. Crawford, who had been in Monroe's cabinet, revealing that in 1818 Calhoun had advocated a court martial for the obstreperous general. The Old Hero was now thoroughly aroused by this evidence of what he regarded as Calhoun's duplicity. He sent the Crawford letter to Calhoun for his denial or confirmation. The latter replied in a 52-page letter, not denying the charge, but observing that this revival of an old and forgotten controversy at this time was an intrigue. The breach between these two leading Southern statesmen became public when the correspondence between them was published early in 1831. The consequences of this quarrel, based on such petty grounds, became far-reaching and tragic, for Calhoun lost his chance to become President, and possibly the course of American history may have thereby been changed.

In the latter part of the 1820's South Carolina, in common

[8] For a defense of Calhoun in this episode, see C. M. Wiltse, *John C. Calhoun, Nullifier, 1829-1839* (Indianapolis, 1949).

with the older Atlantic seaboard states, was suffering an economic decline, a phenomenon that has been called "the rural depression."[9] Cotton sold at the peak of 29.5 cents a pound in June, 1825, thus stimulating heavy planting for the next season, but the price of the staple dropped to 12 cents a pound in 1826 and 9.3 cents during the following year. It was natural that the planters should seek to find some cause for their economic suffering—a scapegoat. Instead of blaming themselves and their forebears for wasteful agriculture that took no thought of the future, and instead of considering the factor of overproduction, they hit upon the protective tariff as the cause of their distress. The tariff was prejudicial to the economic interests of the planters, but the main reasons for their inadequate returns from agriculture were the exhaustion of their soils and their inability to compete in cotton production with the rich virgin soils of the new Southwest.

The policy of a protective tariff, begun in 1816, had led to increases in the customs duties, until in 1828 the Tariff of Abominations stirred deep resentment in the South. Even before this unjust law was passed. Robert J. Turnbull had written letters in the Charleston *Mercury,* entitled "The Crisis," protesting violently against the high tariff policy and threatening secession. Dr. Thomas Cooper, president of the University of South Carolina (then called South Carolina College), declared that the time had come for the people of his adopted state to calculate the value of the Union to themselves. In 1828 a committee of the South Carolina legislature had published an ominous document of warning to the North, entitled the *South Carolina Exposition and Protest.* Calhoun was the author, but this fact was kept secret.[10]

[9] Avery O. Craven, *The Coming of the Civil War* (New York, 1942), chap. 3.

[10] The two standard studies of the nullification movement are D. F. Houston, *A Critical Study of Nullification in South Carolina* (Cambridge, 1896); and C. S. Boucher, *The Nullification Controversy in South Carolina* (Chicago, 1916).

The Carolina leader had radically changed his attitude toward the tariff since 1816. At that time he thought that his native state could develop manufactures under the protection of such a law and thus obtain a more balanced economy. But the years had demonstrated the fallacy of his youthful optimism, and he now believed that the agricultural section of the nation was being exploited by the industrial section through the tariff. In 1827 came the turning point in his public attitude to the protection, or subsidizing, of manufactures. The introduction of the Woolens Bill into the Senate brought forward again the issue of tariff protection. The division of yeas and nays on this measure was equal, which forced him as president of the Senate to cast the deciding vote—a negative vote. In New England Webster had also made a remarkable reversal in his stand on the tariff as the economic interest of his section shifted.

During the next year, yielding to the pressure of lesser political leaders in his state, Calhoun drafted an elaborate argument against the constitutionality of the tariff in the *South Carolina Exposition and Protest.* In this document he pointed out that the South exported two thirds of all domestic products sent to foreign nations by the United States—chiefly cotton, tobacco, rice, sugar, and naval stores. In return for these exports, England and other European countries sent manufactured goods that were taxed at the customs ports for the benefit of New England and the Middle States manufacturers. He observed also that the tariff of 1828, which averaged 45 per cent ad valorem, deprived the South of cheap manufactured goods and thus increased the cost of the production of cotton. Furthermore, this bill was imposed by a two-thirds majority on the one third of the population who produced two thirds of the exports of the country. He proclaimed that the inhabitants of the South were "the serfs" of the tariff system, which extracted $16,650,000 annually from them in duties, whereas the national government disbursed to the South less than $2 million annually. Thus the South was being ruthlessly exploited by the North.[11]

What was the remedy? Not secession, as the radical leaders, Dr. Thomas Cooper, Robert J. Turnbull, and Robert Barnwell Rhett, had suggested. Disunion was abhorrent to Calhoun at this time. His remedy was what he liked to call "State Veto," but others called nullification. This legal doctrine was derived primarily from the Virginia and Kentucky Resolutions of 1798, the last of which had declared that the several states had the right to nullify an unconstitutional law. The South Carolina statesman took a more extreme step of declaring that a single state could nullify a Federal law it regarded as unconstitutional. The Federal government, he maintained, was merely the agent of the states, created by the Constitution, and it could not act legally beyond its written instructions in the compact, or contract, of the Constitution. In the case of grand clashes between the state and the Federal government over a question of the interpretation of the Constitution, there was no common umpire (the Supreme Court could not be considered such, since it was a party of the Federal government). Each state, therefore, had a right to judge whether the Federal government had violated the Constitution. To arrest the operation of an unconstitutional law it was necessary for a specially elected convention to exercise the sovereignty of a state.

Calhoun did not take an active part in the nullification movement until the summer of 1831. The crisis in his career as a national statesman seems to date not from 1828 but from his quarrel with Jackson, which blasted his immediate prospects to become President. His authorship of the *Exposition* was then made public, and on August 28, 1832, he gave a definitive statement of his views on nullification in the "Fort Hill Letter" (*Fort Hill* was the name of Calhoun's home near Pendleton in the up-country of South Carolina). In this document he made important qualifications of the doctrine as expounded

[11] Crallé (ed.), *Works of John C. Calhoun,* Vol. VI.

by the extremists. He recognized an appeal beyond the sovereign state, namely, a three-fourths majority of the states —the ratifying power of the Constitution. If an amendment conferring upon the Federal government the disputed power should be ratified, the dissatisfied state must submit or leave the Union. Calhoun did not believe that a state could nullify a Federal law and remain within the Union. Even in this modified form the nullification doctrine seems to be an impracticable instrument that would permit a state to refuse to obey a national law that it did not like and thus paralyze the action of the Federal government in carrying out the will of the people.

Calhoun refused to recognize that the Constitution had changed since 1789. Actually a new concept of the nation had arisen that reduced the power of self-determination, or sovereignty, of the individual states. The framers of the Constitution and the Americans of 1789 believed that sovereignty could be divided and that the Constitution gave sovereignty to the national government in some departments of political action and to the state government in other fields. But Calhoun accepted a new definition of sovereignty expounded by the English theorist, John Austin, that sovereignty was indivisible, for the ultimate power of decision cannot be divided. This idea was wittily expressed by John Randolph of Roanoke, who compared sovereignty to a woman's virtue, observing that it was just as absurd to ask a state to surrender part of her sovereignty as to ask a woman to surrender a part of her virginity.

The *South Carolina Exposition* was a statement of South Carolina's grievances and a warning, which was considered and published by the legislature but not formally adopted. The state now waited to see what would be the policy of the new administration in regard to the unjust and oppressive tariff legislation. Since Jackson considered himself a native of South Carolina and was a cotton planter and a slave owner, the Carolinians expected sympathy and aid from him. In January, 1830, Senator Robert Hayne delivered a magnificent speech in the Senate, seeking to form an alliance between South and West, and defending the South Carolina doctrines, to which Webster replied, asserting national supremacy. In the following April at the Jefferson anniversary dinner, designed to promote the South-West alliance, Jackson gave a toast which was a sharp warning to those hot-headed Carolinians who might attempt the nullification of a Federal law—"Our (Federal) Union—it must be preserved!" Calhoun replied with a nobler toast: "The Union—next to our liberty, most dear. May we always remember that it can only be preserved by distributing equally the benefits and burthens of the Union."[12]

The first effort to call a convention to nullify, in the autumn elections of 1830, was defeated. Two years later, however, a new tariff law was enacted that continued the high level of duties that had exploited the South. The North rejected a compromise, and Jackson refused to veto. South Carolina decided that the time to resist had arrived. By a two-thirds majority the legislature summoned a convention at Columbia and voted (November 24, 1832) that the Tariff Acts of 1828 and 1832, being unconstitutional, were null and void. The nullification ordinance was to go into effect February 1, 1833, after which date no Federal duties could be collected in South Carolina ports and no appeal from the state courts to the Supreme Court of the United States in regard to the tariff was permissible. The adoption of the nullification ordinance was preceded by a bitter fight between the nullifiers, led by Robert Y. Hayne and James Hamilton, Jr., and the Unionists led by such cool-headed men as James Louis Petigru, Daniel E. Huger, Joel R. Poinsett, and Benjamin F. Perry, editor of the *Greenville Mountaineer*.

[12] R. R. Stenberg, "The Jefferson Birthday Dinner, 1830," *Journal of Southern History*, XIV (August, 1948), 331-356.

South Carolina appealed to her sister states below the Mason and Dixon line to join in this movement of resisting the oppression of the Federal government. But not a single other Southern state came to her aid by nullifying the obnoxious tariff law. Georgia, however, proposed a Southern convention. Disaster then faced South Carolina, especially since Jackson privately announced that he would hang nullifiers on the trees of the state as traitors. Publicly he issued a proclamation written mainly by his Secretary of State, Edward Livingston, declaring nullification to be a destruction of the Union, which he would not tolerate. South Carolinians then began to prepare for defending the homeland from the invasion of Federal forces.

In this crisis Calhoun resigned the Vice-Presidency and was elected to the Senate by the South Carolina legislature. His journey from his plantation at *Fort Hill* to the national capitol has been compared to Luther's journey to the Diet of Worms. Calhoun did not know whether Jackson would order his arrest for treason when he arrived in Washington or permit him to take his seat in the Senate. In the Senate he spoke earnestly in defense of his native state, but his words had little effect. Henry Clay stepped forward and offered a compromise tariff bill, gradually reducing the tariff duties for a period of nine years, until by July 1, 1842, they should stand at a revenue basis of 20 per cent. Privately Clay told his friends that one Congress could not bind later Congresses—a Machiavellian line of argument.

In the meanwhile the South Carolinians had postponed the date of the operation of nullification. On March 1, 1833, the Clay compromise tariff, as well as a "Force Bill," giving the President authority to employ the armed forces of the United States to collect the customs in the disaffected state, were passed. South Carolina then repealed the nullification ordinance, but as a last gesture of defiance, nullified the Force Act. Actually, South Carolina had won in the nullification controversy, for she had accomplished her object of forcing the lowering of the tariff. At the same time the doctrine of nullification received a fatal blow, since South Carolina had been isolated in her struggle against the Federal government. The problem of the state veto has recently been revived on a broader scale in the Council of the United Nations, where it remains as difficult a question to solve as in the time of Calhoun.

Calhoun regarded his nullification, or state veto, doctrine as a Union-saving device that would allay sectional discontent by protecting minority rights. Gradually the former War Hawk lost his enthusiasm for broad national measures and placed the interests of his section above those of the nation. After the subsiding of the nullification movement, he was aroused to a defense of Southern interests by the rise of the Northern abolition movement. The South Carolina statesman was one of the foremost Southern leaders in working for legislation to quarantine his section from the abolition contagion. He appealed to the Northern states to suppress their antislavery societies and the antislavery press. From Congress he demanded that rules be adopted which would prevent the reception of antislavery petitions by Congress—the most thoroughgoing type of gag resolution—and legislation authorizing the Southern states to exclude from the mails publications regarded as incendiary. He believed that slavery was not a national but a local problem which should be exclusively handled by the people of the Southern states, who understood the Negro and who were directly affected by the race problem.

Calhoun had a remarkably prophetic intelligence. Not only did he foresee the War for Southern Independence, but he also predicted that a civil conflict to free the slaves would result in the Negroes becoming, not slaves of individual masters, but slaves of the community. His clairvoyant genius made him gloomy, like Cassandra, for he never quite lost his early nationalism and his love of the Union, which he believed to be in grave danger from the antislavery "fanaticism" of the North. His constant advice to his section was to meet the enemy (the Northern antislavery men) "on the frontier." Making concessions to the abolitionists would not satisfy them, but lead to bolder encroachments on the rights of the South and to more intolerable insults. Therefore the proper course for the South to pursue was not to yield an inch of Southern rights. In order to protect their vital interests, Southerners must give up their party loyalties and unite in an unbreakable phalanx. Realizing that the South's relative strength in the Union was ebbing each day on account of the rapid growth of the North in population and economic resources, he warned that the cause of the South would be lost by pursuing a temporizing course. "If there must be an issue," he said in 1836, "now is our time. We never can be more united or better prepared for the struggle, and I, for one, would much rather meet the danger now, than turn it over to those who come after us."[13] A few years later, he reiterated this advice: "The true policy is to take bold ground and force an issue as soon as possible."

During these years of agitating to arouse the Southern people to realize the dangers of the abolition movement, Calhoun was not unmindful of his frustrated Presidential aspirations. After his return to the Democratic fold during Van Buren's administration, he aspired to win the presidency by forming an alliance between the South and the West. Such a powerful partnership would curb the menace of the industrial Northern states and might elevate him to the presidency. In 1843 he launched his candidacy by publishing a campaign biography he himself wrote, but he induced Representative R. M. T. Hunter of Virginia to assume the paternity of this anonymous panegyric. In April, 1844, his appointment as Secretary of State in Tyler's cabinet gave him a splendid

[13] Crallé, *Works of John C. Calhoun,* II, 486; see Eaton, *Freedom of Thought in the Old South,* chap. 6.

opportunity to win a large political following by championing the annexation of Texas, but he muffed his chance by his foolish Lord Aberdeen letter, in which he maintained that annexation of this region was needed to protect Southern slavery.

His claim to be more than a sectional statesman was bolstered by his renewed interest in internal improvements. On this issue primarily he hoped to base an alliance between the South and West. In 1845 he was invited to attend a Southern Convention at Memphis. Here he proposed a great east and west railroad that would connect Memphis and Charleston, a more appealing project to Southerners than Robert Y. Hayne's plan of a line uniting Charleston and Cincinnati. At this convention he returned to his earlier idea of obtaining the aid of the Federal government in undertaking internal improvements. He announced his doctrine that the Mississippi River and its tributaries were so vast that they should be regarded as an inland sea, and therefore they formed a proper object for the expenditure of Federal funds for the improvement of their navigation. Thus Calhoun anticipated some of the aspects of "regional planning," which as a developed program lay far ahead in the next century.

Although he had opposed the Mexican War, he was determined that the South should be treated fairly in the distribution of the spoils. Consequently he powerfully resisted the adoption by Congress of the Wilmot Proviso (first introduced in 1846), which would have excluded slavery from any territory acquired from Mexico. He elaborated the doctrine that the Constitution protected the establishment of slavery in all Federal territories. Only when a territory had attained the status of a state could it exclude slavery, and Congress had no power to pass legislation prohibiting Southerners from entering the common domain of the nation with their slaves.

When California in the autumn of 1849 drafted a constitution forbidding slavery and applied for admission to the Union,

Calhoun was greatly alarmed by this threat to the preservation of the sectional equilibrium in the Senate—a safeguard to slavery. He sought to form a Southern bloc in Congress to protect Southern rights. For this purpose he composed an "Address of the Southern Delegates in Congress to Their Constituents," which presented the dangers that menaced his section from the antislavery crusade and urged Southerners, regardless of party loyalties, to unite to resist encroachment on their rights by the North. As early as 1845-1847 Calhoun had attempted to organize a third party based on Southern Rights, by which he may have hoped to elevate himself into the presidency via election in the House of Representatives.[14] When the efforts to form a Southern third party and a Southern bloc in Congress failed, he agitated for the calling of a Southern convention which resulted in the assembly of the Nashville Convention of 1850. . . . His last days were spent feverishly trying to alarm and unite the South in order to arrest "the aggression of the North." The only hope for the continuance of the Union, he believed, was for "the South to present with an unbroken front to the North the alternative of dissolving the partnership or of ceasing on their part to violate our rights. . . ."[15]

After Jefferson, Calhoun was the ablest political philosopher produced by the Old South. His ideas of a correct government were formed very much as the political theory of Aristotle was devised, by rationalizing the status quo of the political state in which he lived. Slavery was a social institution Southerners regarded of paramount importance, and it must be protected against an aggressive antislavery movement

[14] J. S. Rayback, "The Presidential Ambitions of John C. Calhoun, 1844-1848," *Journal of Southern History,* XIV (August, 1948), 331-356.

[15] J. F. Jameson (ed.), "Correspondence of John C. Calhoun," *Annual Report of the American Historical Association for 1899* (Washington, 1900), II, 765. Letters to Calhoun have been edited by Chauncey S. Boucher and R. P. Brooks, "Correspondence Addressed to Calhoun." *Annual Report of the American Historical Association for 1929* (Washington, 1931).

based in the Northern states. The South was overwhelmingly agricultural, whereas the industrial interest of the North was becoming increasingly powerful. Politically, the South was a minority group in the nation. How was this section to protect itself within the framework of the Union against a numerical majority that was bent on using its power in Congress to injure the economic interests of the South and its way of life?

Calhoun devoted his magnificent powers of analysis and logic to forge a weapon of defense, a political theory that fitted the needs of the Southern planters. Beginning with a concept of human nature quite different from the romantic idealism of Jefferson or the pessimism of Hamilton, he held that human nature is neither black nor white, but gray—a medium view of human beings. Men are dominated, he thought, by their selfish interests, so that it is essential for a democratic government to provide protection to the minority from the selfishness of the majority. His view of human rights was based on a frank repudiation of the Declaration of Independence, with its equalitarian doctrines. He declared that men are unequal and that liberty is the reward of ability and achievement. Therefore, liberty must not be thrust upon men, but they must earn it by acquiring the ability to govern themselves. Such ideas he expressed in lucid prose in his essays, *A Disquisition on Government* and *A Discourse on the Constitution and Government of the United States,* written at the close of his career.

Calhoun's most significant contribution to political theory was made in dealing with the problem of protecting minority rights against a numerical majority. He was only the most prominent of a group of Southern political thinkers who rationalized the status quo of their section into a political theory. Abel P. Upshur, a Tidewater Virginian, in his *A Brief Enquiry into the True Nature and Character of Our Federal Government* (1840), also gave a remarkable analysis of the dangers of majority rule, maintaining that the tyranny of a majority is more destructive of liberty than the tyranny of the few. Calhoun developed an abhorrence for the uncurbed rule of the majority, declaring that the word *democrat* was usually applied to "those who are in favour of the government of the absolute numerical majority to which I am utterly opposed and the prevalence of which would destroy our system and destroy the South."[16] Although this aspect of Calhoun's political thought fits into an antidemocratic tradition, he was nevertheless a great defender of constitutionalism, an opponent of the totalitarian state, which has a modern validity.

One means of preserving minority rights advocated by Calhoun was the strengthening of the doctrine of state rights, a defense mechanism used by minorities in the North as well as the South. In support of this time-honored device, he proposed the doctrine of the concurrent majority, or of the concurrent voice. The Carolina statesman had observed the working of this formula in the government of his native state. The power of the numerical majority in South Carolina was checked by a compromise in the constitution by which the minority of wealthy slaveholders in the eastern parishes controlled the Senate, which could veto legislation unfavorable to their property interests, whereas the upland areas of the state, in which the slave interest was weak, was given control of the lower house of the legislature.

Calhoun advocated the application of the doctrine of the concurrent majority to fundamental controversies between the states and the Federal government. He held that in all great clashes between the national government and a state, or group of states, the will of the numerical majority should not be put into force unless the minority consented or concurred. He cited historical examples of this principle, such as the working of the jury system, the consuls in the Roman republic, and the Polish diet. He believed that in a nation composed of sections

[16] Jameson (ed.), "Correspondence of John C. Calhoun," 399-400.

with divergent economic interests the doctrine of the concurrent majority should be exercised in order to preserve liberty. The power to check the numerical majority from adopting an unjust course was needed as a Union-saving device, for it would cause the leaders of a dominant section to be more conciliatory and more cautious in disregarding the rights of weaker sections. In other words, fair compromise would be the basis of an enduring marriage between the sections.

The theory that Calhoun proposed for the protection of minority rights sounds admirable, but it had great practical weaknesses. His agency for the operation of the doctrine of the concurrent majority was the state veto of legislation that was deemed unconstitutional. Ignoring the function of the Supreme Court of judicial review, he maintained that a state had the right to hold up the execution of an unconstitutional law until three fourths of the ratifying states—the amending power—could pass on the controversy between the Federal government and the aggrieved state. South Carolina successfully applied this doctrine in the nullification crisis, and Northern states practically nullified the Fugitive Slave Act of 1850 by passing Personal Liberty Acts. Nevertheless, Calhoun's doctrine of a state interposition appears impractical as a working instrument of government. At the close of his life he offered another solution of the problem of protecting the South as a conscious minority, namely, the creation of a dual executive for the Federal government, a Southern President and a Northern President, each having a veto power over legislation hostile to the interests of either section.[17]

Calhoun in his later career became reactionary, rigid in his fixed ideas, absorbed in political abstractions. But his political

[17] Valuable expositions of Calhoun's political theory are found in W. E. Dodd, *Statesmen of the Old South* (New York, 1911); Gaillard Hunt, *John C. Calhoun* (Philadelphia, 1908); J. T. Carpenter, *The South as a Conscious Minority, 1789-1861* (New York, 1930); and Louis Hartz, *The Liberal Tradition in America: An Interpretation of American Political Thought Since the Revolution* (New York, 1955).

theorizing was devoted to the practical task of forging intellectual weapons to protect Southern economic and social interests. Ideas are, in reality, the most powerful of political weapons, which pass by a process of osmosis, or seepage, into the current of political life. The politicians need the slogans, the simplified dogmas, and the imaginative symbols which the intellectuals create. Calhoun furnished these ideas for his section. He was a conservative, however, fearful of the leveling or reforming spirit, and the champion of landed capital against industrial capital. He regarded the rise of Northern capitalism to dominant power in the Federal government as a great menace to the economic interests of the "cotton capitalists" of his section.[18] He believed that the interests of this minority group within the South were also the interests of all Southern people. His argument in behalf of minority rights thus broadened into a defense of the agricultural interest against the exploitation of the industrial interest, which was largely localized in the Northern states. Consequently, there is a definite link between the gaunt, defiant Calhoun of 1850 and the Southern Agrarians of 1930, who in a provocative book, *I'll Take My Stand,* fought a quixotic battle against the industrialization of the South.

The strongest criticism of Calhoun and the Carolina political leaders is that they turned the attention of the people away from progressive reforms within the state to fighting national political issues over slavery. Benjamin F. Perry, the South Carolina Unionist, was sagacious in his comment: "What might not South Carolina now be if her Calhouns, Haynes, McDuffies, Hamiltons and Prestons had devoted their great talents and energies to the commercial and internal improvements of the State, instead of frittering them away in political squabbles, which ended in nothing?"[19] The reforms that

[18] See Richard N. Current, "John C. Calhoun, Philosopher of Reaction," *Antioch Review* (Summer, 1943), 223-234.

[19] L. A. Kibler, *Benjamin F. Perry, South Carolina Unionist* (Durham, 1946), 302.

South Carolina desperately needed were an enlightened system of public schools, good roads, manufactures, a penitentiary for criminals, railroads, and democratic changes in government, such as the abolition of the overrepresentation of the lowland parishes in the legislature and of the aristocratic method of choosing the governor and presidential electors. Perry as editor of the *Greenville Mountaineer* and later of the *Southern Patriot* and as a member of the South Carolina legislature fought bravely for these reforms, but Calhoun was the dictator in South Carolina from 1832 to 1850, and he thwarted all the efforts toward progressive reforms within the state, for he did not wish South Carolina to be distracted by bitter internal fights. Rather, he was determined to preserve the unity of the state and devote its harmonious energies to fighting the battles for slavery in Congress and in presidential elections.

Today we have powerful and articulate minority groups in the United States, notably the Negroes who have multiplied from 4 million in 1860 to nearly 20 million in 1965, or approximately 10 per cent of the population, the Jews, the Catholics, and the Communists, all of whom have found their civil liberties continually threatened or ignored. Our largest and most important minority group is not a racial or religious one but the South, with its population in 1960 of 55 million people within a nation of 180 millions. This self-conscious region has through much of its history strenuously resisted outside dictation. When a strong movement arose in Congress some years ago to pass a federal anti-lynching law, the Southern congressmen violently opposed it. Senator William E. Borah of Idaho supported the Southern position, recurring in his argument to the point of view of the dead Carolina statesman. It was folly, Borah maintained, to force a law upon a great minority section, such as the South, by the majority vote of Northern and Western congressmen; and his position has recently been sustained by the Republican candidate for president, Barry Goldwater. It would be wiser, the Western Senator said, to let the people of the South handle their own local problems. The progress of education, reason, and persuasive argument constituted a better method of reform.

Borah did not perceive—he lived before the time when the influence of the United States in the world was to be jeopardized by the treatment of the Negro—that the issue of emancipating the slaves in the Old South or of according full civil rights to the Negro in the New South is not a sectional but a national problem. Calhoun spoke for the right of self-determination of a section against centralization—to him this meant liberty—but there was and is another fundamental right of the nation that balances his point, namely the preservation of human liberty. The great Catholic historian Lord Acton has observed that one truth is often balanced by an opposing truth; one can rightly act only in behalf of the larger truth. Does Calhoun's doctrine of the concurrent majority and its corollary of "state interposition" have any vital application to the modern problem of protecting minority rights? Was his warning against great centralization the voice of wisdom? The answer must be that although his means were invalid and he was wrong in the particular issue upon which he waged his fight for minority rights, his end was just. Calhoun's warnings against a naïve faith in the justness or wisdom of majority rule has tended to make American political theory more sophisticated. His contribution to posterity was to educate the people of the United States to recognize the need of protecting minority rights, which in the course of our history has often been forgotten.

CHAPTER EIGHT

FREEDOM OF CONSCIENCE IN POLITICS

ALEXIS DE TOCQUEVILLE wrote of a visit to America during the Jacksonian period: "I know of no country in which there is so little true independence of mind and freedom of discussion as in America."[1] The tyranny of majority opinion in the United States, he noted, contrasted with the free political institutions of the Americans. One of these institutions which increased the awesome power of the majority was the doctrine of the right of state legislatures to instruct their Senators and Representatives in Congress how to vote. Were such instructions binding on them, or were they free to cast their votes as their judgment and conscience dictated? The principle involved in this question was considered by Edmund Burke in 1774 in a speech before the citizens of Bristol, who had just elected him to Parliament. Burke maintained that the representative should deliberate for the nation and ought not to sacrifice "his unbiased opinion, his mature judgment, his enlightened conscience" to the will of his constituents or to any set of men. The coercive authority of instructions he rejected as utterly unknown to the laws of England.[2]

This question was also debated at length in the first Congress when Thomas Tudor Tucker of South Carolina proposed to incorporate the right of instruction in the first amendments of the Constitution. Four states, North Carolina, Pennsylvania, Massachusetts, and Vermont, had included in their original constitutions the right of the people to instruct their representatives.[3] During the debate on Tucker's proposal the Federalist senators clearly presented the evils that would flow from the practice of this doctrine. Thomas Hartley of Pennsylvania observed that the exercise of the right of instruction had been attended with bad consequences both in England and America. "When the passions of the people are excited," he warned, "instructions have been resorted to and obtained to answer party purposes; and although public opinion is generally respectable, yet at such moments it has been known to be often wrong; and happy is the Government composed of men of firmness and wisdom to discover and resist popular error."[4] Instructions, he maintained, would embarrass representatives in consultation and in the compromise of differences and would substitute the rule of the partial or local view for the broad view in considering proper legislation for the country. James Madison, who had once violated instructions as a delegate of Virginia in the Continental Congress, also opposed binding the representative by a constitutional amendment to vote according to instructions. Consequently, Tucker's amendment was defeated by a vote of 41 to 10.

Nevertheless, the doctrine of the right of instruction was frequently used in states controlled by the early Republican party. For six years, from 1789 to 1795, the Senate, in contrast to the House of Representatives, sat behind closed doors, and not until 1802 did it permit a record of its debates to be published. Finally, it was compelled to abandon this aristocratic policy as a result of the protests of southern states. The instrument that opened the doors of the Senate to the American

[1] Alexis de Tocqueville, *Democracy in America,* translated by Henry Reeve (New York, 1900), I, 267.

[2] *The Writings and Speeches of the Right Honourable Burke* (New York, 1901), II, 95-97; see also Carl Cone, *Edmund Burke and the Nature of Politics* (Lexington, Ky., 1957), 274-275.

[3] F. N. Thorpe (ed.), *The Federal and State Constitutions . . .* (7 vols., Washington, 1909), III, 1892; V, 2802, 3084; VI, 3764.

[4] *Annals of Congress,* 1 Cong., 1 Sess., 761 (August 15, 1789).

public was the exercise of the doctrine of instruction, for in 1789-1791 the southern states forced the issue by instructing their senators to use "their utmost endeavors" to obtain free admission of the American people to the Senate.[5] Perhaps the staunchest upholder of the right of instruction in the Senate was William Maclay of Pennsylvania, who expressed the Republican doctrine that senators, being servants of the people, were responsible to the will of their states and therefore should follow the instructions of their legislatures.[6]

The doctrine of instruction was elaborated by the legislature of Virgina in 1812 during the course of a controversy with the state's senators over instructions for them to vote against the recharter of the Bank of the United States. One of the Virginia senators, Richard Brent, refused to obey this order; the other, William Branch Giles, acquiesced although he denied the right of mandatory legislative instruction. Thereupon, the legislature adopted a set of resolutions written by Benjamin Watkins Leigh, a young representative from Petersburg, which censured the conduct of both senators. This able document, after reviewing the history of the practice of instruction in England, asserted that it was the indubitable right of the legislature to instruct the state's senators in Congress on all points, either constitutional or political, and that the senators were bound to obey or resign.[7] Likewise, John Taylor of Caroline vigorously affirmed the right of instruction in the sixth section of his *An Inquiry into the Principles and Policy of the Government of the United States* (1814). In approving this work Jefferson wrote to Taylor that "it settles unanswerably the

[5] Elizabeth G. McPherson, "The Southern States and the Reporting of the Senate Debates, 1789-1802," in *Journal of Southern History* (Baton Rouge, 1935-), XII (1946), 228-33.

[6] E. S. Maclay (ed.), *Journal of William Maclay, United States Senator from Pennsylvania, 1789-1791* (New York, 1890), 193, 220, 399-400.

[7] "The Right of Instruction. Preamble and Resolutions," February 20, 1812, in Virginia General Assembly, *House Journal*, 1834-1835, Doc. No. 9, p. 6.

right of instructing representatives, and their duty to obey."[8]

During the decade of the 1830's a violent struggle arose between Whigs and the Jackson party over the question of the legislative instruction of senators. The exultantly victorious Jacksonians were disposed to use their power ruthlessly, without a sense of responsibility, and they found the doctrine of instruction a ready instrument at hand for their purposes. The conservative Whigs, on the other hand, were cast in the role of defender of minority rights and upholders of the federal Constitution, which they thought were threatened by the practice of instruction. The dramatic struggle which occurred over this issue provided the backdrop for a remarkable display of moral courage and independence of thought by certain southern senators, notably Willie P. Mangum, John Tyler, and Benjamin Watkins Leigh. It illustrated the fact that strong conservatives do at times advance the cause of liberalism.

The immediate occasion for the great debate over the right of senatorial instruction in the decade of the 1830's was the bitter controversy between the Jacksonians and the Whigs over the removal of the deposits from the Second Bank of the United States and over the expunging of the censure of the President by the Senate for this action. On February 10, 1834, the Whig majority in the Virginia legislature instructed the senators and requested the representatives from the state to use their best exertions to obtain the restoration of the deposits.[9] John Tyler favored this policy and obeyed orders, but William Cabell Rives, an ardent administration supporter,

[8] P. L. Ford (ed.), *The Works of Thomas Jefferson* (12 vols., New York, 1904-1905), XI, 528. John Taylor argued in favor of instruction of representatives by districts. See John Taylor, *An Inquiry into the Principles and Policy of the Government of the United States*, ed. by Roy F. Nichols (New Haven, 1950), 364-70.

[9] *Congressional Debates*, 23 Cong., 2 Sess., 2840 (February 27, 1834). The Virginia instructions were presented to the United States House of Representatives by William Fitzhugh Gordon.

resigned rather than violate his convictions.[10] Promptly his place was filled by the election of Benjamin Watkins Leigh, a strong opponent of Jackson.[11]

On March 28 the Senate by a vote of 26 to 20 passed Henry Clay's resolution of censure of Jackson for ordering the removal of the deposits. Shortly after the passage of this rebuke of the President, Senator Thomas Hart Benton announced that he would introduce a resolution to expunge the censure from the Senate journal. Furthermore, a bitter Jacksonian protagonist, Senator Isaac Hill of New Hampshire, on June 23 presented resolutions from his state legislature approving Jackson's course in the bank controversy, instructing the senators to vote for an expunging resolution, and requesting Senator Samuel Bell to resign since he misrepresented the opinions of a majority of his constituents.[12] It was a day when partisanship knew no bounds. Jackson's personality, his program, and his methods were as effective in polarizing men into Jackson haters and Jackson enthusiasts as were Franklin Roosevelt and the New Deal a hundred years later.

This violence of faction was demonstrated in North Carolina during the struggle to instruct the senators to vote for expung-

[10] Draft of letter of resignation to the General Assembly, February 22, 1834, in William Cabell Rives Papers (Division of Manuscripts, Library of Congress). In a letter to John T. Brown, December 5, 1834, Rives wrote that he did not resign to make up an issue before the people and the legislature but because the resolutions had instructed him to vote, not for a specific law, but for "*abstract declarations of principles or opinions*" which were contrary to his convictions. *Ibid.*

[11] John W. Murdaugh, a member of the Virginia legislature, described Leigh's hostility to Jackson as follows: "I met Mr. Leigh & Jno. Robertson yesterday, they are unceremonious in the use of their terms when speaking of his Majesty." Murdaugh also reveals the practice in this period of the instruction of state legislators by their constituents. He wrote to John N. Tazewell to oppose all attempts "to instruct me & my colleague to vote approval of the Proclamation or condemnation of nullification—I'll be D——d if I'll do either." Murdaugh to Tazewell, January 16, 1833, in Littleton W. Tazewell Papers (Southern Collection, University of North Carolina Library).

[12] *Cong. Debates,* 23 Cong., 1 Sess., 1813 (March 28, 1834), 2061-62 (June 23, 1834).

ing. The chief Jackson foe in North Carolina was Senator Willie P. Mangum, who until the emergence of the nullification and bank controversies had been a supporter of the President. On December 22, 1833, he wrote to Governor David L. Swain: "The only check to an absolute power as that in Russia is found in the Senate. The policy of the man in power is to destroy that body in public opinion. Every other branch of the Govt. is unquestionably and almost unqualifiedly subservient to the will and passions of one man—or to speak more truly to the will and passions of a cabal that gives a decided direction to the Executive."[13] This "man worship" of Jackson infuriated the Whigs. James Whitaker of Franklin County, North Carolina, wrote to Mangum that there were many people in his county "who seem to think that Andrew Jackson can do no rong [*sic*]."[14] Much of Jackson's power, Mangum observed, was due to the belief that he was invincible. Judge William Gaston, one of the greatest of the North Carolina Whigs, wrote gloomily to Mangum deploring "our thralldom to corrupt and factious misrule," which he attributed to a combination of popular infatuation, the discipline of party, and the bribes of office.[15]

On November 28, 1834, Dr. John Potts threw a firebrand into the legislature by introducing resolutions asserting the right of instruction and instructing the senators to vote for expunging. In the rough and tumble of debate which followed, some Whigs maintained that the legislature did not possess the right of instruction but that this power belonged only to

[13] Willie P. Mangum to David L. Swain, December 22, 1833, in Willie P. Mangum Papers (Division of Manuscripts, Library of Congress).

[14] James Whitaker to Mangum, June 13, 1834, *ibid.*

[15] William Gaston to Mangum, December 3, 1834, *ibid.* At this same period the Virginia Whigs were expressing similar sentiments. Hugh Mercer of Fredericksburg condemned "the glaring usurpations of the Federal Executive over laws & Constitutions" and declared that "this baneful spirit of party will soon or later dissolve the union unless put down." Hugh Mercer to Littleton W. Tazewell, January 20, 1834, in Tazewell Papers.

the people in their sovereign capacity, acting through a specially elected convention. Hugh McQueen of Chatham County introduced a resolution that the people "possess the right of instructing our Senators on questions of national policy connected with their own immediate interest and not upon questions of constitutional law."[16] Senators, he held, should be allowed discretion in deciding on the constitutionality of bills before Congress.

The strongest speech made against the resolutions for instructing the senators to expunge was delivered on December 17 by William A. Graham. Graham was an outstanding leader of the North Carolina Whigs, later to be United States senator, Secretary of the Navy, and vice-presidential candidate of the Whig party. At no point in the speech did he challenge the right of instruction, but he argued against its expediency and justice. His main contentions were that the alarming exercise of executive power by Jackson threatened the independence of the Senate, that Congress had a constitutional right to censure the President, and that it would be futile to mutilate the journal of the Senate. He opposed the instruction of Senator Mangum, for it would make him violate his conscience in revoking his honest opinion as to the preservation of the Constitution.[17]

Notwithstanding, the resolutions to instruct Mangum (the other senator, Bedford Brown, was a Jacksonian and needed no instruction) passed the House of Commons December 11 and the Senate December 27. The vote in the House of Commons asserting the right of instruction was 99 to 28, but the resolution instructing Mangum was carried by the narrow margin of 69 to 57 votes.[18] Graham declared that the Jacksonian majority were first inspired to begin the move for

[16] North Carolina General Assembly, *Senate and House Journals*, 1834-1835, p. 83.

[17] Raleigh *Register and North Carolina Gazette*, January 27, 1835.

[18] North Carolina General Assembly, *Senate and House Journals*, 1834-1835, pp. 188, 189.

instruction by their success in re-electing Bedford Brown over the Whig candidate, Governor David L. Swain, which gave them full confidence.[19] The Whig newspapers, the Raleigh *Register* and the Raleigh *Star,* printed speeches of Graham, John Branch, and Mr. Fleming of Burke County against the resolutions of instruction and protested against the man-worship of Jackson by the party representing King Numbers.[20] After the Whigs were defeated on the instruction issue they tried to discredit the instructions by maintaining that the state senators who voted for the resolutions came from counties containing a minority of the population of the state by the federal ratio. The Jacksonian *North-Carolina Standard,* on the other hand, maintained that this Whig calculation was insulting to the people of the state, for it placed white freemen in the same scale with Negroes.[21] It strongly supported the right of instruction and accused Mangum and the Whigs of being aristocrats.

Mangum now had to make a decision whether to obey, resign, or refuse to heed the instructions. In the Mangum correspondence in the Library of Congress there are numerous manuscript resolutions from various meetings in the state urging him to disregard the instructions. Michael Holt, the pioneer textile manufacturer, wrote, "I hope you will not be drove so easily."[22] Only one prominent man, Burton Craige of Rowan County, advised him to resign, on the ground that public opinion sanctioned the right of instruction and that it would be politically expedient to take such a course and seek to change the composition of the legislature in the summer election, which he predicted would result in his re-election.[23] Among his correspondents was John Chavis, a free Negro,

[19] William A. Graham to Mangum, December 8, 1834, in William A. Graham Papers (North Carolina Department of Archives and History).

[20] Raleigh *Register and North Carolina Gazette,* December 2, 16, 23, 1834, January 27, 1835.

[21] Raleigh *North-Carolina Standard,* January 9, 1835.

[22] Michael Holt to Mangum, December 13, 1834, in Mangum Papers.

[23] Burton Craige to Mangum, January 21, 1835, *ibid.*

who had taught Mangum in a white private school. Chavis bitterly opposed both expunging and the abolitionists.[24]

In two letters to William A. Graham, December 16 and 17, Mangum revealed the inner conflict of his mind over the dilemma presented by the instructions. He declared that were he to consult his pride or his desire to recover his wrecked popularity he would resign instantly. However, regarding the Senate as the only barrier to the virtually absolute power of the Executive, he believed that if he resigned he would give countenance to the perversion of the spirit of the Constitution. The doctrine of instruction, he pointed out, was being used to reduce office in the Senate to a mere tenancy at will and by mining and sapping to convert the Senate to a less stable branch of the legislature than the House of Representatives. If he yielded to the popular infatuation, he would be lacking in moral courage. Therefore, he announced that he had no intention to resign to the present legislature.[25]

In addition to this high moral ground he gave a political reason for refusing to resign: "If I resign Jackson will be able to command the Senate in the *next* Congress—if I stand firmly the opposition will continue in the ascendancy in the *next* Congress."[26] He observed that Senators Gabriel Moore of Alabama and John Black of Mississippi would probably be placed in the same predicament in which he was and that his course would be decisive of their action. They had declared to him that it would be impossible for them to withstand the storm if he yielded. On March 3, 1835, in presenting the instructions of the North Carolina legislature to the Senate, he announced that he would disregard them. He maintained that the legislature had no right to require him to become the instrument of his own degradation.[27]

The Alabama resolutions instructing the senators to vote for

[24] John Chavis to Mangum, April 4, 1836, February 1, 1837, *ibid.*
[25] Mangum to Graham, December 16, 17, 1834, in Graham Papers.
[26] *Id.* to *id.*, December 17, 1834, *ibid.*
[27] *Cong. Debates,* 23 Cong., 2 Sess., 722 (March 3, 1835).

expunging, presented by Senator William R. King on January 28, 1835, touched off an acrimonious debate in the Senate on the subject. A month previously Mangum had written: "Gov. [Senator] Moore of Ala. has this morning recd intelligence of the resolutions having passed the Ala. legislature by so large a majority that the firmness of his friends at home is much shaken; & he in turn is so deeply shaken in his purpose that I think his resignation at the close of this session exceedingly probable."[28] Mangum expressed the gloomy thought that if there should be a general yielding by the Whig senators, "the power of resistance in the Senate would be lost and it will settle practically the Constitution in the South." When Senator King, a Jacksonian, introduced the resolutions of his state in the Senate, and announced that he felt bound to obey them, his colleague, Gabriel Moore, refused to obey. Although Moore acknowledged the right of instruction by the legislature on all questions of policy and the obligation of the senator to obey, he declared that on subjects involving constitutional questions he felt himself not bound by instructions but "by higher and paramount obligations due to his conscience."[29] King yielded to Benton the honor of introducing the expunging resolution, which the latter did on February 18.[30] Calhoun, Clay, George Poindexter of Mississippi, Leigh, and Alexander Porter of Louisiana made bitter attacks on these resolutions which they regarded as stultifying the Senate.

In Virginia the storm center in the fight over instruction and expunging was Benjamin Watkins Leigh. The Virginia legislature was scheduled to choose a senator for the regular term of six years early in 1835, and Leigh was the candidate of the Whigs. The Democrats, under the lead of the veteran editor, Thomas Ritchie of the Richmond *Enquirer,* engaged in a feverish campaign to defeat Leigh and restore Rives by

[28] Mangum to Graham, December 28, 1834, in Graham Papers.
[29] *Cong. Debates,* 23 Cong., 2 Sess., 256 (January 28, 1835).
[30] Thomas Hart Benton, *Thirty Years' View . . . from 1820 to 1850* (2 vols., New York, 1854), I, 524-50.

starting a movement in the counties to instruct their representatives in the legislature to defeat the aristocrat, Leigh.[31] Leigh won by the narrow margin of 85 to 81 votes in a joint ballot of both houses of the legislature. The administration Democrats claimed that Rives had been defeated by the flagrant violation of instructions. Some representatives, they charged, ignored the mandate of a majority of signatures of voters in the county by "swelling" the number of voters and then claiming that the list of signatures did not represent a majority.[32]

It is surprising that a man of Leigh's haughty personality could win high office in Virginia, for he was never popular, particularly in western Virginia.[33] Small in stature, "of striking manly beauty, with hair of silky, soft, chestnut brown, floating in curls," and gray eyes, he was distinctly a patrician in appearance. His voice was "soft, clear, flute-like . . . a murmuring music," and his mannerisms, according to Henry A. Wise, always excited sympathy for his infirmity, a short leg, for which he compensated by wearing a cork on the sole of his shoe.[34] Leigh was a man of commanding intellect, a very able lawyer, cultivated, and master of a style "equal to that of the Elizabethan age of English literature."[35] In the

[31] State Senator Thomas P. Atkinson resigned December 26, 1834, because he could not conscientiously obey instructions of the people of Mecklenburg and Halifax counties to aid in the elevation to the United States Senate of Rives, "an avowed advocate of the Proclamation and Protest." Virginia General Assembly, *Senate Journal*, 1834-1835, p. 39. See also H. H. Simms, *The Rise of the Whigs in Virginia, 1824-1840* (Richmond, 1929), 94.

[32] Alex. Brown to Rives, January 9, 1835; Jno. L. Anderson to Rives, January 30, 1835; A. B. Davies to Rives, February 6, 1835, in Rives Papers.

[33] For a brief biographical account of Leigh, published two years after his death, see *Southern Literary Messenger* (Richmond, 1838-1864), XVII (1851), 123-27, 148-49.

[34] Henry A. Wise, *Seven Decades of the Union* (Philadelphia, 1876), 139-42.

[35] Quoted by Claude G. Bowers, *The Party Battles of the Jackson Period* (Boston, 1922), 321.

Virginia constitutional convention of 1829-1830 he had been one of the leaders of the conservatives. Working for the selfish economic interests of the eastern slaveholders, he had opposed granting fair representation in the legislature to the West and the expansion of the suffrage. During the convention he had made a statement which caused him to be burned in effigy in the West and which plagued him in his later political career. He compared the farmers beyond the Blue Ridge to peasantry who occupied the same position in Virginia's economy as the slaves of the East, and he boldly asserted that those who depended on their daily labor for subsistence could never enter into political affairs.[36] Indeed, he looked with disdain upon the Jackson rabble, its electioneering methods, its elevation of mediocre men into office, and its disregard of constitutions.

The Democrats ardently wished to retire this exponent of aristocratic doctrines from his office as senator. Their victory in the spring elections of 1835 gave them control of the legislature. In the following February they used their recently acquired majority to force through the legislature resolutions instructing the senators, Tyler and Leigh, to vote for Benton's expunging measure. Declaring that it was the solemn duty of the legislature "to re-assert" the right of instruction, they passed the resolution declaratory of the principle of instruction by a vote of 114 to 14 in the House of Delegates.[37] Governor Littleton W. Tazewell, however, refused to forward the instructions to Virginia's senators on the ground that they were "a palpable violation of the Constitution."[38]

Both Tyler and Leigh were uncompromisingly opposed to

[36] Charles H. Ambler, *Sectionalism in Virginia from 1776 to 1861* (Chicago, 1910), Chap. V; Simms, *Rise of the Whigs in Virginia*, 38-39.

[37] Virginia General Assembly, *House Journal*, 1835-1836, p. 111.

[38] Rebecca S. Luttrell, "The Campaign to Expunge the Resolution of Censure, 1834-1842" (M.A. thesis, University of North Carolina). See also Charles H. Ambler, *Thomas Ritchie: A Study in Virginia Politics* (Richmond, 1913), 178.

carrying out the instructions of the legislature, which were really designed to vacate their offices and make way for the election of Jackson men. Most Whigs desired that the two senators should act in unity, but Tyler and Leigh chose different courses in responding to the legislative mandate. According to Leigh, Senator William C. Preston of South Carolina, a native Virginian, jealous because of "a notion he has that there is some rivalry between us as to reputation for oratory," began an intrigue to persuade Tyler to resign and thus discredit Leigh, who had no intention of resigning.[39] In this crisis the Whig leaders gave him conflicting advice. John Hampden Pleasants, powerful editor of the Richmond *Whig*, urged him to resign for political expediency.[40] The Washington *Globe*, spokesman for Jackson, insinuated that a motive for Tyler's resignation was to offer "a small oblation in order to be candidate for Vice President."[41]

Tyler was so devoted to consistency of political conduct that at times he turned a virtue into a vice.[42] The fact that he had in 1811 introduced a motion to censure the Virginia senators for their cavalier attitude to legislative instructions had great weight with him on this occasion. On February 19, 1836, he sent his resignation to the legislature. His letter reaffirmed his belief in the right of legislative instruction. Since he could not obey the instruction to vote for expunging without in his opinion violating the Constitution, he felt obliged to offer his resignation. He declared that he would not resign for every difference of opinion between himself and the legislature but that he would not hold office for an

[39] Leigh to Littleton W. Tazewell, February 18, 1836, in Tazewell Papers. Henry A. Wise offered another explanation for the refusal of Leigh to resign, namely that Leigh had earlier advised Mangum not to resign. Wise, *Seven Decades*, 140.

[40] Lyon G. Tyler, *The Letters and Times of the Tylers* (2 vols., Richmond, 1884-1885), I, 525-27.

[41] Washington *Globe*, March 1, 1836.

[42] Oliver P. Chitwood, *John Tyler, Champion of the Old South* (New York, 1939), Chap. X.

hour against the settled wishes of his constituents. He observed, however, that the right of instruction might degenerate into an engine of faction, an instrument of the outs to get in office.[43] Tyler's resignation gave the Jackson men in the legislature the opportunity to return Rives to the Senate on March 3, 1836.

Seven months before the legislature had passed the resolutions of instruction, Leigh had anticipated the event and had determined neither to obey nor resign. "I will not be instructed out of my seat," he wrote Tyler. "I will not obey instructions which shall require me to vote for a gross violation of the Constitution."[44] After the instructions arrived, he wrote to Tazewell: "I have refrained from all correspondence with the members of our Assembly; because I was resolved that no man should be committed, in any way, to share my fate and sacrifice their [*sic*] political hopes by sustaining me."[45] The Richmond *Enquirer* taunted the political-minded Whigs for changing their opinions in regard to obeying instructions. The editor of the Richmond *Whig*, it observed, belonged to the Resigning School now; with an eye on the polls in April, he was eager for Leigh to resign.[46]

On March 2 Leigh wrote a letter to the legislature explaining his recalcitrant position on obeying instructions. He announced that although he adhered to the right of instruction as stated by the Virginia resolutions of 1812 of which he himself had been the author, he had stipulated in those resolutions that a senator was not bound to obey instructions which required him to violate the Constitution or commit an act of moral turpitude. He could not vote for the expunging resolution, for he regarded it as a clear violation of the Constitution. At

[43] Virginia General Assembly, *House Journal*, 1835-1836, pp. 171-75; and Doc. No. 49.

[44] Tyler, *Letters and Times of the Tylers*, I, 523.

[45] Leigh to Littleton W. Tazewell, February 18, 1836, in Tazewell Papers.

[46] Richmond *Enquirer*, March 3, 1836.

the same time he believed that his duty forbade him to resign. The real motive, he observed, behind the instructions was to instruct him out of his seat in the Senate. If he yielded, he would aid in the establishment of a pernicious practice by which the tenure of the senatorial term of office would be changed from six years to tenure at the pleasure of the legislature. The doctrine which the Jacksonian party wished to impose, he declared, was that the senator "has no right to exercise his own judgment at all, or consult his own conscience; he is not in this case a moral agent."[47] The abuse of the right of instruction, he also pointed out, would give a President who was checked by senatorial opposition an incentive to intervene in state politics and by using the patronage to secure the removal of his opponents in the Senate.

Leigh realized that it would be expedient for him to resign since most Virginians believed in the right of instruction. Nevertheless, he felt that he must "signalize his resistance to unconstitutional instructions" by remaining at his post in the Senate.[48] Thus he deliberately sacrificed his political career to maintain his principles inviolate. On April 4 he made a powerful speech in the Senate against the adoption of the expunging resolution and the surrender to party spirit. Three months later he resigned for personal reasons but reaffirmed his views on instruction. On December 31 the legislature condemned Leigh's letter of March 2 as "sophistical and unsatisfactory" and reasserted that it was the duty of a senator to obey instruction or resign.[49] After Leigh's defiance of popular opinion on this occasion, he never afterwards held political office except from 1839 to 1841 when he served as reporter of the Supreme Court of Appeals in Virginia.

The fate of the Whig senators in the South who opposed Jackson in the expunging controversy was far from happy.

[47] Virginia General Assembly, *House Journal,* 1835-1836, pp. 186-94; and Doc. No. 50.

[48] *Ibid.,* Doc. No. 50, pp. 8-9.

[49] *Ibid.,* 256-57.

Senator Willie P. Mangum resigned his seat in November, 1836, after North Carolina had elected another Democratic legislature.[50] Alexander Porter, Whig senator from Louisiana, who had delivered a long speech against expunging, followed a somewhat similar course by resigning voluntarily in 1836 after a Democratic legislature had been elected.[51] The bitter, vituperative George Poindexter of Mississippi was defeated for re-election by Robert J. Walker. The legislature of Alabama tried to recall Gabriel Moore by passing resolutions requesting him to resign because of his opposition to Jackson policies, but he refused to do so, filling out his term until 1837.[52] The fight of the anti-Jackson senators against legislative instruction to expunge the censure of the President was a powerful force in the growth of the Whig party in the South.[53]

The use of the doctrine of legislative instruction was not confined to the southern states. Both New Jersey and Ohio instructed their senators to support Jacksonian policies, but Senators Samuel L. Southard and Thomas Ewing from those states proved "recreant" to the doctrine of obedience to instruction. The legislature of New York on January 26, 1835, ordered the senators from that state to vote for expunging the censure of Jackson in the manner indicated by the Virginia legislature, namely, "by causing black lines to be drawn around the resolution in the original manuscript journal, and these words plainly written across the face of the said resolution and entry: 'Expunged by order of the senate of the United

[50] For Mangum's career as a Whig leader, see Joseph G. deR. Hamilton, *Party Politics in North Carolina, 1835-1860* (Durham, 1916), 32-33, 41-42.

[51] Wendell H. Stephenson, *Alexander Porter, Whig Planter of Old Louisiana* (Baton Rouge, 1934), 97-100.

[52] *Niles' Weekly Register* (Baltimore, 1811-1849), XLVII (January 10, 1835), 317.

[53] Professor A. C. Cole in his study of *The Whig Party in the South* (Washington, 1913) devotes little attention to the significance of the expunging controversy in developing the Whig party in the South; for recent studies, see Paul Murray, *The Whig Party in Georgia, 1825-1853* (Chapel Hill, 1948), and Clement Eaton, *A History of the Old South* (New York, 1949), Chap. XIII.

States.' "[54] The Vermont legislature two years later instructed the senators and requested the representatives from the state to present antislavery resolutions to Congress and to work toward their fulfillment.[55]

The practice of instructions in the 1830's constituted a standing invitation to the President to intervene in state politics and purge his opponents, as was illustrated in the history of instruction in Tennessee. Senator Hugh Lawson White was conscientiously opposed to expunging although he was willing to vote to repeal or rescind the Senate vote of censure without mutilating the Senate journal. Accordingly, when a Jackson supporter, Joseph C. Guild, introduced a resolution to instruct the senators to vote to expunge, the friends of Judge White, regarding this resolution as an effort to expunge Judge White from his seat in the Senate, bitterly opposed it.[56] President Jackson urged his lieutenants in the state to promote meetings in the counties for the purpose of instructing the representatives to the legislature to vote for instructions to the senators to expunge. The "Old Hero" did not scruple to draft resolutions instructing the Tennessee senators to vote for expunging and to send them to Governor William Carroll to present to the legislature.[57] Thus he hoped to prevent the re-election of Senator White, who had become independent of executive dictation. But the legislature tabled the instructing resolutions and later re-elected White.[58]

The practice of instructions proved to be a double-edged

[54] J. M. Mathews and C. A. Berdahl, *Documents and Readings in American Government* (New York, 1930), 324.

[55] United States Congress, *Senate Journal,* 25 Cong., 2 Sess., 144.

[56] The Nashville *Republican,* February 25, 1836, declared that Jackson used his frank freely to influence the adoption of expunging resolutions. The Nashville *Union,* September 18, 30, and November 24, 1835, on the other hand, urged the legislature to pass the instructing resolutions. See also J. C. Guild, *Old Times in Tennessee* (Nashville, 1878), 145-54.

[57] Andrew Jackson to James K. Polk, August 13, 1835, in John Spencer Basset (ed.), *Correspondence of Andrew Jackson* (6 vols., Washington, 1926-1935), V, 18.

[58] Joseph H. Parks, *John Bell of Tennessee* (Baton Rouge, 1950), 109-11.

sword. In January, 1838, the Whig majority in the Tennessee legislature, for example, tried to drive the old Jackson war-horse, Felix Grundy, from his seat in the Senate by instructing him to vote against the Sub-Treasury scheme of Van Buren.[59] Grundy turned the tables on his opponents, however, by obeying instructions and throwing the responsibility of his act upon the legislature.[60] In a delightful letter of irony, written February 6, 1838, he observed "You, by your instructions, have taken upon yourselves the responsibility of the vote I am required to give, and I am relieved from it. The people will look to you as the principal and to me merely as the agent, in performing an act expressly required by those in whom I recognize the right to instruct."[61] During the next year the Democrats won control of the legislature and instructed the Whig senators, Hugh Lawson White and Ephraim H. Foster (Grundy had in the meantime resigned to become Attorney General of the United States), to vote for Van Buren's Sub-Treasury Bill, in effect forcing them to resign. Foster resigned almost immediately after the passage of the instructing resolutions, and Grundy was re-elected to fill the vacancy. White, however, postponed his resignation until January 14, 1840, when the Sub-Treasury bill was introduced in the Senate. Thus, the doctrine of legislative instruction developed virtually into a form of recall of senators, anticipating the Progressive Movement for the recall in the early twentieth century.

The driving of such a venerable and eminent senator as Hugh Lawson White from his office by the instrument of instructions undoubtedly contributed toward discrediting its use in Tennessee. White was a republican of the old school, noted for his independence of mind and his incorruptible

[59] Tennessee General Assembly, *House Journal,* 1837-1838, pp. 402-403, 515-18; the resolution passed January 23 by a vote of 39 to 19.

[60] Joseph H. Parks, *Felix Grundy, Champion of Democracy* (University, La., 1940), 309-17.

[61] *Niles' Weekly Register,* LIV (March 10, 1838), 20-21.

virtue. Although he sincerely believed in the right of the legislature to instruct and the obligation of a senator to obey or resign, he felt keenly that by the abuse of instructions he had been sacrificed on the altar of his principles. In the Senate he gave his "swan song" reaffirming his principles, and at a farewell dinner he bitterly condemned "that monster, party spirit," which had banished him from the service of his country because he would not recant his principles.[62] For thirty-eight years White had been in public service, and now his abrupt dismissal by the partisan use of instruction was shocking to many in Tennessee who loved and respected him.

In the same year of White's instruction the Whig majority in the North Carolina legislature passed some resolutions hostile to Van Buren's administration and condemning the expunging resolution of 1837. The Democratic senators of the state, Bedford Brown and Robert Strange, refused either to carry out the will of the legislature or to resign. They declared that they regarded resolutions of the legislature which did not explicitly instruct them as advisory only.[63] Senator Henry Clay, on the other hand, maintained that the North Carolina senators should carry out the intent of the legislature without quibbling over technical terms. As for his own position, he stated that he supported the doctrine of instruction "as it stood in 1798," namely that the representative should vote in matters of expediency but not on questions of constitutionality in accordance with the will of his constituents.[64] Yet Clay's record on instructions was variable and

[62] The instructing resolutions were not presented by White until January 13, 1840; the resolutions and a brief summary of his farewell remarks are found in *Cong. Globe*, 26 Cong., 1 Sess., 116-17 (January 16, 1840); N. N. Scott (ed.), *A Memoir of Hugh Lawson White* (Philadelphia, 1856), 397; and L. P. Gresham, *The Public Career of Hugh Lawson White* (Nashville, 1945). See also Powell Moore, "James K. Polk: Tennessee Politician," in *Journal of Southern History*, XVII (1951), 502-503; C. G. Sellers, *James K. Polk, Jacksonian* (Princeton, 1957), 382-85.

[63] *Cong. Globe*, 25 Cong., 3 Sess., 109-12 (January 14, 1839).

[64] Calvin Colton, *The Life, Correspondence, and Speeches of Henry Clay* (6 vols., New York, 1864), VI, 134-38.

inconsistent; he had advised the Kentucky representatives in Congress in 1825 to disregard their instructions and vote for John Quincy Adams for President. In 1842, shortly before he retired from the Senate, the House of Representatives of Kentucky instructed the senators to vote for the repeal of the General Bankruptcy Law which had been recently enacted. Instead of following instructions, the great Whig senator took the opposite course, making a speech in favor of retaining the law; but Congress repealed it, nevertheless.[65]

One of the most independent senators from the slave states who defied legislative instructions was Thomas Hart Benton, senator from Missouri from 1821 to 1851. Benton had many objectionable traits—he was egotistic, bombastic, and given to long and boring speeches in the Senate—but he was courageous, devoted to the interests of the West and the common man, and opposed to the extension of slavery into the free territory of the West.[66] In 1834-37 he led the fight in Congress to expunge the censure of President Jackson from the Senate Journal, during which he upheld the right of instruction.[67] Yet when the two-edged sword of instruction was turned against him, as in 1849 after the legislature had passed the "Jackson Resolutions" ordering the Missouri senators to support the extreme pro-Southern position of Calhoun on the extension of slavery into the territories, he refused to obey.[68] A free-soiler by conviction, he could not obey these instructions without violating his conscience. Instead, he appealed to the people of Missouri to support his position. In a strenuous campaign across Missouri, he denounced the "Jackson Resolu-

[65] *Journal of the House of Representatives of the Commonwealth of Kentucky*, 1841-2 (Frankfort, 1841), 61-63; "On a General Bankrupt Law," in Senate Jan. 17, 1842; Colton, *Clay*, VI, 296-300; Clement Eaton, *Henry Clay and the Art of American Politics* (Boston, 1957), 151.

[66] See William N. Chambers, *Old Bullion Benton* (Boston, 1956).

[67] Benton, *Thirty Years' View*, I, 524, 529, 531.

[68] *Congressional Globe*, 31 Cong., 1 Sess. Vol. XXI, Part I, 97-98. Jan. 8, 1850, Resolutions of Instruction presented by Senator David Atchison. Benton replied that they did not represent the will of the people.

tions" and the pro-slavery group headed by Claiborne F. Jackson and Senator David Atchison, who he believed were trying to instruct him out of his seat in the Senate. His defiance of instruction and his brave fight against slavery extension, however, was not only in vain, but the legislature also selected a pro-slavery Whig to take his place in the Senate.

Mandatory legislative instruction was practiced most frequently in the Southern states, but it was also exercised on occasions by Northern legislatures. In 1834 James Buchanan expressed a view of the binding nature of legislative instruction in a letter to a committee of the Pennsylvania legislature in which he said that in voting contrary to his judgment, "I act merely as their [the legislature's] agent. The responsibility is theirs, not mine."[69] Four years later the Pennsylvania legislature instructed him as senator to vote against the Sub-Treasury Bill, which he had previously sponsored. He could not disobey, for he had publicly stated that the right of instruction was a fundamental article in the creed of the Democratic party to which he belonged. To those friends who urged him to disregard these instructions on the ground that they did not represent popular opinion, he replied that if a senator should look behind his instructions and act according to his own opinion of the popular will, the right of instruction would at once be abandoned.[70] But he temporized by securing a postponement of a decision on the bill.

Another significant instance of legislative instruction by a Northern state was the instruction of Senator Lewis Cass by the Michigan legislature in 1849 to support a Wilmot Proviso law. Cass was widely known as the champion of popular sovereignty and in 1848 he had been the candidate of the Democratic party for president. He strongly protested against

[69] Buchanan to Jacob Kern *et al.*, Dec. 22, 1834, George T. Curtis, *Life of James Buchanan* (New York, 1883), I, 229-31; Philip S. Klein, *President James Buchanan, a Biography* (University Park, Pa., 1962), 102.

[70] John Bassett Moore (ed.), *The Works of James Buchanan* (New York, 1960), III, 380-385.

this instruction, which if he obeyed would cause him to violate his principles. He believed in obeying instructions, notwithstanding, if they were fairly administered; accordingly, he offered to resign if he could not reconcile his duty to follow his conscientious scruples with obeying instructions.[71] Shortly afterwards, he was released from this dilemma by the legislature's rescinding its instructions and leaving him free to vote for the Compromise of 1850. Five years later, the problem again arose when the legislature under the dominance of the Republicans issued a peremptory set of instructions ordering the Michigan senators to vote for any bill prohibiting slavery in the federal territories or repealing the Fugitive Slave Act.[72] This time, declaring that the passage of such laws would lead to "the dissolution of the Confederacy," Cass defied the instructions of a Republican majority in the legislature.[73]

The doctrine of the right of instruction was subjected to a devastating criticism by John Bell of Tennessee in a speech before the Senate, February 23, 1858. Bell had just received instructions from the Tennessee legislature disapproving of his vote four years before against the Kansas-Nebraska Bill (he and Sam Houston were the only Southern senators who had voted against the bill), virtually requesting him to resign, and instructing the Tennessee senators to vote for the admission of Kansas under the Lecompton Constitution. Bell refused to obey instructions and maintained that such a practice had long ago been discarded by the Whig party. He traced the origin of the practice of instruction to the period of the Confederation, when delegates to Congress were regarded as ambassadors. He declared that legislative instruction had no warrant in the Constitution and that it was resorted to chiefly as "an engine of party and to promote party ends." Senators,

[71] *Appendix to the Congressional Globe,* XXII, Part I, 74 (Jan., 1850).

[72] Resolutions of Michigan legislature, presented by Senator Stuart, Feb. 5, 1855. *Congressional Globe,* 33 Cong., 2 Sess., XXX, 555-556.

[73] See Andrew C. McLaughlin, *Lewis Cass* (Boston, 1899); Frank B. Woodford, *Lewis Cass, the Last Jeffersonian* (New Brunswick, 1950).

he argued, did not represent the legislatures but the people, and therefore they were no more responsible to the fluctuating opinions of factions in control of legislatures than was the President to the electoral college.[74]

After the Civil War the doctrine of mandatory legislative instruction became obsolete. The last notable practice of it occurred in 1878 when the Mississippi legislature instructed the senators from that state to vote for the Bland Silver Act. On February 15 of that year Lucius Quintus Cincinnatus Lamar, a man of imposing presence, darkly handsome, eloquent, and aristocratic, arose in the Senate and had the chief clerk read the Mississippi resolutions of instruction, which he announced he should disregard.[75] While he was a professor at the University of Mississippi, he explained, he had taught his students to respect truth and courage; he himself must abide by these precepts and not shrink from his duty. The Silver Bill created a dishonest dollar and he must vote against it as a matter of preserving "unsullied the spotless legacy of Southern honor." To his wife he wrote: "The Legislature has instructed me to vote for the Silver Bill. I cannot do it; I had rather quit politics forever."[76] If he followed the instructions of the legislature against his judgment, he maintained, he would be throwing away the fruit of his previous preparation and study of the subject and become merely an echo of current opinion.[77]

Jefferson Davis, whom Lamar admired and whose leadership he had followed for so many years, took a different view of the doctrine of legislative instruction. In a letter published in the Jackson (Miss.) *Clarion,* January 15, 1879, the former

[74] *Congressional Globe,* 35 Cong., 1 Sess., 804-806, Feb. 23, 1858.

[75] *Congressional Record,* 45 Cong., 2 Sess., Vol. VII, 1061 Senate, Feb. 15, 1878.

[76] Edward Mayes, *Lucius Q. C. Lamar, His Life, Times, and Speeches, 1825-1893* (Nashville, 1896); 347; 333; see also W. A. Cate, *Lucius Q. C. Lamar, Secession and Reunion* (Chapel Hill, 1935).

[77] The then Senator John F. Kennedy in *Profiles in Courage* (New York, 1956), 142-150, cited Lamar's act in disobeying instructions as a distinguished example of political courage.

Confederate president stated his belief that legislative instructions were mandatory on representatives. No representative of the people, he held, "should assume that he had more wisdom than the aggregate of his neighbors."[78] Here was an expression of Jeffersonian faith in the judgment of the democratic majority that was almost mystic in nature. Lamar and the old Whigs, on the other hand, believed that the majority was subject to transient passions and that the statesman should take the high ground of acting for the permanent interests of the people (yet in this instance he was probably wrong on the silver issue), trusting that they would later recognize his action to have been wise and just. In the case of Lamar, the people did vindicate his courageous devotion to his principles in opposing the popular will and through the legislature re-elected him to his seat in the Senate.

The doctrine of mandatory legislative instruction, which had arisen in the early republic, matured during the Jacksonian period when the sovereignty of the people and state rights were at their height. The concept of public office held by the Jacksonians regarded the representative as largely a transmitter of the will of the people, a theory that was vigorously expressed by Peter V. Daniel of Richmond in a letter to Van Buren, Sept. 25, 1835. He criticized both Senators Tyler and Leigh for being "upstart gentry who have dared to place themselves above the people." He had only scorn for "the impudence of Leigh's pretension of referring every thing to *his own sense of right exclusively* whatever his constituents may order, or his statement that altho he may *now* be condemned *futurity* will approve and commend his acts."[79] Although in theory the doctrine of instruction seemed to be a noble expression of representative government, in actual practice it was subject to dangerous abuses which thoroughly discredited it. Hezekiah Niles in 1834 pointed out that the

[78] Mayes, *Lamar,* 363-364.

[79] Peter V. Daniel to Martin Van Buren, Sept. 25, 1835. Van Buren Papers, MSS, Library of Congress.

frequent use of instruction would render the legislation of the country uncertain and would unsettle business and commerce.[80] Indeed, the partisan use of instruction in the 1830's caused thoughtful men to reflect upon the dangers of an unrestrained and irresponsible majority in a democracy. Later, Calhoun was to incorporate this distrust of a partisan majority in his theory of government.

Like the duel and virtually at the same time, the practice of legislative instruction disappeared from the political mores of the American people. One explanation of the passing of this highly democratic doctrine, Professor William E. Dodd has suggested, was the prevalence after the Civil War of the idea that election to office gave a property right in the office which a legislature could not take away by the exercise of repugnant instructions.[81] The adoption of the Seventeenth Amendment in 1913 gave a final blow to the venerable doctrine of instructions which had been transplanted from England. Nevertheless, long before that date the development of the Solid South rendered the practice of instructions below the Potomac an act of supererogation. With the passing of this political practice one of the serious threats to independent thought on the part of legislators was removed. The record of those Southern representatives who disobeyed instructions and followed their consciences forms a sober annotation to the history of freedom of thought in the Old South, a rubric written, not by liberals, but by conservatives who withstood the storm of unpopularity rather than sacrifice their political principles.

[80] *Niles' Weekly Register*, XLVII (Nov. 15, 1834), 61.

[81] William E. Dodd, "The Principle of Instructing United States Senators," *South Atlantic Quarterly*, I (October, 1902), 326-332; see also William S. Hoffman, "Willie P. Mangum and the Whig Revival of the Doctrine of Instructions," *Journal of Southern History*, XXII (August, 1956), 338-354, and Holman Hamilton, "Democratic Senate Leadership and the Compromise of 1850," *Mississippi Valley Historical Review*, XLI (December, 1954), 410.

CHAPTER NINE

THE RELIGIOUS EXPERIENCE

THE ANTE BELLUM PERIOD was probably the most religious age in the entire history of the South. Its spirit was exhibited in various ways—the camp meeting, "protracted meetings," the family altar at which the members daily knelt to offer prayer, the frequent readings of the Bible, the dramatic conversions and baptisms, and the letters of the time filled with a simple faith. Arthur M. Schlesinger, Sr., has noted that the American mind has displayed the remarkable phenomenon of an alternating freezing and thawing of thought resulting in periods of orthodoxy and of liberalism. The ante bellum period in the South was one of the settling of religious thought and feeling into a rigid pattern of orthodoxy.

With the rise of the cotton kingdom, Southern religion took on more and more the character of anti-intellectualism. Rational, relatively nonemotional religions such as the Unitarian church, which had made so promising a beginning below the Mason-Dixon Line during the first quarter of the nineteenth century, declined to a shadow after 1830. Only foreign radicals such as the German Free Societies in Baltimore and Louisville during the 1850's dared to offend the mores of their communities by exercising free thought on religious matters. The German Turners of Louisville called down the condemnation of the community upon themselves when they paraded through the streets of the city in January, 1855, to pay honor to the memory of Thomas Paine, the author of *The Age of Reason.* The editor of the *Louisville Courier,* in criticizing these foreigners for their infidel beliefs, declared that American civilization was based on the acceptance of Christianity. He pronounced deluded those who subscribed to the teachings of *The Age of Reason*, Hume's *Essay on Miracles*, the skepticism of Voltaire and Gibbon, or Volney's *Ruins of Empire.*

By 1830 the deism and skepticism of the eighteenth-century Enlightenment had virtually disappeared in the South. The Great Revival and subsequent waves of evangelism had converted most of the doubters who had grown up in an age when skepticism was fashionable among the gentry. In 1835 John Hartwell Cocke was overjoyed at the conversion of one of the skeptics, Professor J. A. G. Davis of the University of Virginia (the same professor who some years later was elected chairman of the faculty). To his wife Louisa he wrote that the learned professor was until lately "the most outbreaking [*sic*] of all our Infidels," but that now he expected to meet him at the communion table in the Episcopal church in Charlottesville.

The elimination of deism and skepticism from the South was effected by many converging forces. Deism, the religion of a number of the statesmen of the early republic, was already dying a natural death when the evangelists of the Great Revival attacked it, for it was too cold and intellectual for the ordinary man. The spirit of the nineteenth century, moreover, was deeply affected by the enveloping movement of Romanticism, which was the antithesis of eighteenth-century rationalism. And the need to defend slavery against the attacks of the abolitionists fostered a fundamentalist form of religion.

The religion of the Southern masses in the nineteenth century was strongly evangelical. The manuscript diary of Richard Hugg King (which is preserved in the North Carolina Department of Archives at Raleigh) gives a remarkable insight into the evangelical mind of the Old South. Although King had been educated at Princeton, he was close to the common man in his religion and in his techniques of preaching. He was a backwoods farmer and collector of the odious excise tax on whiskey in North Carolina before he was converted in a violent religious paroxysm at a camp meeting during the period of the Great Revival. Since the Presbyterian church would not license him as a preacher because he had not studied theology, he joined the Methodist church and became a circuit rider in western North Carolina for twelve years. At this time the Methodist circuit riders were paid eighty dollars a year, plus traveling expenses, a fact that made it necessary for him to combine farming with riding the circuit.

The Reverend Eli Washington Caruthers, who wrote a manuscript biography entitled "Richard Hugg King and his Times" (also in the North Carolina Department of Archives) has sketched a striking portrait of him. He described this ardent evangelist, whom he had heard preach when he was a young student, as a tall portly man, well over six feet in height, inclining a little to corpulence. He had black hair and black eyes, a dark complexion, and an intellectual and impressive countenance. When he preached, he spoke slowly and calmly at first, in a loud but musical voice. Then he gradually warmed up to his subject until his eyes became fixed apparently on every person in the house, and soon he and his susceptible audience would weep together. The recurrent themes of his sermons were the redemption of sinners from the fate of Hell and the providence of God.

During his latter years in east Tennessee, he was much handicapped in his crusade to save souls by his great weight, for he weighed more than four hundred pounds and was affected by a swollen leg that forced him to preach sitting in a chair. Nevertheless, he was a man of such ardent temperament, who could "in tones of thunder deal out the terrors of the law," that he would at times involuntarily arise to his feet, to the alarm of his hearers, and appeal to sinners until he sank exhausted into his chair. He would on occasion preach in the groves, sitting in his chair, his audience "solemnly attentive." Periodically he went to Knoxville to attend religious services or he would set out in a sulky to administer the sacraments in lonely little places like Baker's Creek and Grassy Valley. Around him sickness raged, especially typhus or epidemic fever, the virulent ague, and after 1833, cholera epidemics, which took people from this earth with dramatic suddenness. These recurring diseases that baffled the puny efforts of the country doctors must have frightened the people and made them susceptible to the kind of religion which the Methodist circuit riders and the uneducated Baptist ministers preached.

The dramatic moment in American religion, in the North as well as in the South, was the experience of "conversion." When the scientist Joseph Le Conte was a student at Franklin College (the University of Georgia) he was converted at a revival. His description of his emotions at this time was typical of most conversions in the ante bellum period: "I passed through all the stages . . . a period of great distress, of earnest prayer, of exercise of faith, followed by a sudden sense of acceptance, and intense ecstatic joy for deliverance. . . ." The greatest effect of his conversion, he believed, was not in the change of his moral life, for he was an exemplary young man, but in his emancipation from "the bondage of the fear of death and the hereafter."

During the period of the Great Revival there was a remarkable cooperation among the various sects, their doctrinal differences being largely ignored in the common cause of saving souls. But after the ebb of the Revival movement, men began to fight over these differences and their attitudes hardened into an unyielding denominationalism. Sectarianism, indeed, often influenced such important decisions as to whether a Methodist should marry a Baptist, or whether to vote for a staunch Baptist or an Episcopalian. The symbol around which the battle lines were drawn was most often the rite of baptism, but there were other matters of violent disagreement, such as closed or open communion, temperance, and missionary activity. A revealing example of the weight attached to denominations in the Old South is found in the letters of a Louisiana private in the Confederate Army to his wife. She had wounded his feelings, he wrote, by becoming a Baptist, and he begged her not to make Baptists of his children. "The ware [war] and the Baptist and the sickness," he declared, "is a nuff to make a man go crazy that dont have fare [far] to go no how. . . ." Later he wrote in a glow of triumph concerning a debate in his company: "It was on the subject of Baptist and clost communion. The scriptures was perused fore proof of the doctrine. The Baptist was as completly wound up as i ever saw in my life. This debate lasted 3 or 4 hours. It wound up by the Baptist saying that wee dident look at the scriptures right."

When the Reverend Neal Gordon of Nicholasville, Kentucky, sought in 1850 to persuade his church, the Associated Reform Presbyterian, to engage in a missionary enterprise to Africa, he ran into difficulties over denominational prejudices. He proposed that the church buy four Negro boys and educate them to go to Liberia as missionaries and to establish a school in Africa. Some of the members were strongly opposed to merging their resources and efforts with other denominations in such a project. Gordon received letters saying that any merger would result in the loss of the distinctive characteristics of their branch of the Presbyterian church and that many of the wealthy members of the church, who were of "the straightest sect" and "sticklers for order and form," would not contribute.

The census statistics in the last decade of the ante bellum period show that the more emotional sects had flourished in the South like the proverbial green bay tree. While population had increased during the decade at the rate, for example, of 24.06 per cent in Alabama, 21 per cent in Georgia, and 12.29

per cent in Virginia, the number of Methodist and Baptist churches increased 50, 34, and 30 per cent respectively. On the eve of the Civil War these churches, which appealed especially to the yeoman families and the Negroes, included well over three-fourths of the churches in the South, ranging in ratio from 70 per cent in Virginia to 90 per cent in Georgia.

The secession convention of Mississippi in 1861, which probably represented the leadership class of the state, presents an interesting picture of church membership. It contained twenty-three Methodists and sixteen Baptists—55.7 per cent of those of the convention who belonged to churches; the other denominations were represented by sixteen Presbyterians, twelve Episcopalians, two Roman Catholics, and one member of the Christian church; thirty of the hundred members of the convention apparently did not belong to a church, though some of these listed themselves as "friendly to all" churches.

The Presbyterians, from all indications, were far stronger among the leadership class than their numerical church membership would rank them. They sought more than any other sect to obtain control over the education of the youth and to mold it along Calvinistic lines. A good example of their strong-minded preachers who united the mystical with the intellectual in religion was James Henley Thornwell, outstanding leader of the Southern Presbyterian church at the end of the ante bellum period. The son of a South Carolina overseer, he became the intellectual interpreter of the religion of the upper middle class. He had received his education as the result of the philanthropy of some gentlemen of Cheraw, and he repaid their confidence by becoming an intense student. At South Carolina College this small, sickly looking youth was graduated at the head of his class. His erudition was such that he astonished people by his ability to recite from memory whole dramas of Shakespeare, numerous verses of Milton, and long extracts from the classic authors. He was a remarkable example of the effect of the classics upon the Southern mind—resulting in an appreciation of classical literature primarily for its value as a mental discipline rather than for its artistic and humanistic content.

In 1834 Thornwell enrolled as a student at Andover Divinity School in Cambridge, Massachusetts, and also studied briefly at Harvard College. Here he was shocked by the rationalistic attitude of professors and students toward the sacred mysteries of orthodox religion. He declared that the Unitarian doctrines of New England were "little better than downright infidelity" and quickly left those ungodly places where they flourished. Underlying his brilliant but dogmatic mind was a deeply passionate nature; religion was an emotional outlet for him and a passport to Heaven. Full of invective and sarcasm, he displayed a Hebraic intolerance toward unbelievers. He also exhibited the same type of puritanical asceticism that characterized the life of Alexander H. Stephens, especially when both men were young schoolteachers. He condemned dancing as "an insult to God," but he himself indulged in the pleasure of chewing tobacco from eleven years of age to his death.

From the time when his polemic career began during the great controversy in the Presbyterian church over the "New School" and the "Old School" until his death in 1862 Thornwell exercised great power in South Carolina and throughout the Southern Presbyterian church. Not only was he an influential preacher, but he served as president of South Carolina College from 1851 until 1855, when he resigned to become a professor in Presbyterian Theological Seminary located in Columbia. A large part of Thornwell's influence on his section emanated from his uncompromising convictions and his eloquence as a public speaker. Joseph Le Conte has observed in his autobiography that Thornwell by his personal eloquence and magnetism created a very high sense of honor among the students. Indeed, in referring to his joining the faculty of South Carolina College in the 1850's Le Conte wrote, "I had never previously seen (nor have I since) so high a sense of honor among students in their relations to one another and to the faculty."

A great polemicist, Thornwell fought mightily against modernism in religion as exhibited by the "New School" faction of the Northern Presbyterian church. He fought side by side with another potent leader of the "Old School" theologians—Robert Jefferson Breckinridge, professor in the Theological Seminary at Danville, Kentucky. These churchmen stoutly upheld the Calvinistic doctrines of the Westminster Confession of Faith, especially the depravity of human nature and Christ's atonement for the ancient sin of man by his sacrifice on the cross. In Thornwell's religious philosophy, sin and God's grace to repentant sinners played a central role; he had no doubt about the existence of positive evil in the world, both in the carnal nature of man and in the Devil being abroad. In these beliefs he reflected the universal faith of the South, as well as of the great majority of the devout rural folk of the North. There was no room in his religion for the toleration of heresy or free thought, such as atheism, unitarianism, or "the abomination of Popery."

A pillar of conservatism in religious matters, Thornwell was also a staunch conservative in the defense of slavery. He had a plantation named Dryburgh Abbey near Lancaster, South Carolina, which he would visit periodically for relaxation and refreshment of his soul. He was a kind and indulgent master who was careful to provide religious instruction for his slaves. Although he made virtually no profit from the slaves, his ownership of a plantation obtained for him the prestige and advantage of a planter in South Carolina society. In the General Assembly of the Presbyterian church in 1845 this doughty debater fought against any condemnation of Southern slavery. He maintained that slavery was not sinful: it was justified by the Holy Scriptures and was a civil relation with which the church had no right to interfere.

An ardent and ruthless expansionist, Thornwell desired to annex Texas and to take California and Mexico. To his wife he wrote from Wheeling, Virginia, on June 14, 1845: "The more I reflect upon the subject, the more I am satisfied that the mission of our Republic will not be accomplished, until we embrace in our Union the whole of this North American continent. If the New England people are disposed to kick up a dust about the annexation of Texas, I am prepared to take the ground that it would be better for this country, and for the interests of the human race, to give up New England, than to abandon any new territory which we may be able to acquire."

Though he had opposed the Nullification movement in 1832 and secession in 1850, he became intensely sectional in his outlook during the decade of the 1850's. He advocated, for example, that Southern youth should be educated in the South and not sent to Northern schools and colleges. In a famous Fast Day sermon on November 21, 1860, he preached a strongly political sermon setting forth the Southern point of view. God was scourging the nation, he declared, for its "national sins"—abolitionism and subversion of the Constitution by selfish Northern interests. He excoriated the free states for refusing to return fugitive slaves and for seeking to exclude slaveholders from federal territories. He seems also to have adopted George Fitzhugh's views, expressed in the latter's books *Sociology for the South* (1854) and *Cannibals All* (1857), that Southern slavery was not based on race but on a natural and beneficial relation between capital and labor. He scorned the recently propounded doctrine of the diversity of the races as opposed to God's word and maintained that the Negroes were of the same origin as white men, having the same heavenly Father and the same everlasting destiny. When the Southern Confederacy was established, he was the leading figure in the organization of the Southern Presbyterian church and until his death at the height of Confederate success in battle was confident that God was on the side of the Southern people.

A comparison of Thornwell with another extremist, Theodore Parker of New England, illustrates the wide difference between the Southern point of view on religion and that of the Northern reformers. Reform was in the New England air during the ante bellum period, as it was not in the South, and a number of its leading ministers were deeply influenced by the reform impulse. Probably the main difference between Southern and Northern forms of Christianity lay in this fact, for the great masses throughout the United States held to an orthodox and traditional religion. While the Southern preachers, in general, centered religion on the "saving of souls," the reform-minded ministers of New England regarded religion as an agent of social reform.

Parker was a product of this reform movement just as Thornwell was deeply influenced by the changing social environment of the Southern states around 1830. Both men came from humble families. Parker was born in Lexington, Massachusetts, into a deeply religious and austere family of farmers and mechanics. By hard physical work on the farm and by teaching school he was able to earn enough money to put himself through Harvard Divinity School. He became a Unitarian minister at West Roxbury, Massachusetts, and when he came under the influence of Emerson and the transcendentalists, he broke completely with orthodox religion. While J. H. Thornwell and most Southerners relied on the authority of the literal word of the Bible as the basis of their religion, Parker shocked the orthodox by maintaining that true religion existed independently of the revelation of the Bible. Thornwell, on the other hand, was a man of conventional and orthodox views. Though he was a scholar, his scholarship was narrow and unaffected by the fresh breezes of the critical study of the Bible that moved European scholars. Parker, in contrast, was a student of tremendous energy who read widely not only works in the English language but also German philosophy and literature. He read so voraciously that Professor Henry Steele Commager has called him an "intellectual gourmand." In Parker's sermons there was little, if any, of the gentlemanly tradition of religion that the Episcopal clergy preached; they were blunt, forthright, uncompromising, appealing to the intellect and the New England conscience. This Boston preacher, deeply influenced by the reform impulse, was a universal reformer, concerned with prison reform and the abolition of capital punishment, the rights of women, free school education, Sabbath reform, temperance, and the improvement of the lot of industrial workers, but the reform in which he became an extremist was the abolition movement and the higher law doctrine.

Quite different from the reformist preaching of New England and the stern Presbyterian faith of Thornwell was the decorous Episcopal church in the South. This church represented the way to Heaven for the Southern gentry. Highly dignified, it was not noted for its evangelical zeal or its missionary activities. The sermons of its well-educated, restrained rectors could not compete with the emotional, hell-fire preaching of the Baptists and Methodists; the practice of charging rent for pews was repugnant to the common man; the latitudinarian ideas of its members in regard to dancing, card-playing and wine-drinking seemed "worldly" to many Southerners, and its ritual smacked of Roman Catholic practices. Though it grew vigorously after 1825, as did the evangelical churches, the Episcopal church never appealed to more than a very small fraction of the Southern people. In 1860 it had only 33 of the 572 churches in Louisiana, only 25 of the 1,441 churches in Mississippi, and only 188 of the 3,105 churches in Virginia where its strength was greatest.

No more admirable leader of this church, according to

Southern standards, existed at the close of the ante bellum period than the bishop of Louisiana, Leonidas Polk. Born in Raleigh, North Carolina, in 1806, he came from a family that had acquired large landed estates. After attending the University of North Carolina for a year he received an appointment to West Point, where he roomed with Albert Sidney Johnston. At West Point, Polk was an exemplary young man, enamored with military life, enjoying the pleasures of the fashionable world—such as attending a dancing school—yet at the same time a good student, ranking eighth in his graduating class in 1827.

Until he was twenty years old, the aristocratic Carolinian paid little attention to religion. Indeed, zealous devotion to religion was derided by most of the cadets. But in the spring of his junior year he was deeply troubled by a mistake that he had made which lowered his standing in his class and darkened his future. Coincidentally he had a dream of the Day of Judgment which disturbed him. He went to the chaplain, the Reverend Charles McIlvaine, for consolation and instruction as to how he might save his soul. The chaplain gave him a textbook on the evidences of Christianity, which aided him in becoming a deeply religious convert. It was a courageous step for him as a cadet to practice his faith openly, but he wrote to his father that he had fortified himself against the opinions of the world and that instead of finding the religious life one of gloom and austerity, he was happy in carrying out the duties of his faith.

Shortly before he was graduated from the academy, he startled his father, Colonel William Polk of Revolutionary fame, by asking permission to resign from the army and accept a position as a teacher at Amherst Academy (the precursor of Amherst College). He gave as his reason his desire to educate himself further, especially in the liberal arts, the classics, and history, in which he felt that his knowledge was only superficial. His father vetoed this request, attributing it to an impulse, a wild and silly scheme which blinded him from following an honorable military career worthy of his family and his station in life. Leonidas accepted this verdict but shortly afterwards announced that he intended to study theology and become an Episcopal rector. His father was unable to dissuade him; he resigned his commission in the army and in November, 1828, enrolled in the Episcopal Theological Seminary at Alexandria, Virginia. After completing his training there, he was ordained in the spring of 1830. He then received the appointment of assistant to Bishop Moore at the fashionable Monumental Church in Richmond.

Ill-health forced him temporarily to abandon the ministry and to seek a cure for a year by travel in Europe. Upon his return he settled as a planter in Maury County, Tennessee, on land which his father gave him. Here, surrounded by his brothers who were prominent planters, he was very happy supervising his plantation, and operating a small hemp bagging factory on his plantation. He also preached regularly to a parish in the nearby village of Columbia and founded a girl's school. Several years passed in this way when in 1838 at the age of thirty-two, he was unexpectedly appointed Missionary Bishop of the Southwest. His territory was vast, including Alabama, Mississippi, Louisiana, Arkansas, the Indian Territory, and the Republic of Texas.

The westward movement of population had uprooted many families from their churches, and in the crude conditions of a newly settled country they often did not have the advantages of regular worship. When Bishop Polk made his first visitation in 1839, he did not find a single Episcopal church in Louisiana west of the Mississippi River, and so absorbed were the inhabitants in worldly affairs and amusements on Sunday that it was difficult to assemble an audience to hear him preach. His appointment as Missionary Bishop was a great break in the established usages of the church, marking an adaptation to western conditions.

Polk was admirably suited to the arduous task before him. A handsome man of imposing appearance, great energy, and decisive character, he accommodated himself to the crude conditions that he met, and fortunately he was not a stickler for ritual and form. He carried into his work the spirit of a soldier, and he was dominated by the evangelical zeal to save souls. He wrote to his mother in 1839 that the urgent calls of Bishop Kemper and himself for coworkers in their respective fields of missionary endeavor had met with little response, so that he must make a tour eastward to recruit; it was useless for him to travel and preach unless there were laborers "to nourish the Seed Sown" and aid in founding and fostering congregations in the Southwest. On his first visitation, he traveled five thousand miles—on horseback, in steamboats, and on stages—preached forty-four sermons, baptized fourteen, confirmed forty-one, and established two churches.

In 1841 he was elected bishop of Louisiana. Accordingly, he decided to leave Tennessee and establish his family on a plantation in the state where his diocese was located. Mrs. Polk, in the meanwhile, had received a large inheritance, with the choice of taking either money or four hundred slaves. The Bishop made the unfortunate decision to take the slaves and operate a large sugar plantation in Louisiana with them. His motives were twofold, as his son explains in his biography—a belief that he could exercise a greater influence with the planters of Louisiana by joining their ranks and a desire to persuade them to a kinder treatment of their slaves by setting the example of paternalism and of ministering to their spiritual needs.

His plantation Leighton on Bayou La Fourche, sixty miles from New Orleans, became a showplace among Louisiana plantations, the scene of an idyllic family life, and a model of the patriarchal slave plantation. Polk would not follow the custom of the sugar plantations of the region by working the slaves on Sundays during the critical grinding season between the harvest and the coming of frost. Thus, because of his scruples, he sacrificed his own financial interest at times. Zealous in holding religious services among his black dependents, he required them to belong to the Episcopal church, although most religious slaves preferred the more emotional sects of the Baptists and Methodists. He appealed to them to do their duties on the plantation out of motives of self-respect, but whenever they persistently erred, he punished them as children were punished in that age. Sometimes instead of whipping, he ordered humiliating penalties such as requiring a chicken thief to stand for several hours on Sunday with the stolen property tied around his neck, to the great amusement of the other slaves.

The good bishop divided his energies between the administration of his diocese and the superintendence of his large plantation. Such a dual role led to the neglect of his plantation and his worldly affairs. Moreover, he suffered extraordinarily bad luck: in 1849 an epidemic of cholera carried away 106 of his slaves; during the next year a tornado destroyed a large part of his property, including the sugarhouse valued at $75,000; and in the fall of that year an early frost reduced his sugar crop by one-third. These misfortunes and the heavy debts which he had accumulated forced him to turn over Leighton to his creditors and move his family to New Orleans.

The great but unfulfilled work of Leonidas Polk was the establishment of the University of the South. Though the Presbyterians, Methodists, and Baptists had founded denominational colleges in the Southern states, the Episcopal church in the 1850's had none. Bishop Polk resolved to establish an educational institution that would go far beyond being a church college and become a truly regional university. He made the first public announcement of his plan in the summer of 1856 in a printed letter addressed to the Southern bishops of the Episcopal church. He dreamed of founding a university in the South that in five years would rival Harvard, Yale, and the University of Virginia.

Polk urged the foundation of a regional Southern university because he believed that an emergency existed, "a stern necessity." Southern youth were being forced to abandon Northern schools and colleges because of their aversion to the antislavery doctrines taught in these institutions. Southern parents, he observed, "would rather their children go half-educated than send them to the North." The good bishop looked with apprehension upon the growth of radicalism, especially of abolition fanaticism, in the Northern states. Writing to Bishop Elliott of Georgia, August 20, 1856, he expressed a fear (in a passage omitted from the letter as published in the biography by his son) that the Northern Episcopal church, which had hitherto resisted fanaticism, would surrender to the antislavery movement and that secession would inevitably follow. The South then, he believed, would be in a bad way for education.

The founder planned to establish the University of the South on the solid rock of conservatism. There would be no Yankee professors on its faculty. In a passage also omitted from the published letter of August 20, he wrote, "We are afraid of Northern domination in our schools and pulpits of the South, 'these Northern men with southern principles.'" He also warned of danger from the influence of Northern seminaries and colleges; his university would protect Southern students from subversive doctrines.

The University of the South, he decided, should be different from the bourgeois schools and colleges of the Northern states; it should incorporate an aristocratic element by training the sons of planters to be Southern gentlemen. Only the Episcopal church was suited, he thought, to found this type of university. "The Baptists and Methodists," he observed in a letter of January 21, 1856, "have not the bearing or the social position or prestige, required to command the public confidence." In the projected university he proposed that there should be thirty-two schools—a far too ambitious undertaking—including architecture, civil engineering, agriculture, commerce, mining, and fine arts. One unique feature of his plan for the university was that its long vacation should be in the winter months and that it should operate throughout the summer when the students could closely associate with their parents who would be spending their vacations in nearby cottages.

His vision began to take practical shape when delegates from all over the South met on top of Lookout Mountain near Chattanooga on July 4, 1857, for the purpose of establishing the University of the South. The following year the legislature granted a charter. A great rivalry then ensued over the location of the projected university. Bishop Polk favored a site on Sewanee Mountain in eastern Tennessee because of its easy rail communication through Chattanooga with the lower South and because of its salubrious climate and charming landscape, which he thought would attract cotton and sugar planters to make their summer homes there. One of the promoters of the Sewanee site was John Armfield of the famous slave-trading firm of Franklin and Armfield; he owned the fashionable summer resort Beersheba Springs, which was located near the Sewanee site. Armfield entertained the Episcopal bishops at the Springs, contributed money to print promotional literature for the site, and built cabins on his land for Bishops Polk and Otey. The Sewanee Mining Company gave 9,500 acres of land for a campus and endowment. When the Sewanee property was finally selected in preference to the town of Chattanooga, its citizens became so vituperative over the loss of a moneymaking project that the good bishop commented: "They are a repulsive set of vulgarians." He devoted his energies until the coming of the

Civil War to fund-raising campaigns; he traveled in the North to observe its universities and corresponded with leading men in Europe in regard to plans for the grand design.

In his efforts to found a religious proslavery university, Polk revealed that he had changed his views on slavery since he was a student at Episcopal Theological Seminary. At that time he had regarded colonization as a means of gradually eliminating slavery from the South. In a letter to his father, dated January 21, 1829, he had written: "Now I believe in the course of not many years one State after another will be willing to abolish slavery. This is proved by the state of things in Maryland and Virginia, the slave states farthest north. . . ." Three years later when he was traveling in England he observed in a letter to his mother: "I confess I am quite charmed with the neatness of the country houses, and the manner in which the fields are arranged, hedged, and tilled; and when I think of our own vast plantations, with our dirty careless thriftless Negro population, I could, and do, wish that we were thoroughly quit of them. The more I see of those without slaves, the more I am prepared to say that we are seriously wronging ourselves by retaining them. . . ."

By 1856, however, his views on the "peculiar institution" seem to have changed decidedly along with the changing attitude of his section. In August of that year he wrote to Bishop Elliott that "those madcaps at the North" did not understand slavery at all. Polk believed that Southern slavery was a patriarchal institution and that his projected university would train the sons of planters to be humane masters and to bring up their slaves in Christianity. The premature emancipation of the slaves, he held, would be a great wrong both to the slaves and to the masters.

For the remainder of his career until he became a general in the Confederate Army, Bishop Polk devoted his main efforts to founding the university. He wrote numerous letters to prominent Episcopalians, studied the organization and government of the best European universities, especially Oxford, and sought for a liberal endowment for the new institution. On October 9, 1860, the cornerstone of the first building was laid. Both the Honorable John S. Preston of South Carolina and Matthew Fontaine Maury spoke at the exercises on Sewanee Mountain. A few months earlier Maury had written to Bishop James Otey that his heart was in the great enterprise of building a Southern university. "You will not have it up a whit too soon," he warned, for the Union was in danger, and in the event of its dissolution the South would have the means of educating its leaders.

When the Secession movement interrupted the great work of his life, the Bishop took a loyal sectional stand on the issue of preserving the Union. Bishop Otey of Tennessee, one of the most important promoters of the university project, rebuked him for following the drift of public opinion instead of opposing the Secession movement. "It is God alone," Otey declared, "that can still the madness of the people. To what quarter shall we look, when such men as you and Elliott deliberately favor secession?"

Polk did endeavor, nevertheless, to prevent the Secession movement from resulting in a civil war. On December 26, 1860, before Louisiana had seceded, he wrote to President Buchanan, urging him to take no step toward coercing the Southern states and thus precipitating a civil war. He declared that in his opinion there was not "the remotest prospect for the reunion of the two sections as long as slave labor shall prove advantageously applicable to the agricultural wants of the Southern Confederacy."

Though the Bishop had no military experience after he left West Point, President Davis offered him a commission as major general in the Confederate Army to take charge of the defense of the Mississippi Valley. Polk conferred with Bishop Elliott and with the venerable Bishop Meade of

Virginia on the advisability of accepting the commission. Upon their approval, he decided that it was his duty to accept the call to arms. On June 25, 1861, he became a major general in the Confederate Army. From then until June 14, 1864, when he was killed at Pine Mountain near Marietta, Georgia, opposing Sherman's advance, he served creditably in high command and was promoted before his death to the rank of lieutenant general. Rejecting the ruthless principles of total war, he believed that fighting men should behave as Christian gentlemen.

The career of Leonidas Polk as a churchman and that of the leader of the Northern branch of the church, Bishop Philander Chase, bear many striking resemblances. Chase was much older than Leonidas (he was born in 1775 in Cornish, New Hampshire), but they had virtually the same attitude toward religion, and their careers as missionaries in the West were similar. After graduating from Dartmouth College, Chase served as a pioneering clergyman in western New York and in 1817 went to the crude, recently settled area of Ohio. Here in 1819 he became the first bishop of Ohio. He found great difficulty, as did Polk, in securing ministers from the East who were willing to serve in the rough settlements of the West, and accordingly he determined to found a theological seminary and college in the West to train native sons for the ministry. In 1824 he was able to raise funds in England for the founding of Kenyon College, which he named after one of his English patrons. The location of the college was called Gambier after another patron, Lord Gambier, to whom Henry Clay had given Chase a letter of recommendation. He decided to locate his college in the woods rather than in a town, a plan which led to bitter opposition.

Bishop Chase had a more puritan attitude toward life than did his Southern counterpart. He fought strenuously in the temperance cause and would allow no drinking of whiskey among the students or even among the workmen who erected the college buildings. Both men seem to have been equally zealous in overcoming obstacles and enduring wilderness hardships to establish the Episcopal church in the West, and both had masterful and dominating personalities. It was this last quality that caused the faculty of Kenyon College to rise in rebellion against the rule of the autocratic Chase and led to his resignation as president in 1831. Both churchmen were warriors fighting under the banner of the Episcopal church against sin in the world. Chase had spent six years as a minister and teacher in New Orleans, and he always entertained a warm friendship for Southern people. In New Orleans he had bought a slave (who ran away from him), and the reminiscences which he composed in 1847 give no indication that he shared the abolitionist zeal of his nephew, Salmon P. Chase. Indeed, the religion of the Northern and the Southern champions of Episcopalianism in the West appear to be almost identical: both were Low Churchmen, who emphasized in their sermons prayer, the confession of sins, the weaning of the soul away from "the world," the preparation of the soul for death, and faith in the literal word of the Bible.

In Leonidas Polk there was a commingling of several religious traditions, as was often the case in both the South and the North. Polk was at the same time a missionary, the founder of a university, an exemplar of plantation paternalism, and an Episcopal clergyman. Not a profound thinker, he was a doer. Nor was he a pulpit orator like Thornwell or the eloquent Presbyterian minister of New Orleans Benjamin M. Palmer, the open advocate of secession. In manner and tastes he seemed far removed from the evangelical leaders, the fervent exhorters of the camp meetings; nevertheless, he did not differ basically in his religious ideas from these simple men—his thoughts, like theirs, were centered on "salvation," the winning of immortality in Heaven.

The Episcopal leader held the belief, common both to the evangelical and the gentlemanly traditions that the Christian life would be rewarded by practical benefits on this earth. To his brother Lucius who had recently joined the church, he wrote in 1843 that God would bless him in mind and estate: "For truly Godliness is profitable for all things, the life that now is as well as that which is to come." But the worldly success of the righteous was not to be compared to the salvation in the life beyond the grave. He warned against the folly of men who delayed the repentance of sins and preparation for death. "The time to prepare to meet death," he wrote to Lucius "is when we are in full health and have all our faculties at liberty to give to the wish."

Both the evangelical and the genteel traditions were obsessed with the idea of man's preparation for death. Throughout Polk's writings, for example, there is a strong sense of the tragic element of life—the lurking of death. Life was short in the Old South, and the presence of death was emphasized by the mourning costume of women. Death would not have been so fearful, had not the sense of sin and guilt been emphasized by the preachers. The concept of sin varied to some degree among different groups but the deadliest sin was the sin of the mind—unbelief in Christian orthodoxy.

In the Petrie Papers at Auburn University is a letter which reveals what Freud might call the guilt complex of Americans of the prewar generation. To George H. Petrie, a student at the Presbyterian Theological Seminary in Columbia, South Carolina, John P. Porcher wrote on December 31, 1831, a description of a protracted meeting in the Presbyterian Church of Charleston, lasting four days, in which a minister from Savannah created a great sensation. As a result of his forceful preaching, wrote Porcher, "many have been convinced of the enormity of Sin and its awful consequence.—He preaches the terrors of the Law, and every one who hears him must feel and tremble."

Wilbur Cash in his *Mind of the South* has argued that the Southern people had a guilt complex because of the immoral relations of Southern men with slave women, and Mrs. Chesnut has lent support to this idea in her *Diary of Dixie*. Some modern liberals have attributed the emotional fundamentalism of the Old South to a guilt complex over the wrongs of slavery, but many Northern people had a similar feeling of sin. The more probable explanation for the great consciousness of sin in ante bellum America was the resurgence of Calvinism with its great emphasis on the depravity of human nature.

The evangelical tradition in Southern religion had generally been opposed to slavery until the decade of the 1820's. Thereafter, with the rise of the cotton kingdom and the renewed profitability of slavery, both the evangelical and the gentlemanly traditions were able to accommodate the existence of slavery in the South with high Christian ideals. This feat was accomplished by a literal interpretation of the Bible, which immeasurably strengthened conservative trends in Southern society. There were so many contradictions in the Scriptures that both North and South could claim its authority for opposing views of the rightfulness of slavery. Probably the vast majority of Southerners after the 1830's came to accept without question the views of preachers, editors, and politicians who sanctioned slavery through the Holy Scriptures, for it seemed a profitable institution and the natural order of life.

Nevertheless, some brilliant and sensitive Southern men were troubled by doubts, such as the cultured former Senator William C. Preston, who had been president of South Carolina College. In 1857 while he was visiting in Virginia, Preston wrote to Waddy Thompson concerning his meeting with Phillip St. George, son of John Hartwell Cocke: "He put into my hands an essay on the *Scriptural* and statistical views of slavery, vastly the best work I have ever read on the subject, especially the *Scriptural.* It has wrought a change in my views which have been worrying me all my life. The work is by a Mr. Stringfellow, a Baptist preacher. Do get it and read it."

The great change in Southern religion in 1860 from that of 1800 arose from the intervening Romantic movement. The romantic aspects of Southern religion of the ante bellum period are indeed striking. Thousands of planter families were fascinated by the allegory of John Bunyan's *Pilgrim's Progress* with its dream of Beulah Land and the Celestial City. In the Fackler Papers at the University of Kentucky there is a letter from young Calvin Fackler, who wrote to his mother in Huntsville, Alabama, April 21, 1850, that he had presented a copy of *Pilgrim's Progress* to his sweetheart. "I have always from childhood admired it more than any work I have ever read, though then I regarded it only in the light of a strange, mysterious piece of romance. I sincerely believe that there is more in it of satisfaction to the young convert than of any work ever published, not of inspiration." In January, 1855, John Hartwell Cocke of Bremo sent word to Lucy Skipwith, the slave teacher on his Alabama plantation, to read *Pilgrim's Progress* to the Negro children in her school. The puritan cavalier was in the habit of opening his Bible at random to seek guidance and encouragement. He almost certainly would have approved of the faith of Maria Fleet, mistress of Green Mount in Virginia, who consulted the prophecies in the Book of Revelation to obtain light upon the troubled times of Virginia during the Civil War.

The religion of William L. Yancey, the great orator of secession, is another illustration of the influence of the Romantic movement on Southern religion. To Yancey religion was a matter of the heart rather than of the mind. To one of his closest friends, the Presbyterian minister William H. Mitchell, he revealed his feelings of guilt and his doubts that he was a Christian. In the Yancey Papers in the Alabama

State Department of Archives is a remarkable letter from Congressman Yancey, who wrote to Mitchell in 1846 from Washington, D. C. He confessed that he was sorely beset with temptations. Though his mind was brilliantly illuminated with a sense of duty, his heart seemed to be cold and torpid. Morning and evening, and sometimes at noonday, he prayed. He also attended a weekly Congressional prayer meeting with "some few praying spirits." Nevertheless, he lamented: "But lo! how little of life—of living and lively faith now dominates me! How feeble is the practice of a Christian duty & oh! how often—too often is that duty neglected, and sometimes shamefully violated!" It was Yancey who moved that the secession convention of Alabama should open its meetings with prayer.

The most apparent difference between the faith of the Old South and modern religion is the changed views of sin. The evangelical preachers, with their eyes turned heavenward, were a powerful force in imposing on the Old South a form of puritanism such as the region had never seen. The novelist William Gilmore Simms, who belonged to the Episcopalian or gentlemanly tradition, believed that this asceticism injured the cause of true religion in the South. In a review of Mrs. Trollope's *Domestic Manners of the Americans* he observed that this denial of wholesome amusements by the evangelical clergy was an important cause of the fanaticism of the revival movements. He also pointed out that the loneliness of the rural population and the rivalry of religious sects to outdo each other in their appeal to the masses contributed to the emotional excesses of the camp meetings.

Among upper class families there was often a conflict between puritan asceticism and cavalier attitudes, as was illustrated by the Fleet family of Green Mount in King and Queen County, Virginia. Originally the family had been Episcopalians, but the generation of 1860 were Baptists. Dr. Fleet could not control himself from periodically going on drinking bouts, and finally, to prevent from being excommunicated, he resigned from the church. While the strict Baptists in the neighborhood were excommunicating some girls for dancing, the Fleets accommodated their religion to the aristocratic tradition. "Pa" Fleet and his teen-age son Benny went to dances; on one occasion they stayed up dancing until morning and Pa was tired out. Mrs. Fleet made currant wine; and Benny read novels, an indulgence which was frowned upon by the devout—such novels as Caruthers' *The Knights of the Horse-Shoe*, the Waverly novels of Scott, and Dickens' *Great Expectations.* He patronized the circus, and when he visited Richmond to sell the plantation produce, he often went to the theater.

At the same time, Benny Fleet's diary is filled with the religious activities of the family. They went to "protracted meetings," where contrite sinners were welcomed at the "Mourner's Bench"; they watched baptisms in the mill pond; and they attended regular services on Sundays, when Benny invariably noted the Bible text upon which the sermon was based. The Fleet diary and letters give an intimate glimpse into the religion of the Old South, especially the strong faith in Providence, the belief that "good works" will not get you to Heaven, the great reliance on prayer, the belief that in order to enter Heaven a man must be "prepared" for death, that is, have his sins forgiven beforehand. The Fleets derived great strength and consolation from their religion, enabling them to meet the disappointments and crises of life with fortitude.

In 1860 there was little disagreement between the fundamental beliefs of the lower and the upper classes of the South, in contrast with the dichotomy that had existed in the early American republic and in many creative periods of history; all classes in the South adhered to a conservative faith, a common orthodoxy. The variations between the different forms of Protestantism—the evangelical, the Calvinistic, and the genteel—were principally in matters of ritual such as baptism and communion, the practice of a decorous religion, the toleration of worldly pleasures, or the policy of sending missionaries to foreign countries. In the beliefs that mattered—the role of the supernatural in life, the efficacy of prayer, ideas of sin, salvation, and an over-ruling Providence—there was virtually no disagreement. This unity of religious belief, as well as the restrictive influence of slavery, may explain why the South, though a strongly religious section, produced no theologian with new ideas (with the possible exception of Alexander Campbell)—no William Ellery Channing, no Emerson, no Joseph Smith—only pulpit orators. Instead of being a reasoned orthodoxy, the religion of the Southern people on the eve of the Civil War was truly a faith, deeply imbued with the spirit of the Romantic movement of the time.

CHAPTER TEN

THE INTELLECTUAL BLOCKADE

IN THE WINTER of 1828 young Henry Rogers, the son of a professor of William and Mary College, listened entranced to a lecture by Frances Wright in the Belvedere Theater, Baltimore. This tall, stately woman, "with her short hair unbound and in ringlets on a head which would have graced Minerva," was engaged in a dramatic attack on the priestcraft and the theology that shackled the human mind.[1] By her eloquence, her prodigious learning, and her bold spirit of inquiry, she made a profound impression on the young scientist fresh from Virginia, and he sought an interview with her. This Scotch reformer was shocking all staid and respectable people by daring to depart from woman's sphere to lecture on the public platform. Moreover, she was an ardent advocate of all those "pernicious isms" which the Southern people heartily loathed and feared. Unblushingly she advocated birth control, easy divorce laws, the equal education of women with men; she urged the gradual emancipation of the slaves; and she was a disciple of Robert Owen, the founder of the communistic society of New Harmony, Indiana.[2]

Henry Rogers's enthusiasm for Frances Wright continued to grow, although he found it necessary to be guarded in his expressions of it. Eventually he joined the reformers and accompanied Robert Dale Owen, the son of Robert Owen, to Europe. Here his interest in geology was awakened, and he gave up his pursuit of the isms to become one of the pioneers in American geology. But the spectacle of a Southerner even dallying with the isms in his youth was a rare phenomenon.

At a period when the rest of the United States was effervescing with experiments of utopias and efforts to eradicate "the evils" of society, the South was strikingly free from reformers. Thornton Stringfellow, a Virginia minister who wrote an able defense of slavery, pointed out that, although isms flourished in New England like Jonah's gourd, one might travel through the Southern States and not find a single ism with an *organized* existence.[3] The Southern press, as well as the powerful influence of the clergy, was almost uniformly opposed to social experimentation or to radical reform movements. W. W. Holden, editor of the Raleigh *Standard*, and later reconstruction governor of North Carolina, described this unity of the ante bellum press as follows: "It has uniformly rejected the isms which infest Europe and the Eastern and Western States of this country. Newspapers devoted to socialism, or to social equality, nihilism, communism or to infidelity in any of its shapes or shades, could not live in the atmosphere of North Carolina."[4] Against such foes of the established order the Southern people set up an intellectual blockade, a *cordon sanitaire.*

What were these ideas which seemed dangerous to the shepherds of Southern minds? "Parson" Brownlow answered the question by proposing an organization called "the Missionary Society of the South, for the Conversion of the Freedom Shriekers, Spiritualists, Free-lovers, Fourierites, and In-

[1] *Life and Letters of William Burton Rogers Edited by His Wife* (Boston, 1896), I, 70.

[2] See Robert Dale Owen, "An Earnest Sowing of Wild Oats," *Atlantic Monthly*, XXXIV, 71-76 (July, 1874).

[3] Thornton Stringfellow, *Scriptural and Statistical View of Slavery* (Richmond, 1856), pp. 119-120.

[4] W. W. Holden, *Address on the History of Journalism in North Carolina*, p. 21.

fidel Reformers of the North."[5] His catalogue of the pernicious ideas beyond the Potomac, however, was far from complete. In the Chardon Street Convention of the Friends of Universal Reform at Boston (1840), the "lunatic fringe" of the reform movement held high carnival. Here was gathered, according to Emerson, a pandemonium of the Northern isms, Muggletonians, Dunkers, come-outers, Seventh-Day Adventists, strident feminists, abolitionists, Unitarians, philosophers, and many persons whose church was a church of one member only.[6] The North had become a germinating center for feverish reform movements and strange cults. Boston was regarded in the Southern States as the capital city of the isms, although western New York was almost as pre-eminent in radicalism.[7]

The South confronted the various extravagances of the reforming zeal of the North with aristocratic detachment, regarding them as middle-class enthusiasms. Both sections were deeply touched by the romantic movement of the time. In the North, romanticism manifested itself in a passion for making over society according to the dreams of perfectionists, Fourierites, feminists, abolitionists, and transcendentalists. In the South, on the other hand, the romantic movement looked to the past for its inspiration, to the dream of a Greek democracy, or to the feudal charm of Sir Walter Scott's novels.[8] Consequently, the Oneida Free Love Colony, the Village of

[5] W. G. Brownlow, *Ought American Slavery to be Perpetuated?*, a debate between Brownlow and Prynne (Philadelphia, 1858), p. 167.

[6] R. W. Emerson, *Lectures and Biographical Sketches* (Boston, 1887), pp. 351-354.

[7] Governor Henry A. Wise of Virginia, who had never stepped upon the soil of New England, wrote to his cousin in Boston, a son-in-law of Edward Everett: "Why don't he [Everett] and such as he in New England wield such pens against the wild 'isms' of Massachusetts. Their moral influence would overthrow the monster. Boston seems to be a center of 'isms'" (Wise to Lieutenant Wise, Sept. 11, 1855, Henry A. Wise MSS in Library of Congress).

[8] Parrington, *The Romantic Revolution in America*, pp. 99-108, 317-434.

Modern Times on Long Island, and Trialville in Ohio were unthinkable below the Potomac. They furnished a happy label, indeed, for use against the Republicans in 1856, "Free Love and Frémont."[9] When the Fox sisters began to give their séances in New York about 1850, they were irreverently referred to in the South as the "Knocking Girls of Rochester."[10] The spiritualist craze in the North, leading to numerous spiritualist circles and the establishment of the *Spiritual Telegraphy,* found hardly an echo of credulity in the South.[11] The planters and the yeoman farmers were content to enjoy its rural simplicity, almost wholly free from disturbing social adventures.

The woman's rights movement that was developing in the North struck an almost impenetrable barrier when it attempted to gain converts in the South. There were at least five good reasons why the Southern people would have nothing to do with this Yankee fad. In the first place, the feminist movement in the North had grown up in close alliance with the abolitionist movement. Many of the most odious abolitionists were also aggressive champions of the rights of women. In the second place, Pauline theology, which had a tenacious hold on the Southern churches, was hostile to feminine assertiveness. Moreover, the prevailing romanticism of the South was incompatible with the attempt of the feminists to equalize the sexes. Although the first woman's college in the United States, Wesleyan Methodist College, was founded in the South at Macon, Georgia, Southern women as a class were not sufficiently educated to demand equality of rights with men. Finally, the energies of so many Southern women who might have grown restive under masculine rule were used up in

[9] Richmond *Enquirer,* Sept. 13, 1856.

[10] *Southern Literary Messenger,* XVII, 1-7 (Jan., 1851), a review, "The Night-Side of Nature."

[11] *Ibid.,* XIX, 385-394 (July, 1853), an article, "Spiritual Manifestations"; *ibid.,* XX, 343-344 (June, 1854), an article, "The Credulity of the Times."

childbearing. Take, for example, Mrs. Calhoun with her nine children, Mrs. Henry Clay with her eleven children, and Mrs. Robert E. Lee, who presented her husband with a new baby at frequent intervals. These women, typical Southern matrons of the upper class, could hardly have had much leisure or desire to crusade for woman's rights. There is probably a genuine correlation between the spread of the practice of birth control and the growth of woman's rights. Those Southern women who were childless or unburdened by large families, such as Mrs. Chesnut, Mrs. Clement C. Clay, Mrs. Pryor, Octavia LeVert, Julia LeGrand, Mrs. Jefferson Davis, found an outlet in the glamour of social life, in the absorption of religious duties, or in writing *belles-lettres*.[12]

The few organized groups of radicals in the South, such as Frances Wright's colony of Negroes and whites at Nashoba, Tennessee, the Spiritualist community at Mountain Cove, Fayette County, (now West) Virginia, the Icarians, and the Free German Societies, were all sporadic adventures of foreign radicalism on Southern soil.

Like William Lloyd Garrison, Frances Wright was a universal reformer, cherishing an exquisite dream of a world renovated and swept clean of all impurities and injustices. One of the visions which she sought to realize was the banishing of slavery and the elevation of the Negro to the plane of his white master.[13] Buying a large plantation in Tennessee in 1826, she proposed to purchase some slaves and allow them to work out their emancipation. The white members of the colony were to teach the slaves and live on

[12] See especially Mrs. Chesnut, *op. cit.;* Eron Rowland, *Varina Howell, Wife of Jefferson Davis* (New York, 1927); Schlesinger, "The Role of Woman in American History," *New Viewpoints in American History*, chap. vi; and Elizabeth Cady Stanton, Susan B. Anthony, and Matilda Joslyn Gage, *History of Woman Suffrage* (New York, 1881), I, 39-406, "Angelina Grimké."

[13] Trollope, *Domestic Manners of the Americans*, pp. 33-42; see also Robert Dale Owens, *Threading My Way* (New York, 1874), pp. 298-302.

a basis of communism with them. Those left in charge of the experiment eventually avowed the doctrines of free love and shocked their Southern neighbors by the unabashed iniquity of their conduct with the Negroes and mulattoes. These slaves of yesterday were treated as though they were highly refined white persons. The indolent darkies, accordingly, loafed and malingered on the plantation until the experiment was an economic failure.[14]

On the fringe of the South, in Fayette County, Virginia, a group of more than a hundred Spiritualists settled in 1852, to await the second coming of Christ. One of the leaders of this strange cult was Rev. Thomas Lake Harris, a brilliant poet with a Dr. Jekyl and Mr. Hyde personality.[15] The community published a journal entitled the *Mountain Cove Journal and Spiritual Harbinger,* which claimed to be "dictated by Spirits out of the flesh, and by them edited, superintended, and controlled."[16] The colony was abandoned in 1853, when the neophytes realized that they had been dupes to their autocratic leaders.[17]

Another abortive attempt of foreign radicals to secure a lodgment in the South was the settlement of the Icarians in Fannin County, Texas. The Icarians were chiefly natives of France who had been deluded by the impractical visions of Etienne Cabet. This reformer had written a book entitled *Voyage en Icaria* (1839), in which he described his magnificent dreams of utopian communism. In 1848 a part of his followers emigrated to an undeveloped section of Texas, where they had bought a million acres of land. The colony lasted

[14] W. R. Waterman, *Frances Wright* (New York, 1924), pp. 92-133. See James Madison's letter to Frances Wright, expressing sympathy for her desire to abolish slavery but disparaging the Nashoba plan (Hunt, ed., *Writings of James Madison,* IX, 224-229).

[15] *Dictionary of American Biography,* VIII, 322.

[16] Mott, *A History of American Magazines, 1850-1865,* p. 210.

[17] Sir Arthur Conan Doyle, *The History of Spiritualism* (New York, 1926), I, 119-120.

no longer than a few months in its unfriendly environment, the survivors moving to Nauvoo, Illinois.[18]

After the ill-fated revolution of 1848 some German settlers who held very radical ideas entered the South. In 1850 a certain Mr. Steinmetz came to Richmond to organize a Free German Society. But the society he founded, numbered only twenty-two persons and was regarded with hostility even by the majority of the German residents. Being threatened with disagreeable consequences if he remained in Richmond, he left the following year. The platform of the Free German Society of Richmond included such revolutionary ideas as the right of the people to change the Constitution when they liked, the abolition of the Presidency, the right of the people to recall their representatives at their pleasure, compulsory education, abolition of capital punishment, repeal of the laws enforcing the observance of the Sabbath, and the support of the program of Cassius Clay for the abolition of slavery.[19] The Free Germans of Louisville, Kentucky, advocated government ownership of railroads, abolition of land monopoly, the rights of woman, complete religious freedom, and the adoption of the program of Cassius M. Clay in regard to slavery.[20] Likewise the Germans of western Texas harbored some vigorous radicals. Olmsted observed that among the faults of the Germans of Texas were a tendency to freethinking and a devotion to reason which were often carried to the verge of bigotry.[21]

A very few native Southerners displayed an active interest

[18] For an account of these communistic societies see J. H. Noyes, *History of American Socialisms* (Philadelphia, 1870); W. A. Hinds, *American Communities; Brief Sketches of Economy, Zoar, Bethel, Amora, Amana, Icaria, the Shakers, Oneida, Wallingford, and the Brotherhood of the New Life* (Oneida, N.Y., 1878); and Charles Nordhoff, *The Communistic Societies of the United States* (New York, 1875).

[19] Schuricht, *op. cit.*, II, 36.

[20] M. W. Cluskey, *The Political Text-Book, or Encyclopedia* (Washington, D. C., 1857), pp. 253-254.

[21] Olmsted, *A Journey Through Texas*, p. 430.

in the isms. The Grimké family of Charleston, belonging to the aristocratic circle of that city, presented an interesting group of radicals. Angelina and Sarah were converted to the Quaker faith as a result of a visit to Philadelphia. They abandoned Charleston to live in the North, where they could advance their antislavery and feminist enthusiasm unmolested.[22] After Angelina had published her antislavery pamphlet, *Appeal to the Christian Women of the South* (1836), the mayor of Charleston notified her family that she would not be allowed to return to her native city. Thomas S. Grimké, brother of Sarah and Angelina, remained in Charleston and continued to hold slaves, but he was a leader in the temperance and peace movements. Senator Hammond of South Carolina, whose father was a New Englander, also was lured by some of the radical movements in the North. Hammond had a curious interest in spiritualism and became a convert to its doctrines. He wrote William Gilmore Simms that he intended to give a lot in Aiken to the first congregation of Spiritualists who would erect a church on it.[23] Not only did he read books on occult science, but he gave Simms ten dollars with which to consult some mediums in New York and obtain answers to a set of questions that he had prepared.[24] The Virginia liberal, Nicholas Trist, was sympathetic to the radical ideas of Robert Dale Owen, whom he consulted about the education of his children.[25]

One of the most extreme of these isolated Southern radicals

[22] Nevertheless, Northern public opinion was shocked when Sarah and Angelina stepped out of the bounds of female propriety to lecture to mixed audiences. Angelina humorously observed that her audiences literally sat with "mouths agape and eyes astare" (*Weld-Grimké Letters*, I, 414).

[23] Hammond to Simms, Dec. 27, 1853 (James H. Hammond Papers, MSS in Library of Congress).

[24] Hammond to Simms, Oct. 2, 1856 (*ibid.*).

[25] Robert Dale Owen to Trist, Feb. 12 and March 24, 1832 (Nicholas Trist Papers, MSS in Library of Congress). See also L. M. Sears, "Nicholas P. Trist, a Diplomat with Ideals," *Mississippi Valley Historical Review*, XI, 90 (June, 1924).

was a Jewish youth named Marx Lazarus, who eventually joined the North American Phalanx at Red Bank, New Jersey. The disapproval of his family was voiced in an ironic letter of Sam Mordecai to Marx's guardian, George Washington Mordecai. "Marx is enjoying the delights of a sort of Fourier association," Sam wrote, "they have made him a menial and a drudge, but as it is according to the principles of the association, he enjoys it, cleans cow stables, waits on the table, takes orders from the cook, ploughs, helps the Ladies iron clothes, etc."[26] At the same time the enthusiastic reformer was writing an article on capital. Later he was practicing homeopathy and translating Fourier's works. Another member of the Mordecai family, Ellen, became a member of Edger's Village of Modern Times.[27]

The pacifist movement, which attained a respectable following in the North, made little headway in the South. As early as 1819 there was a peace society at Raleigh, North Carolina, whose president, Calvin Jones, had resigned from his position as commander of the state militia on account of his convictions. The Georgia Peace Society, at Augusta, was for a while an auxiliary of the Pennsylvania Peace Society. The outstanding advocate of pacifism in the South was Thomas S. Grimké, who became a member of the American Peace Society, and a contributor to the society's journal, *Calumet.* Grimké was converted to a belief that all war, even defensive war, was incompatible with Christianity. He prepared an American edition of *Inquiry into the Accordancy of War with the Principles of Christianity,* by the British Quaker, Jonathan Dymond. Grimké even boldly challenged the rightfulness of the American Revolution.[28] Although the organized peace movement received little support below

[26] Sam Mordecai to G. W. Mordecai, Oct. 17, 1849 (Mordecai Papers).

[27] E. L. Allen to George Mordecai, Jan. 15, 1860 *(ibid.).*

[28] Merle Curti, *The American Peace Crusade, 1815-1860* (Durham, N. C., 1929), pp. 32, 61, 69-72.

Mason and Dixon's line, individual Southerners, like Alexander Stephens and Calhoun, stood courageously against the war fever that swept the nation into the Mexican War.

There was one ism that attained a wide popularity in the South, the temperance movement. It harmonized with the religious and puritanical feeling of many Southern people. Such ardent fire-eaters as Robert Barnwell Rhett and Governor Henry A. Wise, whose mouth was frequently stained with tobacco juice, drank only cold water and were prominent as temperance advocates. Rhett was vice-president of the Young Men's Temperance Society of Charleston.[29] In 1839 the state of Georgia was the dramatic scene of a prohibition movement led by a wealthy planter, named Josiah Flournoy. With indomitable zeal he drove from county to county in his buggy to secure signatures to a monster petition that was presented to the legislature in 1839—a petition which proposed that the legislature should prohibit the retailing of liquor within the state. The movement became involved in a bitter political struggle that resulted in the defeat of a prohibition law by a vote of ninety-eight to fifty-four. During the excited campaign for its adoption Flournoy was subjected to many indignities and died a martyr to the cause.[30] In 1851 the Sons of Temperance in Georgia had reached a maximum growth of over thirteen thousand members, but by the close of the ante bellum period the membership had declined to fifteen hundred. The outstanding advocate of temperance in the Upper South was General John Cocke of Bremo, Virginia, who was elected president of the American Temperance Union in 1836. A cavalier Puritan, he abhorred the use of both tobacco and liquor. He symbolized his devotion to the cause of temperance by erecting a small stone building in

[29] Laura A. White, *Robert Barnwell Rhett: Father of Secession* (New York, 1931), p. 32.

[30] H. A. Scomp, *King Alcohol in the Realm of King Cotton* (New York, 1888), pp. 330-331.

the form of a Greek temple on his plantation with the superscription, "Dedicated to the Sons of Temperance."[31] The Washington revival of the 1840's, based on a pledge of total abstinence, was started by six reformed drunkards of Baltimore.[32]

Many complex factors explain the momentum of the ante bellum South toward conservatism during the time that New England was becoming a center of radicalism. D. R. Hundley, educated at the University of Virginia and at Harvard, suggested an explanation in his *Social Relations in Our Southern States:* the Southern planter lived out-of-doors, riding and hunting, and thus developed a sanity of outlook which made him immune to the fanaticism of the North.[33] In a land where it is so pleasant to be out-of-doors a large part of the year both literature and wild theories are not likely to find favorable soil. The predominantly rural condition of the South undoubtedly contributed to the resistance to Northern radicalism. Yet this point should not be overstressed, for in colonial days and during the Revolutionary period, when the South was even more bucolic, the leaders of liberalism were Southerners. In New England and the Middle States lyceums were an important instrument in disseminating radical doctrines. The lyceum movement in the South, on the other hand, attained comparatively a feeble foothold. In 1838 a lyceum was started at Richmond modeled on the Franklin Institute of Philadelphia.[34] The Fredericksburg lyceum founded for mutual improvement in 1837 secured a special column in the *Southern Literary Messenger* for the literary productions of its members.[35] Lexington had a Franklin Society in 1847 before which John Letcher debated the proposition, "Should the people of

[31] *William and Mary College Quarterly* (Second Series), XIII, 143-154 (July, 1933).

[32] See J. L. Krout, *The Origins of Prohibition* (New York, 1935), chap. ix.

[33] Hundley, *Social Relations in Our Southern States,* pp. 40-41.

[34] *Southern Literary Messenger,* IV, 8 (Jan., 1838).

[35] *Ibid.,* III, 461 (July, 1837).

western Virginia delay any longer in taking steps to bring about a division of the state?"[36] Charleston, although a city of only twelve thousand white people in 1842, had sixty-three different societies, most of them religious in nature, but including such organizations as a Young Men's Debating Society and a Literary and Philosophical Society.[37] An attempt was made to establish a lyceum in Augusta, Georgia, for regular lectures, but it failed.[38] In the little college community of Washington, Mississippi, a lyceum existed between 1835 and 1838, of which the amateur scientist, Benjamin L. C. Wailes, was an active member.[39] The lyceum movement in the South affected only a few people in the cities. It did not serve, as in the North, as a means of adult education and of popularizing the novel ideas and reforms that came from Europe.

Indeed, many of the radical movements that agitated the North originated across the Atlantic. The South of 1850, however, shared only slightly in this importation of foreign ideas. Not only did European immigrants avoid the South, but Southerners who went abroad were chiefly interested in recreation or in the more romantic aspects of European culture. There was no movement in the South to correspond with the transcendental school of New England, which was stimulated in part by German thought and Oriental literatures.[40] Southern importations, whether of ideas or of goods, came largely by way of the North. It is a significant cultural fact that the principal railroads in the Upper South ran north and south, rather than east and west to Southern seaports. The unceasing efforts of Southern commercial conventions to change these trends of commerce, by establishing direct steam-

[36] Prettyman, "John Letcher," III, 314.

[37] Buckingham, *Slave States of America,* I, 80.

[38] *Ibid.,* p. 167.

[39] C. S. Sydnor, *A Gentleman of the Old Natchez Region: Benjamin L. C. Wailes* (Durham, N. C., 1938), pp. 144-148.

[40] See W. P. Trent and others (eds.), *The Cambridge History of American Literature* (New York, 1917), Vol. I, chaps. viii and ix.

ship lines with Europe, were realized only in pipe dreams and the imagination of orators.[41] Furthermore, European nations considered Southern slavery as a repellent anachronism, a fact which tended to preclude any sympathetic consideration of foreign radical ideas by Southerners.

One of the appeals to Southern prejudice which the Know-Nothing party adopted was the assertion that foreign immigrants brought dangerous ideas into the country. Said Alexander H. H. Stuart, a leader of the party in Virginia: "Many of the educated foreigners bring with them the most distorted views of the ends and aims of social organization. Many of them are infidels, atheists, socialists, and agrarians, and by their wild and demoralizing ideas corrupt the very fountains of liberty."[42] Since the Southern States received only a small percentage of these immigrants, its prevailing conservatism of thought was relatively unaffected.

In New England the way was prepared for radical movements by the breakdown of Puritanism. The land of Dixie, on the other hand, remained the great stronghold of puritanical feeling in nineteenth-century America. In general, the Southern yeomanry had puritanical prejudices, frowning upon the indulgent society of the aristocrats. "Parson" Brownlow summed up the narrow creed of these unsophisticated country people: "I have never been arraigned in the church for any immorality. I never played a card. I never was a profane swearer. I never drank a dram of liquor until within a few years—when it was taken as a medicine. I never had a cigar or a chew of tobacco in my mouth. I never was in attendance at a theatre. I never attended a horse-race, and never witnessed their running save on the fair-grounds of my county. I never courted but one woman; and her I married."[43] Men

[41] Wender, *Southern Commercial Conventions*, chaps. ii and vii.

[42] Robertson, *Alexander Hugh Holmes Stuart*, p. 120.

[43] W. G. Brownlow, *Sketches of the Rise, Progress and Decline of Secession; with a Narrative of Personal Adventures Among the Rebels* (Philadelphia, 1862), p. 19.

like "Parson" Brownlow or Stonewall Jackson were as militant Puritans as John Endicott ever was.

Even the well-to-do planter, despite the myth of the gay cavalier, was frequently affected by this mood of puritanism. Colonel Richard Malcolm Johnston has related how his father, after his conversion, gave up dancing and card playing, and, above all, denied to himself his former luxury of a delicious bowl of toddy.[44] When the correct Senator Clement C. Clay of Alabama visited the Creole country, he revealed his puritanical prejudices in a letter to his daughter: "The Creoles—especially French and English—are the most unchristian, ungodly, devilish, pleasure-seeking people I have yet seen. The stores, drinking saloons, workshops, etc., are kept open on Sunday, as on any other day; and everybody who can spare time from business goes fishing or hunting or to play billiards or ten pins. Sunday is the chief day for circus, theatre, other shows."[45] Such a strict attitude toward morals was not conducive to an open mind in regard to the new social propositions that were fermenting Northern society.

The fact that abolitionists were the most prominent advocates of the isms constituted a strong motive for repelling such vagaries from the South. The Richmond *Examiner* in an editorial, "Our Enemies, the Isms and their Purposes," pointed out the close alliance between the abolitionists and the advocates of free love and infidelity. Horace Greeley was described as the leader of the abolitionists and also "the autocrat and prophet of the northern isms."[46] The career of Garrison undoubtedly lent support to this view, for he gradually made the *Liberator* an organ of universal reform, championing abolition of the Sabbath, woman's rights, temperance, the

[44] *Autobiography of Col. Richard Malcolm Johnston* (Washington, D. C., 1900), p. 13.

[45] Clay to Celeste, New Iberia, La., Dec. 5, 1860 (C. C. Clay Papers, MSS in Duke University Library). For a Northerner's equally severe condemnation of Creole laxity see Whipple, *Southern Diary,* p. 119.

[46] Richmond *Examiner,* Sept. 5 and 9, 1856.

peace movement, and so on. Harriet Beecher Stowe, the author of *Uncle Tom's Cabin,* was often cited as typical of the alliance between feminism and abolitionism.[47] The Northern reformers seemed to the Southern clergy to be fanatics because they would not wait for the slow action of Providence. Said Rev. Benjamin Palmer in an ironic allusion to these immediatists: "the sun must be stricken from the heavens if a spot be found upon his disk and the stars swept from the skies if their courses be erratic."[48]

The Southerners greatly exaggerated the numbers and importance of the Northern radicals. The *Free Enquirer,* edited by Frances Wright and Robert Dale Owen, had a subscription list of only one thousand names.[49] The *Liberator* had less than four hundred white subscribers in 1833 and was sustained largely by the Negroes of Philadelphia, New York, and Boston.[50] The aversion toward the isms among the overwhelming majority of Northern people was expressed by B. D. Silliman, of New York City, who had been asked by the Jewish lawyer, Mordecai, to investigate the Village of Modern Times. He wrote: "I am sorry to learn that 'Modern Times' is a rendezvous of 'isms.' Whether Fourierism, Transcendentalism, communism, or which of the crazy isms predominate I am uncertain. The accounts which I hear of it are in every way unfavorable, and I fear Mrs. Allen will not find it a desirable residence."[51] When Judge John W. Edmonds of the New York Supreme Court became prominent in the advocacy of spiritualism, he was pointed at on the street as a crazy spiritualist and was forced to resign from his judicial position.[52] The distorted idea that Southerners enter-

[47] See G. F. Holmes's review of Mrs. Stowe's famous novel in *Southern Literary Messenger,* XVIII, 631 (Oct., 1852).

[48] Thomas, *The Carolina Tribute to Calhoun,* pp. 250-251.

[49] Owen, "An Earnest Sowing of Wild Oats," p. 73.

[50] Barnes, *The Antislavery Impulse,* p. 50.

[51] B. D. Silliman to G. W. Mordecai, April 25, 1860 (Mordecai MSS).

[52] Doyle, *op. cit.,* pp. 130, 141.

tained of the Northern radicals and of their number was an important cause of the intellectual blockade.[53]

George Fitzhugh, a brilliant and trenchant writer of Virginia, published two volumes in which he tried to rationalize and justify the conservative prejudices of his section. These two works, *Sociology for the South and Cannibals All,* however, must not be taken as representative of Southern thought, except that of the extreme right wing. Fitzhugh advanced the idea that slavery had saved the South from the unhealthy radicalism of the North. Southern civilization, he maintained, was founded on Aristotelian principles, by which the inequality of man was recognized. Consequently, Southern society was well ordered and serene, while the North was constantly in turmoil. "Mormons and Oneida Perfectionists," he said, "would no sooner be tolerated in Virginia than Pyrrhic dances and human sacrifices to Moloch."[54] With characteristic exaggeration, he affirmed: "In the whole South there is not one Socialist, not one man, rich or poor, proposing to subvert and reconstruct society."[55] Likewise, in articles for *De Bow's Review* and in his books, he praised the South for its freedom from skepticism in religion and for its resistance to the Woman's Rights Movement which sought to drive women from their sphere (the angelic).[56] Rejoicing in this conservatism of his section, Fitzhugh transmuted the *status quo* of Southern society into an extremely brittle philosophy.

In a chapter on "The Philosophy of Isms," Fitzhugh offered an ingenious theory to explain why the North was the home of radical ideas and social experiments. Free society,

[53] Governor Wise revealed a typical Southern viewpoint: "We can't be made to comprehend here how it is that the Sumners and Wilsons and Burlingames of Massts. should not be in a majority of the masses when they are so strong in the offices and in the influence of the North" (Wise to Lt. Wise, Oct. 6, 1856, Wise MSS).

[54] George Fitzhugh, *Sociology for the South* (Richmond, 1854), p. 110.

[55] *Ibid.*, p. 306.

[56] *De Bow's Review*, XXVIII, 7 (Jan., 1860).

he contended, had proved a failure. This was due to excessive individualism, which had led to cutthroat competition and exploitation. A result of this unhealthy condition was the emergence of the phenomena of strikes, trade unions, phalansteries, communistic establishments, Mormonism, and other excrescences. Isms arose to redress the evils of excessive individualism. "Man's nature is social," said Fitzhugh, "not selfish, and he longs and yearns to return to parental, fraternal, and association relations. All the isms concur in promising closer and more association relations, in establishing at least a qualified community of property, and in insuring the weak and unfortunate the necessaries and comforts of life."[57] Examine the communism of the Mormons, the socialism of Fourier and Owen, the free love villages of Trialville and Modern Zion, he declared, and you will find this trend toward closer and more organic association. Fitzhugh cleverly pointed out the evils of Northern industrialism in exploiting the lower classes and reducing them to wage slaves. Despite his bitter condemnation of Yankee industrialism, he advocated the South's developing manufactures. The inconsistency of this program with the maintenance of slavery was pointed out in the *Southern Literary Messenger* in an able, and on the whole favorable, review of Fitzhugh's *Sociology for the South.*[58]

Henry W. Ravenel, a South Carolina scientist, also attempted to explain the causes that gave the South immunity from "the isms." In an address before the Black Oak Agricultural Society, he observed that the Southern people were dominated by a spirit of conservatism, which saved them from excesses on the one hand, and at the same time caused them to uphold law and order. The South, he declared, was "the breakwater which is to stay that furious tide of social and political heresies now setting toward us from the shores of

[57] George Fitzhugh, *Cannibals All* (Richmond, 1857), p. 332.

[58] *Southern Literary Messenger,* XXI, 137 (March, 1855). Nevertheless, the Tredegar Iron Works, some tobacco factories in Richmond, and some cotton factories in Georgia successfully employed slaves.

the old world." The rural life of the Southerners gave an attachment to the soil, a serene habit of mind, and an indisposition to excesses. The institution of African slavery and the relative freedom from foreign immigrants contributed to this end. "We should shrink intuitively," he warned, "from all the novel and revolutionary notions which are infecting the masses in Europe and the free states of the North."[59]

The Southerners of the ante bellum period preferred the old patterns of life, the path of conservatism. This preference was the natural choice of an agrarian society. But sectionalism, lack of European contacts, a puritanical religious background, the influence of slavery, intensified the distaste for radicalism or utopian experiments. Calhoun pointed out that this conservatism of the South was the salvation of the nation, acting in the capacity of a makeweight against radicalism. "The balance of this system is in the slaveholding States," he declared. "They are the conservative portion—always have been the conservative portion—always will be the conservative portion; and with a due balance on their part may, for generations to come, uphold this glorious Union of ours."[60] The ripe experiences of mankind, what the race had learned by innumerable trials and errors, was not to be lightly set aside. The Southern planters had learned this lesson, which made them cautious of disturbing old social moulds.

Only an atmosphere of good will and understanding could have led to an interchange of ideas and fruitful reforms between the radical North and the conservative South. The Virginia liberal, William Alexander Caruthers, pointed out a method of cultivating intersectional comity and the open mind. "Every southern should visit New-York," he wrote in *The Kentuckian in New-York.* "It would allay provincial prejudices and calm excitement against his northern country-

[59] "Address of Henry W. Ravenel delivered before the Black Oak Agricultural Society, April, 1852" (H. W. Ravenel MSS in possession of Professor W. C. Coker, University of North Carolina, Chapel Hill, N. C.).

[60] Crallé, *Works of John C. Calhoun,* IV, 343-344.

men."[61] Lucian Minor after his trip through New England was also convinced that great benefit would result to Southern farmers, planters, and their wives if they would follow his example. He traveled with an open mind and reported that New England was as far above the South in the achievement of comfort, as the latter section was above the Hottentots or Esquimaux.[62] But the bitter feeling of sectionalism continued to grow, exacerbated by politicians, fire-eaters, and antislavery crusaders, until an intellectual blockade was set up by the South not only against abolitionism, but also against many associated isms that were destined to triumph in the future.[63] Aversion to things Northern even precluded the development of a lively interest among the book readers of the South in the contemporary literature of New England. Emerson's works, representing the best thought of the country, were scarcely read below the Potomac.[64] At the height of the excitement against the North during the resistance movement of 1850, R. S. Holt wrote to Joseph Holt that it had become a question "Whether Southern chivalry will hereafter condescend to cool its Mint Juleps with Northern ice?"[65] Instead of following the advice of Caruthers, Southerners of the prewar years listened to the admonition of Calhoun to meet the pernicious ideas "on the frontier." The dynamics of Southern thought moved, after the death of Jefferson, in the direction of defense, a trend which explains much in the cultural history of the Old South.

[61] Parrington, *The Romantic Revolution in America,* p. 42.

[62] *Atlantic Monthly,* XXVII, 684 (June, 1871).

[63] See Clement Eaton, "The Resistance of the South to Northern Radicalism," *New England Quarterly,* VIII, 215-231 (June, 1935).

[64] Fredrika Bremer wrote: "It is remarkable how very little, or not at all, the authors of the Northern States, even the best of them, are known in the South. They are afraid of admitting their liberal opinions into the Slave States." She found that Joel Poinsett, one of the most cultivated of Southerners, was unacquainted with Emerson's philosophy, which he condemned as "unpractical" when Fredrika discussed it with him (*The Homes of the New World,* I, 298).

[65] R. S. Holt to Joseph Holt, Benton, Miss., Oct. 27, 1850 (Joseph Holt Papers, MSS in Library of Congress).

CHAPTER ELEVEN

THE CONSERVATIVE REVOLT

On December 22, 1859, a special train arrived at Richmond bringing more than two hundred medical students from Philadelphia. It was the hegira of Southern students from the North following the excitement of John Brown's raid. The faculty and students of the Richmond Medical College, the town council, and the Southern Rights Association exultantly welcomed them. All formed in procession and marched, behind the armory band, past the beautiful capitol designed by Jefferson to the governor's mansion. Here Governor Henry A. Wise, standing on his porch, delivered a tirade of incandescent Southern oratory. One of the students gracefully responded. Then they retired to the Columbian Hotel, where the hospitality of the Old South had prepared "a beautiful collation" for them.[1]

Governor Wise, fond of magniloquent phrases, said, "Let Virginia call home her children!" He assured the students that they had acted wisely in leaving a hostile community to build up Southern schools and rebuke the North for its fanaticism. Thus the reproach so often made against the South that Negro slavery paralyzed learning and science would be proved untrue. In that perfervid way of his, he said:

"Let us employ our own teachers [applause], especially that they may teach our own doctrines. Let us dress in the wool raised on our own pastures. Let us eat the flour from our own mills, and if we can't get that, why let us go back to our old accustomed corn bread." [Loud applause.][2]

The John Brown raid threw the Southern people off balance emotionally and gave them a sense of crisis. Instead of assessing the raid as the isolated act of a little band of fanatics, they attributed it to a conspiracy of the Northern abolitionists to instigate servile insurrections in various places in the South. The sympathy for John Brown which was widely manifested in the North made Southerners feel that Northerners hated their section. Out of this jittery state of mind, or popular hysteria, arose numerous vigilance committees to ferret out the emissaries of servile insurrection. As a result, Northern travelers, schoolteachers, peddlers, and workmen in the South were in constant danger of being brought before vigilance committees, flogged, and expelled from the country on the basis of unfounded suspicions.[3] Such a flagrant violation of civil liberties, moreover, was sanctioned by the legal authorities and by public opinion in general.

One of the most unfortunate consequences of the John Brown raid was that it nipped in the bud the revival of a promising Opposition or Old Whig party in the Upper South.[4] This group, led by John J. Crittenden and Joshua F. Bell in Kentucky, Congressmen Alexander R. Boteler and A. H. H. Stuart in Virginia, John Bell and John Netherland in Tennessee, and William A. Graham and George Badger in North Carolina, was seeking moderate solutions of sectional problems. The John Brown raid played into the hands of the fire-eaters in the South, the men who were determined to destroy Stephen A. Douglas's chance to be the Democratic candidate for President in 1860. To achieve this aim, as well as to unite the South by agitation, they had introduced a

1 Richmond *Semi-Weekly Enquirer,* Dec. 23, 1859, Va. State Library.

2 Richmond *Daily Dispatch,* Dec. 23, 1859, Va. State Library. See Clement Eaton, "The Resistance of the South to Northern Radicalism," *New England Quarterly,* VIII, 215-216 (June, 1935).

3 Clement Eaton, "Mob Violence in the Old South," *Mississippi Valley Historical Review,* XXIX, 351-370 (Dec., 1942).

4 See Allan Nevins, *The Emergence of Lincoln* (2 vols., New York, 1950), II, 58-68.

new and indefensible demand upon the North; namely, the passage by Congress of a slave code protecting slavery in the Federal territories.[5]

The high state of emotionalism in the South induced by the John Brown raid was further stimulated in the summer and autumn of 1860 by a prolonged scare, or panic, over rumors of the insurrection of slaves. Beginning in Texas, the fear of servile insurrection spread from state to state as newspapers reported the discovery of slave plots.[6] In December, 1860, when the secession convention met in South Carolina, many Southerners were still alarmed over the danger of slave revolts inspired by Northern emissaries. It was at this time that Major J. M. McCue of Augusta County, Virginia, arrived in Columbia to sell a rifle which he had designed to the South Carolina Convention. The model of the weapon was being fashioned in the Federal armory at Harpers Ferry, and the enterprising Major (of Virginia Militia), who directed that he be addressed as Colonel, planned to begin production of it in a plant to be located in the Shenandoah Valley. Four days after South Carolina seceded, he met Professor Charles S. Venable of South Carolina College on the street and heard a remarkable story of the dread of slave uprisings in the low country.

The professor of mathematics explained to him the excited state of the public mind which had preceded the decision to secede. If South Carolina had not taken things entirely into her own hands and withdrawn from the Union, Venable observed, "she was to be St. Domingois'd."[7] During the convention he had offered the hospitality of his home for the night to a delegate from one of the lower parishes; but the

[5] Robert Toombs expressed such a demand in a letter to Alexander H. Stephens, Feb. 10, 1860, opposing the Davis Resolutions in Congress. U. B. Phillips, *The Life of Robert Toombs* (New York, 1913), 184.

[6] Clement Eaton, *Freedom of Thought in the Old South* (new ed., New York, 1952), chap. iv.

[7] J. M. McCue to J. L. Imboden, Dec. 26, 1860. James Blythe Anderson Papers, MSS, University of Kentucky Library.

delegate had politely declined, saying that it was imperative for him to return home because, just before he left for the convention, his overseer had found some barrels of gunpowder hidden by his slaves. Venable also had heard from his sister in Alabama of her fear of the Negroes as a result of a recent discovery of an insurrection plot below Montgomery, and he mentioned the discovery of another plot in the vicinity of Wilmington which had alarmed members of the North Carolina legislature. McCue commented on these recent instances of danger to the Southern people: "The insidious means used by those wretches of the North who apotheosize Jno. Brown will leave no step of this kind unaccomplished to carry out their malignant purposes–This whole country [the South] will find, I am inclined to believe, that this Virginia rifle will be the surest defence."[8]

All over the South volunteer military companies were organized as a result of excitement over the John Brown raid. On "Looking Glass Plantation," in a placid little community in eastern North Carolina, Catherine Ann Edmondston kept a diary which reflected the emotional disturbance of many Southerners caused by the Harpers Ferry affair. On June 6, 1860, she recorded that her husband Patrick, who was a South Carolina aristocrat, had been out all day drilling his troop in the hot sun–"so much for John Brown and Northern philanthropy." Two weeks later he went with his troop to Enfield by invitation of the Enfield Blues to witness the presentation of a flag by the ladies of that community to the company. On July 16 he attended a military convention at Goldsboro to draw up a code for the organization of militia of the state. Mrs. Edmondston's father, Thomas Pollock Devereux, a prominent Whig planter, scoffed at all this military activity as folly–"no need of preparation for war," he would declare, and "he always winds up with abuse of

[8] *Ibid.* See also letters of McCue to Imboden, July 23, Nov. 22, and Dec. 4, 1860, and Imboden to McCue, Dec. 4 and 7, 1860.

South Carolina for her extreme views." Catherine Ann, who was a spirited sectional patriot, did not share his moderate views. "I do not see him in the present attitude of the North, [the] sample they have given us in the John Brown Raid," she wrote, "he can be so indifferent to our preparation for a future one"; her husband, however, "is on the other extreme, he is like the War Horse in the Bible who 'sniffs it afar.' He is sure that Abraham Lincoln will be elected and we plunged into a civil war before the year is ended. God arrest it!"[9]

In this inflamed state of Southern feeling the election of Lincoln on November 6, 1860, by a completely sectional vote, representing only 39.9 per cent of the popular vote, acted as the detonator of a secession movement. Lincoln, we now know, was disposed to follow a moderate course; but Southerners in 1860 had a distorted view of his personality and policies. The President-elect was regarded as an uncouth countryman who would be a figurehead in an administration controlled by Seward and the radical antislavery wing of the party. It was widely rumored among the ignorant classes of the South that Hannibal Hamlin, the Republican Vice President, was a mulatto. Southerners believed that Lincoln's real intention was to use his power of office to destroy slavery within the Southern states.

Some of the old Whig leaders and moderate newspapers in the South pointed out that Lincoln would be powerless to destroy slavery in the Southern states even if he had such a design.[10] The Supreme Court, under the lead of Taney, they argued, would shield Southern interests. Moreover, in the Thirty-seventh Congress elected in November, 1860, the Republicans would have twenty-nine Senators while the opposition would have thirty-seven; in the House of Representatives

[9] MS Diary of Catherine Ann Edmondston, June 6 and July 16, 1860, in North Carolina State Department of Archives and History.

[10] New Orleans *Bee*, Nov. 8, 1860, and Lexington *Kentucky Statesman*, Nov. 20, 1860, quoted in Dwight L. Dumond, ed., *Southern Editorials on Secession* (New York, 1931), 221-223, 253-255.

the opposition could defeat the Republicans by a vote of one hundred and twenty to one hundred and eight. Yet there was no guarantee that the Northern Democrats would vote for the preservation of slave interests, and the victorious Republican party would necessarily exclude the South from all share in the administration of the national government, for no representative Southerners would accept office from a "Black Republican." Thus the South had come to the end of a long period of control over the Federal government, which had been maintained by the mastery of the Democratic party, by the domination of the Supreme Court, and by the election of "doughfaces" such as Pierce and Buchanan to the Presidency.

The political crisis came at a time when the South was enjoying a period of great prosperity. The approach of the Presidential election broke this spell of economic euphoria. On September 26, 1860, a Kentucky mule trader wrote that "money matters are tighter in Kentucky than I ever saw them," for the planters of the lower South were not buying the Kentucky exports of Negroes, mules, and horses. One Kentucky slave trader, he reported, had recently taken forty-one slaves to Natchez but had been unable to sell a single one. The price range at the time of writing was $1,200 to $1,300 for No. 1 male slaves, and $1,000 for prime girls. In the summer the range had been $100 to $150 higher. "Politics," he declared, "is the cause of all the trouble."[11] After Lincoln was elected, business came virtually to a standstill in the South. A stock breeder of Paris, Kentucky, who was trying to sell mules in Virginia, found such a miserable market that he wrote to his wife on February 6, 1861, "It makes me sick to look at a mule."[12]

[11] F. G. Murphey to George, Sept. 26, 1860. B. F. Buckner Papers, MSS in University of Kentucky Library.

[12] W. B. Rogers to his wife, Feb. 6, 1861. W. B. Rogers Papers, MSS in University of Kentucky Library.

Certain that Lincoln would be elected President, Governor W. H. Gist of South Carolina on October 5 asked the governors of the cotton states what action they would take in the approaching crisis. He wrote that South Carolina preferred that some other state should take the lead in a secession movement, for the Palmetto State had a reputation for ultraism. As to the course of South Carolina, he predicted: "If a single state secedes she will follow her. If no other state takes the lead South Carolina will secede (in my opinion) alone if she has any assurance that she will be followed by another or other states; otherwise it is doubtful." The governors of Georgia, North Carolina, Alabama, Louisiana, Florida, and Mississippi replied that none of these states would take the lead in seceding. Three of the governors were of the opinion that a Southern convention should or would be called. Governor Thomas Moore of Louisiana, whose sugar planters were opposed to separation from a Union which granted them favorable tariff protection, flatly said: "I shall not advise secession of Louisiana if Lincoln is elected. . . . I do not think that the people of Louisiana will ultimately decide in favor of that course. . . . Louisiana is totally unprepared for any warlike measures. Her arsenals are empty." North Carolina's governor, John W. Ellis, himself a secessionist, said that the majority of the people of his state would not regard the election of Lincoln as a justification for secession. Governor Joseph E. Brown of Georgia wrote that Georgia would not go out of the Union simply on account of the election of Lincoln but would wait for an overt act. The most encouraging replies for secession came from the governors of Mississippi, Alabama, and Florida, who declared that, although their states would not secede alone, they would follow if some other state seceded.[13]

[13] These letters are published in John G. Nicolay and John Hay, *Abraham Lincoln: A History* (10 vols., New York, 1904 ed.), II, 306-314.

There was a considerable difference of opinion in South Carolina whether she should take the lead in the secession movement. The informed leaders knew she was distrusted as hot-headed and arrogant among the more conservative Southern states. North Carolinians especially had a profound jealousy and dislike of their southern neighbor. The Raleigh *Register* declared on November 20, 1860, that South Carolina in her zeal for free trade and cheap Negroes ignored the welfare of other Southern states.[14] Consequently, one of the most talented of South Carolina's sons, William Henry Trescot, Assistant Secretary of State in the Buchanan administration, wrote to a leading fire-eater of the state, Representative William Porcher Miles, that every effort should be made to induce Georgia to take the lead in the secession movement: "Give her all the glory, take her men and her measures" to secure joint action of the Southern states. In order to accomplish this concert, with Georgia leading, he observed, "we must cut up by the roots some home ambitions and much home selfishness."[15]

On the other hand, the youthful Congressman Lawrence Keitt, most enthusiastic of the South Carolina firebrands, believed that his state must take the lead in the secession movement. "If we wait for Alabama," he wrote to Miles, "we will wait eternally." He thought William Lowndes Yancey, the foremost secession leader in that state, lacked the elements of real leadership. Keitt gave a most interesting reason for secession by South Carolina after the election of Lincoln, in the need to preserve conservatism in the South against the modern spirit of radicalism. "If we submit," he wrote, "the South is done. The concentration of absolute power in the hands of the North will develop the wildest democracy ever seen on this earth—unless it should have been matched in

[14] Raleigh *Register,* Nov. 20, 1860.

[15] W. H. T. to Miles, Nov. 8, 1860. William Porcher Miles Papers, MSS, Southern Collection, University of North Carolina.

Paris in 1789. What of conservatism? What of order? What of social security or financial prosperity can withstand Northern Republican license?"[16] Keitt was undoubtedly thinking of the disruptive influence on Southern society which he believed the antislavery policy of the victorious Republican party would have. Furthermore, he equated a Union party at the South with an abolition party—"not at first it may be, but through quick transitions."

By recent experience South Carolina had learned that it was impossible to get the Southern states to cooperate in a resistance movement through an All-Southern Convention. In the previous December after the John Brown raid, she had issued a call for a Southern Convention to meet at Atlanta, and early in 1860 she had sent Christopher Memminger, a Charleston lawyer and banker, as a commissioner to persuade Virginia to send delegates; but the leader of the upper South turned a cold shoulder and the movement toward cooperation failed.[17] But after the election of Lincoln South Carolina received assurances from commissioners sent by Mississippi and Alabama that those states would follow her lead in seceding from the Union. South Carolina resolved now to put into practice the doctrine long advocated by Robert Barnwell Rhett and the Charleston *Mercury,* edited by his son, that the secession movement of the Southern states could be accomplished only by the bold action of a single state withdrawing from the Union.

Disunion sentiment was strongest in the parishes of the coastal plain containing a large slave population, but the fear of all classes that Republican rule would destroy the control

[16] Lawrence Keitt to Miles, Oct. 3, 1860. *Ibid.* In the Lawrence Keitt Papers at Duke University is a letter from Keitt to Mrs. Frederick Brown, Mar. 4, 1861, which describes the Republicans as "a motley throng of Sans Culottes and Dames des Halles, infidels, and free lovers, interspersed by Bloomer women, fugitive slaves, and amalgamists."

[17] Ollinger Crenshaw, "Christopher G. Memminger's Mission to Virginia, 1860," *Journal of Southern History,* VIII, 334-349 (Aug. 1942).

of the whites over the Negroes, or the maintenance of white supremacy, was the dominant motive behind secession.[18] In the parishes the planters were haunted by the fear expressed in the diary of the wealthy J. B. Grimball (Dec. 17): "The prospect before us in regard to our Slave Property, if we continue to remain in the Union, is nothing less than utter ruin."[19] By December 1860 there was not a Unionist newspaper in the state. The Charleston *Daily Courier,* edited by Aaron Willington, formerly of Massachusetts, had abandoned its earlier opposition to a headlong movement into secession. The few prominent men who dared to oppose the strongly flowing current, James Louis Petigru of Charleston and Benjamin F. Perry and Chief Justice John B. O'Neall of the upcountry, had virtually no following. Justice O'Neall's plea to wait to see whether Lincoln would injure Southern interests did not suit the inflamed Carolinians.[20] Yet undoubtedly there were citizens, publicly mute, like the German artisan Jacob F. Schirmer of Charleston, who shared the belief confided to his diary that the state had acted hastily in "the dissolution of our glorious Union" and who feared that a civil war would follow.[21]

The quality of the South Carolina mind in 1860 explains much in the enactment of the drama of secession. The

[18] A recent scholarly monograph, H. S. Schultz, *Nationalism and Sectionalism in South Carolina, 1852-1860* (Durham, 1950), 233, concludes: "The movement for Southern independence in South Carolina during the period 1852-1860 was primarily a process by which the conciliatory group in the state became convinced that the antislavery party must eventually gain the ascendancy in the federal government."

[19] John Berkley Grimball Diaries, 1832-1883, MSS in University of North Carolina Library; Charleston *Daily Courier,* Nov. 3, 8, 9, Dec. 21, 1860.

[20] Lillian A. Kibler, *Benjamin F. Perry, South Carolina Unionist* (Durham, 1946), 325, 336-346; O'Neall wrote to J. H. Hammond Sept. 22, 1860, "If Lincoln is elected, *I would say wait,* let us see fully developed his course of action." James H. Hammond Papers, Vol. 28, MSS in Library of Congress.

[21] MS Diary of Jacob F. Schirmer, Dec. 20 and 31, 1860, in South Carolina Historical Society archives.

institution of slavery had engendered in the master class a fierce and quixotic pride. The evolution of their society had nourished a romantic spirit, which placed honor and prestige high among human values and developed perhaps the most uncompromising sense of localism in America. For a generation the Carolinians had felt power slipping from them—a fact which made them ready for desperate measures. The Chesnut diary records a conversation in Columbia in which the Hampton family, who owned fifteen hundred Negroes on Lake Washington, Mississippi, were reported to hate slavery. Some one commented: "Then what are they fighting for? 'For Southern rights,' whatever that is! And they do not want to be understrappers forever to those nasty Yankees."[22] The temper of the lowland aristocracy is also reflected by Catherine Ann Edmondston, who on November 16, 1860, noted the remark of her sister Frances: "You slaveholders have lived so long on your plantations with no one to gainsay you and the negroes only look up and worship you that you expect to govern everybody & have it all your own way—I can see it in Father—in brother John—in Brother Patrick and in you."[23] The South Carolina mind was eminently conservative, believing in class distinctions, the right of gentlemen to rule, and the sacredness of property. The witty Columbia Jewess Miriam Cohen observed: "All good Carolinians are entitled to take the rank of Colonel if they have property enough. In Alabama, if the boat takes a hundred bales from a man's plantation, he is a Colonel. Before the war it required from three hundred to a thousand bales to make him a general."[24] South Carolinians had talked so long about seceding and not submitting to Yankee rule that in 1860 their pride would not permit them to walk humbly down the hill.

[22] Mary Boykin Chesnut, *A Diary from Dixie*, ed. Ben Ames Williams (Boston, 1949), 218.

[23] MS Diary of Catherine Ann Edmondston, Nov. 16, 1860.

[24] Chesnut, *A Diary from Dixie*, 244.

Aristocratic South Carolina was the only state in the Union in 1860 whose Presidential electors still were chosen by the legislature instead of by popular vote. After casting the state's vote unanimously for Breckinridge, the legislature remained in session to learn the outcome of the election. On November 9, shortly after the news of Lincoln's victory was received, the Senate passed a bill calling a convention to meet on January 15. Thus those who wished the state to cooperate with other Southern states before making a decision as to leaving the Union won a temporary victory. The delay would give the people of South Carolina time to learn the will of other slave states and also provide more opportunity for the compromisers to work.[25]

But fate played into the hands of the extremists. Two days prior to this vote the Federal district judge, Andrew G. Magrath, son of an Irish exile, had heightened the secession sentiment by impulsively resigning. Mrs. Chesnut noted in her famous diary that after his resignation pictures of the judge "in the frightfullest signpost style of painting" were suspended across various streets in Charleston. "The happy moment seized by the painter to depict him," she wrote, "was while Magrath was in the act of dramatically tearing off his robes of office in rage and disgust at Lincoln's election. . . . He is depicted with a countenance flaming with contending emotions—rage, disgust and disdain."[26] On November 10 Senator James Chesnut resigned from his Federal office and the next day Senator James H. Hammond, who had previously opposed secession, did likewise.

The resignation of Hammond is a remarkable example of popular pressure in a hitherto aristocratic state. For years

[25] Laura A. White, *Robert Barnwell Rhett: Father of Secession* (New York, 1931), 179-181; Charles E. Cauthen, "South Carolina's Decision to Lead the Secession Movement," *North Carolina Historical Review*, XVIII, 360-372 (Oct., 1941). Prof. Cauthen thinks that Georgia's actions largely explained the advancing by the South Carolina Legislature of the date for the assembly of a convention.

[26] Chesnut, *A Diary from Dixie*, 3.

Hammond had been foremost in advocating Southern independence; but in 1860 he was very conservative in supporting such a movement. When a committee requested his views on the crisis produced by Lincoln's election he replied in a thirty-four-page letter in which he said that the constitutional election of Lincoln should not be a cause of withdrawing from the Union by a people who had always prided themselves on being constitutionalists. He feared that the Southern states could not be unified until they had suffered two defeats at the hands of the Black Republicans in Presidential elections. This letter was so far "behind the times" that the committee prudently suppressed it. On November 11, three days later, Hammond reversed his position and resigned his seat in the Senate. To a relative he apologized for this dramatic act by writing: "I thought Magrath and all those fellows were great apes for resigning and have done it myself. It is an epidemic and very foolish. It reminds me of the Japanese who when insulted rip open their own bowels. . . . People are wild. The scenes of the French Revolution are being enacted."[27]

South Carolina indeed surrendered to a wave of fanaticism. Minute Men of Columbia and the Association of 1860 agitated for quick action in calling a convention. An inflammatory telegram was received in Charleston on November 9, stating that the governor of Georgia had recommended the immediate summoning of a convention and Robert Toombs had resigned from the Senate. The latter item was false, but the telegram touched off a wild demonstration of secession sentiment in the hitherto conservative city of Charleston. Under such excitement the legislature, without a dissenting vote, called a convention, advancing the date of its assembly from January 15 to December 17.

So strong was the emotionalism of the hour that thousands

[27] Hammond to the committee, Nov. 8, and to J. W. Hayne, Sept. 19, and to Major M. C. M. Hammond, Nov. 12, 1860. James H. Hammond Papers, Vol. 28, MSS in Library of Congress.

wore the blue cockade in their hats and formed companies of "Minute Men." The upcountry Congressman John D. Ashmore, who had formerly opposed the fire-eaters, now embraced their views, declaring that Southerners would never permit "Abe Lincoln's banner"—inscribed with such slogans as "The higher law," "Negro equality," "Irrepressible conflict," and "Final emancipation" to wave over them nor submit to the logical results of this victory, "amalgamation."[28]

The campaign for the election of delegates to the convention was conducted with great fervor by the secessionists. On November 12, 1860, William Gilmore Simms the novelist urged that the secession party should place on their ticket candidates of old Revolutionary lineage, a Rutledge, a Middleton, a Heyward, or "a Gadsden if one can be found of the right lineage and decent ability." He wrote to Porcher Miles that the excitement of the time was difficult for him to forbear: "We shall carry the South, I trust, through what the Germans call the Landsturm. It will be a popular rush, as I always predicted as soon as the national party should perish. The momentum given to the people being such as no popular leader or politician would venture to head, or heading which would be sure to run over him."[29]

The secessionists organized a great demonstration at Pendleton in extreme western South Carolina, at which some of the most prominent leaders of the state were invited to make speeches. The object, wrote Ashmore, was to carry Pickens, the adjoining county, "Where we have more tender-footed voters than anywhere else & make the State a unit."[30] A week later he wrote of the tie between the ambitions of certain politicians and their support of the secession movement. "Already," he observed, "have some of the most violent and ultra men seized upon the movement to ride rough shod into

[28] Roy F. Nichols, *The Disruption of American Democracy* (New York, 1948), 372-373.

[29] William Gilmore Simms to W. P. Miles, Nov. 12, 1860, Miles Papers.

[30] John D. Ashmore to Miles, Nov. 13, 1860, Miles Papers.

power and my task is and has been no small one to have to encounter their folly on the one side and Perry's course on the other. Throughout the summer I have labored incessantly to get our people up to the right mark."[31]

In the election of delegates to the convention the secessionists of South Carolina won an overwhelming victory. Even in the extreme west where Unionism had been strongest, under the leadership of Benjamin F. Perry, the opponents of secession were badly defeated. The old Cooperationists, or Unionists, of 1850-1851 now voted for secessionist delegates. Nevertheless, it is interesting to note that a majority of the people of the state did not vote in this critical election for delegates, and it is reasonable to conclude that some of them stayed away from the polls because they were afraid to vote in the negative and thus be branded as "Submissionists." The convention, composed predominantly of elderly men, met first at the capital, Columbia, but adjourned because of smallpox to Charleston, where on December 20, 1860, it passed an ordinance of secession by a unanimous vote.

Beyond the wave of emotionalism that took South Carolina and later the other cotton states out of the Union lay a great glacier of conservative thought. From being the most liberal section of the nation in the period of Jefferson and Madison the Southern states had become one of the most conservative areas of civilized life in the world.[32] Moreover, the leaders of the South regarded this conservatism with pride as an evidence of a superior civilization, forming a balance wheel of the nation, a counterpoise to Northern radicalism. The American Revolution and the French Revolution of 1789 were led by radicals and opposed by conservatives. The secession movement in the South, on the other hand, was truly a conservative revolt in that the South would not accept the nineteenth century.

[31] Ashmore to Miles, Nov. 20, 1860, *ibid.*

[32] See Clement Eaton, *Freedom of Thought in the Old South,* chaps. ii, xii.

By 1860-1861 many invisible bonds which held the Union together had snapped—one by one. The division of the Methodist and Baptist churches in 1844-1845 over the slavery question was prophetic of a political split. The great Whig party which had upheld the national idea so strongly had disintegrated; Southern students attending Northern colleges had returned home; and Northern magazines and newspapers were being boycotted in the South. As Carl Russell Fish has observed, "The Democratic party, the Roman Catholic Church, the Episcopal Church, the American Medical Association, and the Constitution were among the few ties that had not snapped."[33]

The tensions between the North and the South had become so great that the admirable art of compromise, which had hitherto preserved the American experiment of democratic government, failed to function in 1860-1861. Neither the victorious Republicans, with the exception of the business interests in the party, nor the leaders of the lower South were in any mood for compromise. Only in the border states was there a strong movement for conciliation. Too often had the Republicans heard Southerners threaten secession to be alarmed for the safety of the Union. The evidence indicates that Lincoln and the Republican party leaders entertained serious misconceptions about the strength and nature of Union sentiment in the South. They were not disposed therefore to appeasement.

The leaders of secession in the lower South also were in no mood for compromise. Indeed, they were determined to rush the secession movement through before the excitement over the recent presidential election subsided. Representative David Clopton of Alabama, for example, wrote to Senator Clement C. Clay of that state on December 13 strongly opposing compromise. "Many and various efforts," he reported from

[33] Carl Russell Fish, *The American Civil War: An Interpretation* (New York, 1937), 11.

Washington, "are being made to compromise existing difficulties and patch up the rotten concern. They will all be futile." He and several Alabama colleagues, Curry, Pugh, Moore, as well as some other secessionist congressmen had declined to vote on certain issues, "believing that we ought to keep ourselves clean of all compromises." He declared that the general impression in Congress among all parties was that a dissolution of the Union was inevitable. As for himself, he was determined to die a freeman rather than live a slave to Black Republicanism. "I would be an equal, or a corpse," he wrote. "The argument is exhausted, further remonstrance is dishonorable, hesitation is dangerous, delay is submission, 'to your tents O! Israel!' and let the God of battles decide the issue."[34]

Shortly before the Georgia Convention Howell Cobb, Secretary of the Treasury under Buchanan and one of the most influential leaders of the lower South, revealed his uncompromising spirit in a letter to William Porcher Miles. Referring to rumors of coercion, he attributed much of this talk to "the false position of southern men at Washington struggling for an adjustment in *the Union.* We ought to let it be distinctly understood that we will accept no settlement and if that position had been firmly taken at Washington from the beginning the trouble would now be all over."[35]

Nevertheless, there was much conservative sentiment in the lower South as well as in the border states which would have welcomed a compromise designed to preserve the Union and at the same time give guarantees for the safety of slavery. In the election of 1860 Georgia and Louisiana, as well as the states of the upper South, had given a majority of their popular vote to Bell and Douglas, the Union candidates—a fact which indicated that the people of these states had no desire

[34] David Clopton to C. C. Clay, Junior, Dec. 13, 1860. Clement C. Clay, Junior, Papers. MSS in Duke University Library.

[35] Howell Cobb to W. P. Miles, Jan. 10, 1860. Miles Papers.

to follow the lead of the fire-eaters. Breckinridge had polled only 44.7 per cent of the vote of the slave states. Undoubtedly many of those who voted for Breckinridge, the candidate of the Southern extremists although he himself was a Unionist, desired to remain in the Union if a settlement protecting Southern rights could be secured.

Whatever chance there may have been for a compromise was frustrated by late timing. South Carolina had already seceded when the Senate Committee of Thirteen met on December 22 and considered the Crittenden Compromise presented by the venerable Senator from Kentucky, the successor of Henry Clay. The crucial issue in Crittenden's proposals was the restoration of the Missouri Compromise line in the federal territories. The Republican members voted against this concession, which would have meant a surrender of one of the main planks of the Republican platform. The representatives on the committee from the lower South, Robert Toombs and Jefferson Davis, also voted in the negative because the Republicans had done so. Consequently, on December 31, nine days after its first meeting, the committee reported to the Senate that it was unable to agree on any plan of adjustment. When the Crittenden Compromise was presented directly to the Senate, it was brushed aside by the Clark substitute, affirming that there was no need for new amendments to the Constitution or new guarantees to the South.[36] The vote on the Clark resolution was 25 to 23, with six Senators from the lower South abstaining from voting.[37] Thus these Southern Senators contributed to the defeat of the plan of adjustment that had the best chance of acceptance.

Other last-minute efforts for an acceptable compromise that

[36] *Journal of the Senate of the United States,* 36th Cong., 2nd Sess. (Washington, 1860-1861), Vol. 78, p. 76.

[37] Clinton E. Knox, "The Possibilities of Compromise in the Senate Committee of Thirteen and the Responsibility for Failure," *Journal of Negro History,* XVII, 457-458 (Oct., 1932), *Journal of the Senate,* Vol. 78, p. 107.

would prevent the disruption of the Union were also failures. The House of Representatives Committee of Thirty-three appointed by the Republican Speaker Pennington to bring about a solution of the sectional crisis revealed only the partisanship and disharmony of Congress. When the Washington Peace Conference met on February 4 at the call of the Virginia legislature representatives from the states of the lower South and from Arkansas, Michigan, Wisconsin, Minnesota, California, and Oregon absented themselves. It recommended an amendment to the Constitution that would have met Lincoln's main objection to the Crittenden Compromise—a fear of Southern efforts to acquire additional slave territory south of the Missouri Compromise line—by requiring that the addition of any new territory to the United States must obtain the sanction of a majority of the Senators from the free and a majority of the Senators from the slave states. Perhaps the best avenue toward a compromise would have been a national convention, which was proposed by President Buchanan and some others; but this proposal was never seriously considered.

While moderates in Congress were desperately fighting to save the Union by compromise, the states of the lower South were assembling in conventions and hastily passing secession ordinances.[38] Had they delayed action until Lincoln and his party had come into power and actually hurt them, secession might not have occurred. Mississippi, on January 9, was the second state to leave the Union; Florida seceded the following day; Alabama, January 11; Georgia, January 19; Louisiana, January 26; and Texas, February 1. The secessionists were in favor of quick measures in precipitating a revolution. They wished to take advantage of the emotional reaction of the

[38] For general studies of the secession movement in the lower South, see Clement Eaton, *A History of the Old South* (New York, 1949); Dwight L. Dumond, *The Secession Movement, 1860-1861* (New York, 1931); and J. G. Randall, *The Civil War and Reconstruction* (Boston, 1937).

people toward the election of Lincoln. Consequently, they were more active and better organized than their opponents, whom they branded as "submissionists." They promised that secession would be peaceful, and that it would bring the South freedom from economic vassalage to the North, and prosperity. The secession movement, moreover, was accelerated by interstate commissioners who acted as ambassadors to urge sister states to secede.

In every state there was a group known as cooperationists, who were opposed to immediate secession. They wished to call a Southern convention to discuss grievances; and, if secession became necessary, they proposed cooperation instead of separate state action in seceding and forming a new nation. They advocated, moreover, submitting the question of secession to popular vote.[39] Some cooperationists hoped by these tactics to produce delay, so that compromise and sober second thought would prevent the dissolution of the Union. Most of these moderates admitted the legal right of secession, but questioned its expediency. They were strong in the Piedmont and mountainous sections of the South, where slavery was relatively weak.

In northern Alabama, for example, the opposition to secession was strenuous, with violent threats of separating from the rest of the state and creating the state of "Nickajack," to be called after the old Indian name for this region. Hugh Lawson Clay wrote to his brother, Senator Clement C. Clay, about a protest meeting in Huntsville on the day before the secession of the state which passed resolutions instructing the delegates from northern Alabama to retire from the convention if the ordinance of secession was not submitted to the vote of the people. "The people have been so aroused by Red republican harangues," Clay wrote, "that they are in *advance of their leaders* and prepared for anything." He feared that an attempt would be made "to excite the people of N. Ala.

[39] W. R. Smith, *History and Debates of the Convention of the People of Alabama* (Montgomery, 1861), 445-447.

to rebellion vs. the State and that we will have a civil war in our midst. *'The State of Nickajack'* looms grandly in the future in the imaginations of some of the leaders of the Union party."[40]

Although it seems probable that a majority of the people of the lower South were opposed to secession in November, 1860, the desire to leave the Union developed strongly during the next two months. Such an accentuation of the secession fever was not the result of a conspiracy of a few leaders, but was brought on by emotionalism, the failure to obtain a reasonable compromise, and the contagious example of the more extremist states. Nevertheless, large minorities in Alabama, Georgia, Louisiana, and Texas were opposed to immediate secession. Only in Texas did the people have the opportunity to vote directly on the issue of separating from the Union, and here the vote was 46,129 affirmative and 14,697 negative. Secession was rushed through its last stages without a thorough canvass. Yet the Southern people had contemplated dissolving the Union for ten years and had discussed the pros and cons in countless debates. The wave of rejoicing throughout the lower South which followed the passage of the secession ordinances indicated a deep popular approval. The common people of the South, except in the mountain and hill area which jutted down from Pennsylvania, agreed with the aristocrats that the victory of the Republican party was a danger to Southern society which must be met by secession. Rejecting the sagacious advice of the little statesman Alexander H. Stephens, "Let us not anticipate a threatened evil," six states of the lower South dissolved their connection with the Union and sent delegates to a convention at Montgomery, Alabama, February 4, 1861, which created the Southern Confederacy.[41]

[40] Hugh Lawson Clay to Senator Clement C. Clay, Huntsville, Ala., Jan. 11, 1861. Clement C. Clay Papers. MSS in Duke University Library.

[41] Speech before the Georgia House of Representatives, Nov. 14, 1860. See Frank Moore, ed., *The Rebellion Record* (New York, 1861), I, 220, Doc. 147½.

The rise of this new nation was a part of that romantic nationalism of the mid-nineteenth century which was agitating Europe. At last the dream of Southern nationality which the fire-eaters had cherished seemed to be realized—the romantic vision expressed by Langdon Cheves ten years earlier at the Nashville Convention: "Unite and you shall form one of the most splendid empires on which the sun ever shone."[42] The decline of the tradition of American nationality below the Mason and Dixon line which began in the decade of the 1830's was one of the great tragedies of our history. Loyalty to the Union, however, survived in the upper South until Fort Sumter was fired upon, and the states of this border belt were forced to decide whether to fight for or against the Confederacy.

Secession was carried out in a wave of emotionalism. The secessionist leaders used various devices to appeal to the emotions of the rural folk of the South, such as alarming telegrams from Washington, misrepresentations of Lincoln and his party, parades, cockades, the mustering of "Minute Men," and, above all, the branding of cool, sensible persons who opposed their designs as "submissionists." Fiery orators inflamed the electorate, and even the pulpit was employed to bring people over to the secession cause. John Brown's raid and the slave insurrection scare of 1860 so upset the emotional balance of the Southern people that they could not view the election of Lincoln with common sense and reasonable perspective.

The role of agitators in the break-up of the Union was made possible by real grievances and anxieties in both sections. Agitators are powerless unless the tinder is ready for the spark, although they can contribute toward accumulating the tinder.

[42] R. G. Osterweis, *Romanticism and Nationalism in the Old South* (New Haven, 1949), 7. Lawrence Keitt wrote to his wife from Montgomery, Feb. 19, 1861, of his delight over the vision of a great new nation coming into existence. Lawrence Keitt Papers, MSS, Duke University Library.

In the North editors like Horace Greeley of the New York *Tribune,* writers such as Harriet Beecher Stowe, antislavery ministers, and demagogic politicians as well as sincere but fanatical Congressmen, such as Joshua R. Giddings of Ohio, emotionalized the problem of dealing with Southern slavery and created pernicious stereotypes of the Southern people.[43] Below the Mason and Dixon line the fire-eaters aroused acrimonious feelings in the Southern people, fears of the future, and propagated misconceptions of "the Yankees" which contributed to the creation of an emotional chasm between the two sections. Because the United States was a land of frequent elections and of multiple state parties, the politicians had abundant opportunities to arouse the passions of the electorate for their personal aggrandizement and the victory of the party.[44] The indiscriminating indictment of Southern society by the abolitionists stirred up so much ill will between the sections that there is some truth in the exaggerated remark of Mrs. Mary Boykin Chesnut of South Carolina on the psychological reason for the secession movement: "We separated from the North because of incompatibility of temper; we are divorced, North from South, because we have hated each other so."[45]

Some modern students of the Civil War have emphasized economic factors as the most important reason for secession and the subsequent outbreak of war. Charles A. Beard minimizes slavery as a cause of the conflict and interprets the Civil War as produced by the struggle between rival industrial and agricultural societies to control the Federal government for their selfish economic ends.[46] But the Beard thesis

[43] See Avery O. Craven, *The Coming of the Civil War* (New York, 1942) and *The Growth of Southern Nationalism, 1848-1861* (Baton Rouge, 1953), and J. G. Randall, "The Blundering Generation," *Mississippi Valley Historical Review,* XXVII, 3-29 (June, 1940).

[44] Nichols, *The Disruption of American Democracy,* 6-7.

[45] Chesnut, *A Diary from Dixie,* 20.

[46] Charles A. and Mary R. Beard, *The Rise of American Civilization* (2 vols., New York, 1927), II, chap. xviii.

neglects the role of the agricultural West in the sectional controversy and fails to explain the behavior of the Northern businessmen during the secession movement. It also does not take account of the determination of the South to keep the South a "white man's country."[47]

At the beginning of the secession crisis a severe financial panic in Wall Street frightened businessmen. Consequently, they and their mouthpiece, the *Journal of Commerce* of New York, favored compromise on the slavery issue, and huge Union-saving conventions were held by the businessmen in New York, Boston, and Philadelphia. Southern merchants owed to Northern suppliers and bankers, it has been estimated, approximately one hundred and fifty million dollars, which might become a total loss in case of war.[48] It is notable, however, that the businessmen stoutly opposed any compromise on economic matters that affected their profits. They refused to yield on the question of abolishing the Northern monopoly of the coastal trade by repeal of the laws excluding foreign competition, they declined to give up the Federal subsidy to New England fishermen, and they insisted on raising the tariff by the Morrill Act.[49]

The South had a strong sense of being exploited by the Northern merchants, shippers, and factors. Southern commercial conventions had on numerous occasions protested against this exploitation, and in the last few years of the ante bellum period a movement had developed to boycott Northern goods and Northern universities, textbooks, and magazines. Resentment over such economic grievances, both real and imagined, was an incalculable element in Southern nationalism —a desire to be free from economic vassalage. Although the

[47] See U. B. Phillips, "The Central Theme of Southern History," *American Historical Review*, XXXII, 30-43 (Oct., 1928).

[48] P. S. Foner, *Business and Slavery: The New York Merchants and the Irrepressible Conflict* (Chapel Hill, 1941), 218, 302.

[49] Kenneth M. Stampp, *And the War Came* (Baton Rouge, 1950), 159-165.

South was not suffering from a high-tariff policy in 1860, the victory of the Republican party presaged the adoption of such a policy.

Most writers on this period of American history have overlooked the importance of sectional pride or "Southern honor" in motivating the secession movement. Because of pride men at times deliberately act against their own economic interest or comfort. As a matter of self-respect Southerners with few exceptions insisted on "equality in the Union," which they interpreted to mean the right to take their slaves into Federal territory purchased by common blood and common treasure. In 1857 the Supreme Court adopted the Southern point of view in the Dred Scott decision by declaring that neither the Federal government nor a territorial legislature could exclude slaves from the Federal territories. It was only a logical step for the proslavery interest to demand a Congressional slave code to protect slavery in the national territories.

Such a demand did not represent a real pressure of slavery expansion, for it was recognized by many leaders in the South that the territory remaining unoccupied in 1860 was economically not suited to slavery. How far the common people, with their ignorance of geography, realized this fact is, of course, impossible to determine. If slavery expansion into the Federal territories in 1860 was largely an abstract question, why then did the Southern leaders insist on it? The answer, at least partly, was Southern pride, for the Republican program of excluding slavery from the Federal territories placed a stigma on slave-holding in the Southern states. Such a program also struck a blow at Southern political prestige and power.

On the other hand, to many Northern voters in 1860 the South as a section seemed to be acting in an aggressive fashion to advance proslavery interests. George Fitzhugh and some of his fellow extremists were predicting the enslavement of the white masses of the North, following a collapse of free industrial society.[50] A small minority of Southerners also were advocating the opening of the African slave trade, and the pro-Southern Buchanan administration was favorable to the acquisition of Cuba and other territory from which slave states could be created. At the same time the leaders of the Cotton Kingdom made serious mistakes in opposing the adoption of a free homestead law, in trying to force the proslavery Lecompton constitution on Kansas, and in demanding a Congressional slave code for the Federal territories.

Consequently the masses of voters in the North were stirred to take a stand against the extension of slavery into the territories as a moral duty, as "a principle." They could not have had the benefit of reading Professor Ramsdell's essay "The Natural Limits of Slavery Expansion" and thereby realize that they were contending for an abstraction.[51] Certainly a tremendous moral force was generated, particularly in New England and the Northwest, by the antislavery crusade which implemented the program of the Republican party and a coercion policy. A philosopher might observe, however, that this moral fervor on the part of Northerners did not involve great sacrifices such as a prospective loss of property, a serious disturbance of race adjustments, or the deprivation of dominant political power. It should also be remembered that a large segment of Northern public opinion, the Northern Democrats, did not succumb to this moral zeal.

To the South the real issue which the victory of the Republicans in 1860 raised was the safety of the institution of slavery within the old states. Although the Republican platform and Lincoln clearly renounced any intention to disturb this archaic institution within the states, Southerners as a whole were skeptical, knowing how often platforms were forgotten after

[50] See Harvey Wish, *George Fitzhugh: Propagandist of the Old South* (Baton Rouge, 1943).

[51] Charles W. Ramsdell, "The Natural Limits of Slavery Expansion," *Mississippi Valley Historical Review*, XVI, 151-171 (Sept. 1929).

elections. Regarding the race problem in the South as a strictly local concern they violently resented Northern attempts to interfere, as a minority of their descendants did in the Dixiecrat movement of 1948.

How could the election of a Republican President endanger the security of slavery within the old states of the South? In the first place the President could force the free circulation of abolition literature through the Federal mails below the Mason and Dixon line. From 1835 to 1860 the Presidents, who were either Southerners or Northern "doughfaces," had sanctioned the Southern censorship of the mails. If this censorship were removed, Southerners believed, inflammatory literature might instigate a servile insurrection and also might eventually affect the white non-slaveholders.[52] The victory of the Republicans threatened to lead to the abolition of slavery in the District of Columbia and eventually to the repeal of the fugitive slave laws. The President could use the patronage to appoint violent antislavery men to Federal offices in the South. In many indirect ways the Federal power could be used by the Republicans to weaken the institution of slavery. Southerners in 1860-1861 did not know that Lincoln was a moderate; they believed that the administration would be controlled by Seward, whom they erroneously regarded as a dangerous fanatic.[53]

Today we can see that the dominant public opinion in the North in 1860-1861 was based on something deeper than preventing the extension of slavery into territory where it would not naturally go anyway. The real purpose of the Northern majority was nothing less, as a recent historian has pointed out, than "the containment" of slavery geograph-

[52] Clement Eaton, "Censorship of the Southern Mails," *American Historical Review,* XLVIII, 266-280 (Jan., 1943), and *Freedom of Thought in the Old South,* chaps. v, vii.

[53] J. G. de Roulhac Hamilton, "Lincoln's Election an Immediate Menace to Slavery in the States," *American Historical Review,* XXXVII, 700-711 (July, 1932).

ically and politically with a view to its ultimate destruction.[54] This determination represented a part of the movement of enlightened world opinion, which had already abolished slavery in the Western hemisphere with the exception of Brazil, Cuba, and Dutch Guiana. Lincoln had clearly expressed this objective of his party in the famous House-Divided speech of 1858; namely, that the opponents of Southern slavery "will arrest the further spread of it, and place it where the public mind shall rest in the belief that it is in the course of ultimate extinction."[55]

Southerners realized the danger to their way of life in the victory of the Republican party, animated by a purpose of weakening slavery in every legal way possible. Disturbed by a profound sense of insecurity, the black belts of the South looked with fear not merely toward the loss of valuable property, but toward the social consequences of liberating the Negro in districts where black people outnumbered the whites.[56] Political rights, Southerners recognized, would eventually have to be given to the freed Negro, as was actually done in the reconstruction period to the great temporary injury of the Southern states. They believed that emancipation would lead ultimately to the breakdown of all racial barriers and taboos and to the final degradation of amalgamation—a theme that was used widely in the campaign of emotionalism which preceded secession. These apprehensions over the future alarmed all classes of Southern society, nonslaveholders as well as masters, and seemed to justify secession and in the last extremity a resort to war.

[54] Allan Nevins, *The Emergence of Lincoln,* I, chap. v.

[55] Abraham Lincoln, *Complete Works,* ed. Nicolay and Hay (New York, 1905), III, 2.

[56] See Howard K. Beale, "What Historians Have Said About the Causes of the Civil War," in Social Science Research Council Committee on Historiography, *Theory and Practice in Historical Study: A Report* (New York, 1946).

CHAPTER TWELVE

THE LOSS OF THE WILL TO FIGHT

DISCERNING MEN in the South realized that the sun of the Confederacy which had reached high noon at Chancellorsville had begun to sink in midsummer of 1863. Lee and his soldiers had been regarded in the Confederacy as invincible until the defeat at Gettysburg. Kean commented in his diary, July 26, 1863, that "Gettysburg has shaken my faith in Lee as a general," and that the loss of men and material in that battle was less disastrous than the loss of prestige of the army. On November 5 he noted that the Southern people were getting tired of the war, that they lacked confidence in the President and were hopeless about Confederate leaders, and that impressment and the bankruptcy of finances were depressing their spirits. On November 9 he wrote: "The prospect is very gloomy. Men of the most hopeful temper are getting discouraged."[1]

Yet there was a chance that the Northern people would also become war-weary and willing to negotiate a peace recognizing the independence of the Confederacy. As a matter of record, the ghastly defeat at Fredericksburg, December 13, 1862, Sherman's failure to take Vicksburg, and the inconclusive fighting at Murfreesboro made Northern public opinion deeply despondent. The able historian of the Copperhead movement has entitled this period lasting until July 4, 1863, "the period of despair."[2] In April, 1863, General Ambrose Burnside ordered the arrest of the leader of the Ohio Copperheads, Clement Vallandigham, who was tried by a military court and sentenced to imprisonment for the duration of the war. This arbitrary act greatly strengthened the peace Democrats of the Ohio valley; and they captured the Democratic party convention in Ohio, which without a dissenting vote nominated Vallandigham for governor. Even the elation over the victories of Gettysburg and Vicksburg was temporary. In the summer and early fall of 1864 Northern morale seemed to have reached its lowest point. Gloomy over the news that Grant was stalled at Petersburg and Sherman was stopped before Atlanta, many Northerners envisaged the war ending in a stalemate. This was the period of fluctuating sentiment described by Wood Gray as "the period of weariness."[3]

In the Confederacy public sentiment also fluctuated between hope and despair. Many a Confederate soldier must have felt like George Woodward of Wilson, North Carolina, who wrote to his brother from camp near Orange Court House, Virginia, December 27, 1863, "I am bare footed." The dispirited soldier also mentioned that he suffered from the cold and had diarrhea. Out of this bleak prospect, he wrote, "I think the Southern Federacy is broke, for it seems so to me."[4] The poor fellow died of diarrhea a few months afterwards. J. R. P. Ellis, who had been conscripted in North Carolina, wrote to his wife from Kinston, North Carolina, June 8, 1864, that he had recently seen seven deserters hanged, that some of the boys were nearly naked, that he was dirty and "mighty tired of the war."[5] On the other hand, young Sidney Lanier wrote from his signal station at Petersburg, August 2, 1864, that he was confident of Confederate success, for the Northern people now realized that they could not

[1] Kean MS Diary, I, July 26, 1863; II, Nov. 5 and 9, 1863.

[2] Gray, *The Hidden Civil War: The Story of the Copperheads,* chap. vi.

[3] *Ibid.,* chap. viii.

[4] George Woodward to his brother, Dec. 27, 1863. MSS in possession of Hugh Buckner Johnston, North Carolina.

[5] J. R. P. Ellis to his wife, Feb. 15 and June 8, 1864. MSS in possession of Hugh Buckner Johnston.

defeat Lee and conquer the South.[6] Also a son of Senator William A. Graham of North Carolina wrote from Petersburg, September 25, 1864, that his men were in good spirits and confident of whipping Grant if he attacked them in the trenches.[7]

But the hopeful spirit of the Southern people which seems to have revived by midsummer of 1864 began to vanish in the autumn after the reelection of Lincoln and the defeat of McClellan, the candidate of the antiwar Democrats. In the following winter the stress and privations of war, the loss of Atlanta, disillusion over the failure of King Cotton diplomacy, and the realization of the tremendous odds accelerated the growth of dissension among Confederates, and a movement for peace arose. As Professor Edward Channing observes, the Southern people lost "the will to fight."[8]

Although the Confederate government spent much money and effort in foreign propaganda, it gave slight consideration to domestic propaganda, to buoy up the sinking spirits of the people.[9] It is true that the scattered rural population could not be reached easily through the printed word; but much more could have been done than was undertaken to keep up the morale of the civilian population. The chief methods of propaganda used in the Confederacy were proclamations by the President and the governors, editorials depicting the horrors of defeat, particularly racial amalgamation, schoolbooks—between four and five hundred different texts were published during the war—and exhortations of Southern ministers and patriotic societies of devoted women. One of the

[6] Sidney Lanier, *Works*, Centennial ed., VII, 162.

[7] Robert D. Graham to Senator William A. Graham, Sept. 15, 1864. William A. Graham Papers, MSS in North Carolina State Department of Archives and History, Raleigh; for other evidence of high morale in 1864, see Freeman, *Calendar of Confederate Papers*, 181-184, 388.

[8] Channing, *History of the United States*, VI, 612-616.

[9] See J. W. Silver, "Propaganda in the Confederacy," *Journal of Southern History*, XI, 487-503 (Nov., 1945).

most interesting forms of propaganda was the proclaiming of days of fasting and prayer. Jefferson Davis was so engrossed with military affairs that he did not devote adequate attention to inspiring the people to heroic endeavor, and Alexander H. Stephens, although he made more than forty speeches in the first year of the war when enthusiasm for the cause was high, made hardly any during the period of reaction.

Atrocity stories have formed a staple of propaganda in almost all wars, and the history of the Confederacy conforms to the pattern. Jefferson Davis tried on occasions to inflame the Southern people to fight by atrocity stories regarding the behavior of Northern soldiers. In his proclamations and messages he accused the North of waging uncivilized warfare, of atrocities again women and children, and contrasted the conduct of the Confederate soldiers during their invasion of Pennsylvania, acting as "Christian warriors," with the ruffianly conduct of Northern soldiers.[10] His most bitter indictment of military misbehavior was reserved for his proclamation ordering the immediate hanging of Ben Butler if captured, on account of his felonious conduct as military governor of New Orleans. Lawrence Keitt, the South Carolina fire-eater, wrote to his vivacious wife Suzanna just after the battle of Bull Run that ten wagonloads of handcuffs were among the spoils of the battle. "Isn't it atrocious," he exclaimed.[11] Kean's diary, August 2, 1863, cites the cruel treatment of Southern prisoners at Fort Delaware and the episode of a smallpox Negro forced to swim across the Rappahannock River to spread the dread disease among the army.[12]

From the very beginning of the war the morale of the Southern people and the effectiveness of the Confederate government in coping with its tremendous difficulties were weakened by the disruptive effect of the state-rights doctrine. Some

[10] Richardson, ed., *Messages and Papers of the Confederacy*, I, 232.
[11] Lawrence Keitt to his wife, 1861. Lawrence Keitt Papers.
[12] Kean MS Diary, II, Aug. 2, 1863.

writers have overemphasized the importance of state rights in the defeat of the South while failing to recognize that this factor also hampered the North in its prosecution of the war. One student of the weakening effect of state rights on the Confederacy has gone to the extreme of proposing an epitaph for the Confederate cause, "Died of State Rights."[13] Most Southerners would have denied that they were fighting to preserve slavery but would have maintained that they were fighting for constitutional liberty and state rights. The doctrine of state rights was especially strong in the old states which had roots in the colonial past. The newer states of the Southwest were inclined to take a broader view of Southern nationalism, and to some extent President Davis represented this point of view.

The vigorous prosecution of the war required teamwork and a high degree of centralization. The more realistic Southerners, thinking in terms of the Confederacy as a nation fighting for survival, were willing to accept the measures necessary to win independence without scrutinizing their constitutionality too closely. But Southerners of 1860 were an individualistic people, and their agrarian economy and the defense of slavery had led them violently to oppose centralization. The stresses and strains of the Civil War caused one class of Southerners to use the doctrine of state rights to oppose the centripetal policies of the Confederate government. Consequently, serious conflicts occurred between the government of Jefferson Davis and the various state governments over conscription, suspension of the writ of habeas corpus, the control of blockade running and manufacturing, the state militia and local defense, and the impressment of supplies and slaves.[14]

When Braxton Bragg wrote a caustic letter to Secretary of War Benjamin criticizing the state governments for placing

[13] Owsley, *State Rights in the Confederacy*, 1.
[14] See Stephenson, *The Day of the Confederacy*, chaps. iv, x, xi.

local defense above Confederate military policies, Benjamin replied on November 4, 1861: "The difficulty lies with the Governors of the States who are unwilling to trust the common defense to one common head. . . . Each Governor wants to satisfy his own people and there are not wanting politicians in each State to encourage the people to raise the cry that they will not consent to be left defenseless–The voice of reason is stilled."[15]

The first important flare-up of state-rights feeling against the Davis administration occurred over conscription. Georgia was the center of disaffection, and its governor, Joseph E. Brown, led the obstructionists. Brown had been an ardent secessionist; but during the war he was so stanch a defender of state rights that he came close to treason. The aristocrats of Georgia, like Howell Cobb, the owner of a thousand slaves, and Benjamin H. Hill, hated this plebeian whom they regarded as a demagogue. Condemning the conscription law as unconstitutional, unnecessary, and a destruction of personal liberty, Brown suspended the operation of the draft in Georgia until the legislature and ultimately the Supreme Court of his state could pass on its validity. When the Supreme Court refused to declare the conscription law unconstitutional, the obstinate governor tried to hamper the operation of the law in every possible way. He created superfluous state officers in order to evade the effect of conscription, especially by placing in the exempt class approximately two thousand justices of the peace and one thousand constables.[16]

Governor Brown acted as though the defense of the state from invasion was more important than cooperation with the Confederacy to destroy the armies of the enemy. He enrolled

[15] Judah P. Benjamin to Braxton Bragg, Nov. 4, 1861. MSS in University of Rochester Library. Photostat in North Carolina State Department of Archives and History.

[16] Burton J. Hendrick gives a vivid description of Brown's recalcitrance in *Statesmen of the Lost Cause* (Boston, 1939). See also Louise B. Hill, *Joseph E. Brown and the Confederacy* (Chapel Hill, 1939) and Bryan, *Confederate Georgia*, chap. vi.

ten thousand men in the Georgia militia, sometimes called "Brown's Ten Thousand," whom he forbade the Confederate conscription officers to enroll or molest. Such state troops, which Governor Pettus of Mississippi and other governors also tried to establish and protect, were practically useless to the Confederate cause. When Sherman invaded Georgia, the governor condescended to place his "Ten Thousand" under nominal control of General Joseph E. Johnston; but Johnston was not allowed to appoint their officers, or incorporate them in his army. In September, 1864, during one of the most critical periods of the war, Brown granted a thirty-day furlough to the "Ten Thousand." As Sherman sarcastically reported, "Governor Brown has disbanded his militia to gather the corn and sorghum of the state."[17] After Atlanta fell the governor demanded that President Davis send reinforcements to General Hood: if the request were ignored he would recall the troops of the state from the Virginia front; he would order "all the sons of Georgia to return to their own State and within her own limits to rally around her glorious flag."[18] The masses in Georgia supported their recalcitrant executive, whom they had overwhelmingly reelected governor in 1863.

His course of obstruction was also approved by Vice President Stephens, Linton Stephens, and Robert Toombs. A. L. Alexander, a prominent planter of Washington, Georgia, wrote to his daughter, wife of the Confederate Chief of Engineers, in January, 1865, describing the disaffection of Georgia: "Toombs knows no bounds to his vituperation of the administration, and I heartily wish he would leave the country. You know how great his influence *has been* and men find it difficult now to shake that influence off. I don't think it is the purpose of these men to return to the old Govt. but to withdraw if

[17] Gen. William T. Sherman, *Memoirs* (2 vols., New York, 1891), II, 138.

[18] H. A. Fielder, *A Sketch of the Life and Times and Speeches of Joseph E. Brown* (Springfield, Mass., 1883), 324.

possible this and two other States from the Confed. and set up for themselves. Such I think is the scheme now on foot—Brown is only the tool in the hands of the two others—while Toombs is in my opinion the 'primum mobile and ultimum moriens' of it all. Stephens has always been traitorous at heart, but is more wary and reticent—Toombs drinks and then it all comes out. It is sad to see the influence he has over men better than himself."[19]

Next to Brown, the most obstreperous war governor opposing the centralizing policies of the Confederacy was Zebulon Baird Vance of North Carolina. This tall, bushy-haired mountaineer from Buncombe County was extremely popular.[20] His followers regarded him as a "rough diamond" partly on account of his robust and often obscene sense of humor and his marvelous oratorical power. Although he had been a firm Union man during the crisis of secession, he later raised a volunteer company and joined the Confederate Army. In 1862, at the age of thirty-two, he was elected governor on a platform urging the prosecution of the war. As governor he was a dynamic leader of a people who had been lukewarm in the secession movement.[21] He actively cared for the North Carolina soldiers and also tried to give generous relief to the families of poor soldiers. He purchased a blockade runner, the *Ad-Vance,* as well as an interest in other blockade runners to import military and essential supplies for the North Carolina troops and the civilian population. In a lecture entitled "Last Days of the War in North Carolina" he enumerated later some of the supplies which his ships had brought through the blockade: 60,000 pairs of hand cards, 10,000 grain scythes, leather for 250,000 pairs of shoes, 50,000 blankets, gray woolen

[19] A. L. Alexander to Mrs. Jeremy F. Gilmer, Jan. 20, 1865. Jeremy F. Gilmer Papers.

[20] See Clement Dowd, *Life of Zebulon B. Vance* (Charlotte, N. C., 1897).

[21] See R. E. Yates, "Zebulon Vance as War Governor of North Carolina," *Journal of Southern History,* III, 43-76 (Feb., 1937).

cloth for 250,000 uniforms, 12,000 overcoats, 2,000 Enfield rifles, 100,000 pounds of bacon, $50,000 worth (at gold prices) of medicine, and cotton- and woolen-mill machinery.

Yet this energetic leader was provincial in his point of view and quarreled often with the central government. He demanded that it allow conscripts the privilege of selecting the regiments to which they would go. When Secretary of War Seddon appointed a native of another state, Colonel T. P. August, as conscription officer in North Carolina, Vance vehemently protested. He declared that the pride of North Carolina was wounded by the appointment of "strangers" (citizens of other states) as officers over North Carolina troops and as collectors of the tax in kind when some of "her noblest sons" could be utilized for this purpose.[22] The masterful governor forbade the central government to distill thirty thousand bushels of grain into whisky for the Medical Department as a violation of the laws of the state. He quarreled with the central government over its attempt to regulate blockade running, especially the requirement that all ships leaving Southern ports should reserve one-half of their cargo space for the Confederacy. Also he and the legislature monopolized the product of the cotton mills of the state for North Carolina troops and civilians. While Lee's troops in Virginia were ragged and suffering from lack of shoes, Vance hoarded 92,000 uniforms and large supplies of leather and blankets for North Carolina troops.

The opposition of Vance and Brown to the centralizing policies of the Richmond government should be viewed in its true perspective. Anyone who reads the numerous letters written to Vance, preserved in his correspondence in Raleigh, will perceive the tremendous pressure exerted on him by the public opinion of his state to act as he did. Senator George Davis, for example, wrote to him from Richmond, April 16,

[22] Dowd, *op. cit.*, 489.

1863, "I have for a long time been very indignant at the appointment of persons from other states to command North Carolina troops."[23] He complained that the recommendations of the North Carolina Congressmen for military appointments were ignored and only recommendations of generals were accepted. The governor received letters from the western part of the state protesting against stationing Confederate cavalry in that area, for the horses ate up the corn necessary for the sustenance of the people; letters complaining that the textile factories at Fayetteville were charging more than 75 per cent profit, that poor soldiers' families could not buy provisions in competition with the factories, and letters describing bushwhackers terrorizing neighborhoods.[24]

Letters came also from army officers, such as D. H. Hill and Johnston J. Pettigrew, urging him to suspend the writ of habeas corpus and proclaim martial law to deal with suspected persons who were dangerous to the Confederate vedettes. D. H. Hill raved against skulkers and vile speculators, declared that the people of North Carolina did not have the unconquerable will to win, and that the North Carolina newspapers and Judge Pearson were causing men to desert.[25] Johnston J. Pettigrew declared that the soldiers felt dissatisfaction with the legislature because it gave no word of encouragement and manifested none of "that enthusiastic detestation (or hatred) of the enemy for his outrages which animates us who witness them."[26]

The opposition of some Confederate governors to the growing power of the central government was not unlike the struggle between President Lincoln and some Northern gover-

[23] George Davis, Richmond, Apr. 16, 1863, to Vance. Zebulon B. Vance Papers, II, MSS in North Carolina Dept. of Archives and History.

[24] Letters to Vance from A. S. Merrimon, Asheville, July 31, 1863; Samuel Wilkinson, Rutherfordton, Mar. 16, 1863; W. M. Poisson, Fayetteville, Feb. 23, 1863; and A. C. Cowles, Feb. 24, 1863. Vance Papers, II, 4, 22, 25.

[25] Gen. D. H. Hill to Vance, June 4, 22, and 25, 1863. *Ibid.*

[26] Johnston J. Pettigrew to Vance, Feb. 5, 1863. *Ibid.*

nors. Furthermore, those executives who overemphasized state rights during the conflict were in a minority among the Southern governors. Governor Thomas O. Moore of Louisiana and Governor J. J. Pettus of Mississippi had some friction with the War Department in their zealous efforts to defend their states by retaining a considerable body of militia; but Pettus rendered valuable service in strengthening the defense of Vicksburg and in other ways. Governors Francis Lubbock of Texas, Milledge Bonham of South Carolina, Henry W. Allen of Louisiana, Charles Clark of Mississippi, and John Milton of Florida cooperated well with the central government.[27]

South Carolina went through a rather drastic revolution of sentiment toward the Confederate government. During the first two years South Carolinians were zealous participants in the war. After the sea islands were captured in November, 1862, the convention that had passed the secession ordinance reassembled and appointed an executive council, consisting of the governor, the lieutenant governor, and three members, with practically unlimited war powers. The council became very unpopular when it enforced the conscription act vigorously and began a state-wide impressment of slaves. Accordingly, popular pressure forced both the dissolution of the convention and the abolition of the executive council at the close of the year. Benjamin F. Perry, the old Unionist but now loyal Confederate, observed that many of the leading movers of secession failed to volunteer to fight and were reluctant to furnish their slaves for defense projects.[28] The Impressment Act of 1863 and Confederate military reverses caused a revulsion of feeling against President Davis so that in 1864 the Charleston *Courier* alone among the newspapers of the

[27] See J. K. Bettersworth, *Confederate Mississippi* (Baton Rouge, 1943); K. T. Abbey, *Florida, Land of Change* (Chapel Hill, 1941); J. D. Bragg, *Louisiana in the Confederacy* (Baton Rouge, 1941), and Francis R. Lubbock, *Six Decades in Texas* (Austin, 1900).

[28] Kibler, *Benjamin F. Perry*, 362.

state remained pro-Davis. Congressman William W. Boyce, in partnership with Foote of Tennessee, led a revolt against the President; and in October, 1864, Boyce publicly proposed a convention of states, North and South, to discuss peace terms, hoping thus to help the Northern Democrats elect a peace candidate for President.[29] In December of that year the anti-Davis state-rights faction elected Andrew G. Magrath governor.

After the disasters of Gettysburg and Vicksburg the peace movement developed rapidly, especially in Georgia and North Carolina. In the latter state the leader was the former Union editor W. W. Holden, whose support came largely from the western part of the state. Governor Vance, although he had been feuding with the Confederate government, strongly opposed the various peace meetings held in the state, declaring that they would cause the army to melt away by desertion, would produce civil war, encourage the enemy, and lead to the subjugation of the South. "No living man," he wrote to Senator Graham August 13, 1863, "is more anxious for peace than I am"; but it would have to be upon the basis of separation and independence.[30] He sternly opposed the movement which was then gaining momentum to take North Carolina out of the Confederacy through the calling of a convention by the legislature.[31] Nevertheless, on December 30, 1863, he

[29] White, *Robert Barnwell Rhett*, 225, 237-238.

[30] Vance to William A. Graham, Aug. 13, 1863. William A. Graham Papers.

[31] John H. Houghton was advocating a speedy peace. On Aug. 17, 1863, Vance made an eloquent and moving appeal to him and the people of the state. His letter referred to the recent failure of Alexander Stephens's efforts to negotiate with the enemy, and pointed out the results of the conquest of the South by the North, confiscation of estates, hanging of the principal leaders—a ruinous tariff, and four million Negroes let loose on society. He declared that the Northern people were weary of fighting also, and that it was impossible to restore the Union after all the hate generated by the war. The people of the South could not be conquered if they had the will to resist, and he declared that he himself would never submit on the basis of the restoration of the Union. Rather than peace meetings, meetings should be held to aid the poor and persuade deserters to return. Vance Papers, II.

suggested to President Davis that an effort to obtain peace would help the morale of the people of his state, for when they realized that only ignoble terms would be granted they would support the prosecution of the war more wholeheartedly.

The peace movement in North Carolina became involved in internal politics and personal ambitions. In 1863-1864 the scars of the fight over secession still remained, and the citizens were divided roughly into the Secessionist party (the old Democratic party) and the Conservatives (the old Whig party). Vance was a conservative, but he bitterly opposed the efforts of the turncoat Holden to seize the leadership of the Conservative party and use it to advance the peace movement. To Senator Graham he wrote: "I will see the Conservative party blown into a thousand atoms and Holden and his under-strappers in hell (if you will pardon the violence of the expression) before I will consent to a course which I think would bring dishonor and ruin upon both State and confederacy. We are already ruined almost, but are not yet dishonored. Is Holden the leader of the Conservative party? If so, I don't belong to it—a known demagogue and a man of bad character."[32] Vance spoke vehemently to the people against the movement to surrender and he was sustained by them. On April 9 he wrote to Graham that he had visited the North Carolina soldiers in camp, a journey which he regarded as very profitable, and which he hoped would not give the impression in the state that he had "gone over" to the secessionists.[33] In August, 1864, he ran for reelection against Holden, the peace candidate, and won an overwhelming victory by a majority of nearly four to one.

The hill country of Georgia, Alabama, and Mississippi was another area where the peace movement was most active. In Georgia a powerful core of leadership regarded President Davis as a "despot," and opposed many laws of Congress necessary for vigorous prosecution of the war, including con-

[32] Vance to Graham, Jan. 1, 1864. Graham Papers.
[33] Vance to Graham, Apr. 9, 1864. *Ibid.*

scription, the impressment act, and the suspension of the writ of habeas corpus. These leaders, who maintained that they were fighting for "Constitutional liberty," threatened by the centralizing and consolidating policies of the Davis administration, included Robert Toombs, embittered because he had not been elected President of the Confederacy and because he had failed as a general; Governor Joseph E. Brown; Vice President Alexander Stephens; and Linton Stephens. Toombs resigned his military commission and ran for Congress in 1863, but was defeated, partly as a result of the opposition of the President.

Alexander H. Stephens, also a great egotist, became the brains behind the anti-Davis movement in Georgia, the abettor of Governor Brown in his state-rights policies, and instead of attending to his duties as Vice President he spent much of his time in Georgia, agitating against the policies necessary to a vigorous prosecution of the war. His half-brother Linton, eleven years younger and Harvard-educated, faithfully cooperated with him in political policies. As a member of the Georgia legislature, Linton was in a strategic position to influence the action of the state. Governor Brown and Alexander Stephens opposed the policies of the Davis administration so strenuously that General Sherman sent messages to them to arrange a meeting to discuss Georgia's secession from the Confederacy, which they declined.[34]

The loss of the will to fight became pronounced in the Southern people after the reelection of Lincoln in November, 1864. The conflict had entered upon a stage of attrition, wearing down the weaker military machine of the Confederacy. King Cotton diplomacy had failed miserably, and thus the South was deprived of such foreign recognition and aid as had immeasurably strengthened the American colonies in the struggle of 1776. The morale of the civilian population

[34] Rabun, "Alexander H. Stephens and Jefferson Davis," *American Historical Review,* LVIII, 290-321 (Jan., 1953).

also must have been deeply affected after 1863 by the large number of women in mourning. The role of the anti-Davis newspapers in destroying confidence in Southern success and the will to fight cannot be measured. Economic disintegration was profoundly important in the deterioration of morale, but the most important factor seems to have been military reverses. The realization in the last year of the war of the overwhelming odds against them made the people definitely war-weary and eager to end hostilities by negotiation.

Yet the laws and resolutions of the last Congress of the Confederacy, November 7, 1864, to March 18, 1865, show scarcely a trace of defeatism. In this last year of the struggle Congress received many patriotic resolutions passed by the army, such as those of Stewart's Brigade of Virginia infantry "to dedicate themselves anew to the sacred cause of Liberty and Independence and to prosecute the struggle in which they are engaged with redoubled energy and an unfaltering purpose." Congress in reply voted its cordial thanks and declared that such examples of heroic self-sacrifice were well calculated "to revive the hopes of the despondent and to stimulate the Congress and the people at home to cultivate that spirit of harmonious and unselfish cooperation which can alone impart to our cause the irresistible strength which springs from united councils, fraternal feelings and fervent devotion to the public weal."[35]

As the shadows of war began to darken the lives of the women of the Confederacy, many of them longed for peace and meditated on the dubious value of war. Their sons, husbands, and lovers began to come back to them in coffins, causing them to put on deep black mourning, a custom rooted in old folkways that now became depressing to Southern morale. Mrs. Chesnut voiced the feeling of many of her sex when she contemplated the death of so many fine young men:

[35] Ramsdell, ed., *Laws and Joint Resolutions of the Last Session of the Confederate Congress*, 37-38, 43.

"Is anything worth it—this fearful sacrifice; this awful penalty we pay for war?"[36] Another wife of a Confederate officer wrote from Richmond to Mrs. Roger A. Pryor during the dark days of the war, "I am for a tidal wave of peace—and I am not alone."[37] In contrast to these yielding women, others strongly opposed surrender. Augusta Jane Evans, the Mobile novelist, wrote July 15, 1863, that she mourned over the fall of Vicksburg like Queen Mary over the loss of Calais, and that she would rather see Mobile destroyed than polluted by the presence of Yankees.[38]

The breakdown of Southern morale in the latter years of the war was registered in the appalling amount of desertion in the Confederate armies. The official reports fixed the number of deserters at 103,400, but actually the number was greater. In addition to the loss of strength from desertion the remarkable laxity of the authorities in granting furloughs depleted the army. Modern studies indicate that there was one desertion to every nine enlistments in the Confederate armies and one to every seven in the Union armies.[39] North Carolina with 23,694 deserters and Virginia with 12,071 led the Southern states; but they also furnished the largest numbers of troops. Alabama, with 1,578 deserters, had the lowest record. The widespread absenteeism in the Confederate armies is indicated by the fact that at the beginning of the war 21 per cent of the soldiers were absent, and by December, 1864, the number had increased to 51 per cent. In a speech at Macon, Georgia, September, 1864, President Davis bluntly told the people (and Sherman also) that two-thirds of Hood's army were absent, most of them without leave. The Northern

[36] Chesnut, *A Diary from Dixie,* 422.

[37] Mrs. Roger A. Pryor, *Reminiscences of Peace and War* (New York, 1905), 293.

[38] Augusta J. Evans to J. L. M. Curry, July 15, 1862. J. L. M. Curry Papers.

[39] See Ella Lonn, *Desertion During the Civil War* (New York, 1928) and Bessie L. Martin, *Desertion of Alabama Troops from the Confederate Army: A Study in Sectionalism* (New York, 1932).

armies suffered more extensively from desertion, having more than two hundred thousand offenders; but their surplus man power made the loss less serious than the Confederate desertions.

The causes of Confederate desertion were numerous, perhaps the greatest being the decline of morale after the defeats of Gettysburg and Vicksburg. Many mountaineers and backwoodsmen who disliked slavery and the cotton aristocracy were forced into the army, and hence deserted when a chance arose. Other men absented themselves temporarily to look after wives and children who were suffering severe hardships, or were called home by pitiful letters from wives and relatives to protect them from bushwhackers and outlaws. Augusta Jane Evans wrote from Mobile in the second year of the war that courts martial condemned soldiers who pleaded "in palliation of desertion the cries of hungry wives and starving children. Officers state that they see letters from wives received by privates in which their families plead for them to come home at every hazard . . . women selling their last extra dress for food."[40] Minor causes of desertion were cowardice, shortage of rations, discomforts of camp life, tyranny of officers, and lack of money to pay the railroad fare to return after a furlough. A more important factor may have been the resentment of non-slaveholders over the exemption of owners of twenty slaves.

The relative impunity for absences without leave encouraged desertion. Although some offenders were shot, Southern courts martial generally were lenient and imposed light penalties for this dangerous crime, such as flogging with thirty-nine lashes. The Federal authorities were also merciful, executing only 121 soldiers for desertion. On August 1, 1863, following the disasters of Gettysburg and Vicksburg, President Davis issued a proclamation which portrayed the disasters that would befall the Southern people, including servile insurrec-

[40] Augusta J. Evans to J. L. M. Curry, Dec. 20, 1862. Curry Papers.

tion and confiscation of property, if the Federal government conquered the South, and implored absentees and deserters from the army to return to their posts. He declared that the absentees, if they returned, would "suffice to create numerical equality between our force and that of the invaders," and that their return would insure victory. He promised a general amnesty to all who would return within twenty days, and he urged the women of the country not to shelter the deserters. The Confederate government offered three general amnesties to deserters if they would return to the ranks, but the offers did not accomplish much in recouping the losses by desertion.

The story of Newton Knight of Jones County, Mississippi, is a revealing case history of a deserter. A manuscript sketch of his career by his son gives a vivid impression of a frontier individualist. Newt grew up in the piney woods of southern Mississippi, where it took six days by oxcart to make a trip to the nearest trading town, Shubuta. One of twelve brothers, he received no education until his wife taught him to read and write. He had a frontier versatility of skills which he employed in farming, making shoes for his neighbors, and building log houses. When secession came to a vote the people of Jones County voted 376 to 24 to remain in the Union. Newt was drafted, and told the authorities "that he would go with them since he had to go, but he would not fight the Union." He was made a hospital orderly in the Seventh Mississippi Battalion. After the passage of the "20 nigger law" many soldiers from his relatively slaveless home community deserted; and when a letter from Mrs. Knight told Newt that the Confederate cavalry had taken his horse and were taking other private property and mistreating women and old men he also deserted.

Returning to Jones County, he organized the Unionists and deserters into a company "to fight for their rights and the freedom of Jones County." These men bound themselves by an oath never to surrender to the Confederacy until the last man was killed. Their password was, "I am of the Red, White, and Blue." A natural leader, Knight was elected captain of the irregular Unionist company, which sustained itself partly by capturing Confederate supplies and partly by the labor of the women in the fields with hoe and plow. A company of cavalry came into the county from Louisiana to restore Confederate authority. According to Newton's son, they were "mighty ruff on the boys they caught in Jones County," hanging one of Newton's brothers. When bloodhounds were sent to track down deserters the women would poison the dogs. Newt's company attacked and defeated Lowery's Cavalry.[41] After the war the tradition arose that Jones County had seceded from the Confederacy and set up the "Free State of Jones."

The great number of absences without leave from the Confederate armies in the last two years of the war was an indication of the loss of the will to fight and had grave effects on the war effort. One serious result of desertion, which was particularly common after battles, was that the soldiers carried away precious guns and other military equipment; another was that the loss of man power prevented at times the following up of victories. Deserters hid in caves, in deep mountain fastnesses, in swampy areas, and in the debatable land between the opposing armies, often becoming plunderers and murderers.

As desertion depleted the ranks of the army and enlistments declined the Southern people in desperation began to consider the use of Negro troops. The Union Army had set an example by recruiting Negro troops in invaded territory. The recently discovered diary of James T. Ayers, a Northern recruiter in Tennessee and northern Alabama, illustrates the methods of recruiting Southern Negroes for military service. This lay preacher would go to plantations behind the Union lines, announce to the slaves that they had been freed by President Lincoln, and offer the inducements of food, clothing, and ten

41 Short Sketch of Life of Newton Knight Told by His Son, T. J. Knight. MSS in Louisiana State University Library, Manuscript Division.

dollars a month to enlist. On occasions he would display posters and lure the Negroes to volunteer with the music of a fiddler, the example of a detachment of Negro soldiers, and his own fervid oratory.[42] Despite such enticements, he found the slaves exceedingly reluctant to join and finally gave up in discouragement. Nevertheless, 186,017 Negroes served in the Union Army, of whom 104,387 were recruited in Confederate territory.

The South could very well have profited by the example of the North in using Negro troops. In November, 1862, Thomas Wentworth Higginson, an ardent abolitionist and admirer of John Brown, was placed in command of the first slave regiment employed by the United States, the "First Regiment of South Carolina Volunteers," which was used in fighting in that state. Later Colonel Robert Gould Shaw of Massachusetts commanded a regiment of Negro troops from Massachusetts, losing his life and many of his men in a night attack on Battery Wagner, Charleston Harbor, July 18, 1863. Led always by white officers, the Negro recruits made brave soldiers; and they had a prominent part in the capture of Port Hudson, the battle of Milliken's Bend on the Mississippi, and the fighting at Petersburg, Virginia. Northern soldiers, however, were almost as bitterly hostile as Southern to Negro troops.[43]

President Davis, December 23, 1862, practically threatened death to slave troops and their white officers, in a proclamation which turned them over to the states to be dealt with as agents to excite servile war. The Confederate Congress on April 30, 1863, voted that white officers leading Negro soldiers should be "deemed as inciting servile insurrection" and, if captured,

[42] *The Diary of James T. Ayers, Civil War Recruiter,* ed. J. H. Franklin (Illinois State Historical Society, Springfield, Ill., 1947).

[43] Even Charles Francis Adams, Jr., while stationed at Hilton Head, S. C., opposed using Negro troops; he wrote to his father that the white troops were very anti-Negro and hailed with joy the breaking up of Hunter's Negro regiment. He revised his views later and even commanded Negro troops. Ford, ed., *A Cycle of Adams Letters,* II, 170-174, 212-219.

should be put to death. Lincoln retaliated by promising that, for every Union soldier killed in violation of the laws of war, a Confederate prisoner would be executed. In the spring of 1864, when Forrest recaptured Fort Pillow on the Mississippi River in Tennessee, his men were accused of massacring the Negro troops in the garrison, refusing to accept their surrender. This assault became the "atrocity" of the war. A Congressional investigation headed by Senator Ben Wade branded the action as beyond the pale of civilized warfare. Actually the Confederates captured 226 of the garrison of 577, about half the Federal troops having been killed during the battle. The primary cause of so much loss of life in the assault was the havoc produced by Confederate sharpshooters before the attack and the retreat of the garrison to the protection of the gunboat *New Era* without lowering the flag of the fort. There must have been some individual atrocities, but Forrest should be acquitted of the charge of ordering a brutal murder of the Federal garrison without quarter.[44]

At Dalton, Georgia, in 1864, General Patrick Cleburne circulated among the officers under the command of Joseph E. Johnston a document advocating the recruiting of Negroes for the Confederate Army. A council of officers considered this audacious project and voted against it by a large majority. Some of them condemned the proposal as incendiary and contrary to chivalric warfare. Johnston, acting under orders from President Davis, persuaded Cleburne to suppress his memorial. After the fall of Atlanta, however, Secretary of War Seddon advocated not only employment of slaves as soldiers but emancipation as a reward for military service.

Such revolutionary proposals were debated with great excitement and vehemence in the fall and winter of 1864-1865.[45]

[44] Henry, *"First with the Most" Forrest,* chap. xvii.

[45] See T. R. Hay, "The South and the Arming of Slaves," *Mississippi Valley Historical Review,* VI, 34-73 (June, 1919), and N. W. Stephenson, "The Question of Arming the Slaves," *American Historical Review,* XVIII, 295-308 (Jan., 1913).

Governor William ("Extra Billy") Smith proposed that Virginia and the other Confederate states, not the central government, should arm the slaves and later emancipate them as a necessary measure to save Southern independence. In a letter of January 11, 1865, Lee favored this plan and advised that it be adopted immediately in order to allow time for training the Negroes. However, he refused to intervene to force the issue. After a long debate the Virginia legislature voted to permit the arming of slaves without promising emancipation. Judah P. Benjamin in a speech, February 9, 1865, in the African Church at Richmond urged the enlistment of slaves with the grant of freedom, and this was one of the reasons for an attempt to drive him from the cabinet. President Davis, who had opposed the arming of the slaves, now became an ardent advocate of it, not only to fill the depleted ranks of the army but to influence European diplomacy.

The influential Richmond *Enquirer* on February 24, 1865, strongly urged the recruiting of Negroes for the army. The fact that Lee favored the use of Negroes was sufficient reason for its adoption, according to the editor; "by all means let him have them." He pointed out that, regardless of Southern prejudice, Negroes had made respectable soldiers in Grant's army, that President Davis favored using Negroes as cooks, teamsters, servants in the hospitals, and laborers for the army, and that Lee and the army desired them; "yet the Senate deliberates, and that is all it does—deliberates, *deliberates*."[46] The editor urged the Virginia legislature to arm a large body of slaves.

On the other hand Howell Cobb, one of the largest slaveholders, opposed this measure, declaring, "If slaves will make good soldiers, our whole theory of slavery is wrong."[47] Rhett came out of retirement to write a powerful letter arguing that the proposal violated state rights by removing slavery from

[46] Clipping in the Jeremy F. Gilmer Papers.
[47] Hay, *op. cit.*, 63.

state control. Robert Kean of the Confederate War Bureau thought that it would be "a colossal blunder" because it would dislocate society and for every Negro recruit the Confederacy got the enemy would get four.[48]

On February 10, 1865, bills to arm the slaves were introduced both in the Senate and the House of Representatives. After much debate a compromise bill was passed and signed by the President one month before the surrender at Appomattox. It gave him the power to ask slave owners for Negroes to serve in the army and, if enough were not offered, to call on each state for its quota of 300,000 troops "irrespective of color." This reluctant decision to use Negro troops was tremendously weakened by a proviso in the law that emancipation of slave soldiers should take place only with the consent of the owners and of the states which furnished them. A consideration that was urged against Negro troops was the strong aversion of white troops to fighting side by side with Negroes. Several companies of Negroes were organized in Richmond as decoys to encourage volunteering by other members of the race; but they were ridiculed, and their gaudy uniforms were pelted by small boys.

In World War I the German people lost the will to fight after four years of deprivation with the prospect of military defeat. Somewhat similarly the Southern people became war-weary after three years of fighting for independence, and a peace movement developed. One of the most popular songs in the South at this time was "When This Cruel War Is Over." John Dimitry, chief clerk in the Post Office Department, attributed the loss of enthusiasm among Southerners to fight for independence to a lack of moral principle. "Want of Moral Principle in the People," he wrote, "has done more to injure the Cause than either Grant or Sherman. . . . I am, honestly speaking, disappointed in our people. They are not up to the mark of the times. They have failed to rise to the grandeur

[48] Kean MS Diary, II, Dec. 25, 1864, and Jan. 1, 1865.

of the War. . . . If we lose, the Posterity of the actors in this war . . . will decide that while the President did his full duty honestly and conscientiously, the cause was lost because there was no Wisdom in Congress and no Public Virtue among the People." Senator Clement C. Clay likewise wrote to Wigfall that he was "sick of the selfishness, demagogism and bigotry that characterize a large portion of those in office," and when he saw "how many are growing rich in the Commissary and Qr. Masters Departs. by defrauding the Government and the people and yet are unchecked," and how many "cheating impressing agents" there were, he wished to leave public life.

Throughout the great Allegheny peninsula which jutted far into the South, the Unionists began to make trouble for the Confederacy.[49] They formed secret organizations such as the Heroes of America, peace societies, and constitutional societies, with rituals, grips, and passwords. Kean noted in his diary, June 20, 1864, that there was a curious secret society in North Carolina which extended into Alabama and the army, whose principles were the second and sixth chapters of Joshua; namely, to obtain peace and preserve their property by betraying their country.[50] The commissary stationed at Dublin in southwestern Virginia wrote to Bragg, September 21, 1864, that he was amazed at the extent of disloyalty in that part of the state—he was informed that in Montgomery County there were no fewer than eight hundred "heroes of America," who had elected the sheriffs and the justices of the peace, and there had been a meeting in Floyd County of fifty-one deserters armed with Enfield rifles who planned to destroy a section of the Virginia & Tennessee Railroad.[51]

These revolutionary associations protected deserters and engaged in "fifth column" activities. Some of the members

[49] See Georgia L. Tatum, *Disloyalty in the Confederacy* (Chapel Hill, 1934); Martin, *Desertion of Alabama Troops from the Confederate Army;* and Bryan, *Confederate Georgia,* chap. ix.

[50] Kean MS Diary, II, June 20, 1864.

[51] Henry J. Leroy to Gen. Braxton Bragg, Sept. 21, 1864. Jefferson Davis Papers, MSS in Duke University Library.

were bushwhackers who plundered and murdered loyal Confederates. The illegal trade in cotton between the lines contributed to the growth of disloyal sentiment, and the mountain vendettas and private feuds, intensified by the Civil War, led some clans to side with the Union forces. But the main cause of disaffection in North Carolina, Georgia, and Tennessee stemmed from Unionism in 1860-1861.

The passing of the Impressment Act in March, 1863, aroused a storm of opposition that injured the morale of the people. The purpose was to legalize a practice of military officials and to protect the people from impostors. According to the law, if the impressment officer and the producer could not agree on a price, the price was to be decided by local arbitrators, with an appeal by the Confederate officer to a board of impressment commissioners in the state appointed jointly by the President and the governor. This board was required to fix, every two months, a schedule of prices for goods taken within the states by the Confederate government. In addition to impressment by the Confederate authorities, there was impressment by state governments for public defense or poor relief. Indeed, the depreciation of the currency made such practices almost imperative.

The enforcement of the impressment law contributed much toward turning loyal sections into Unionist districts. The Confederate cavalry would often stir hatred and dread by their seizure of food and horses under the law. The people bitterly resented the fact that corn and other agricultural produce were impressed at about half the market price. The law was carried out by agents who could not be closely supervised, who were susceptible to bribery, and who followed the line of least resistance; and, according to an able student of the Civil War, "No other one thing, not even conscription, caused so much discontent and produced so much resentment toward the Confederacy."[52]

[52] Ramsdell, *Behind the Lines in the Confederacy*, 93, 117.

The suspension of the writ of habeas corpus at intervals by the Confederate Congress was another important factor that lowered the morale of the people. Although President Davis used it conservatively, chiefly to rid Richmond and other cities of spies, traitors, and deserters, he was violently attacked as a despot. In the spring of 1864 the Georgia legislature adopted resolutions introduced by Linton Stephens declaring the suspension of the writ to be "a dangerous assault upon the Constitution" and recommending peace offers after every Confederate victory.[53] When the last suspension expired in August, 1864, a long and bitter struggle took place in Congress over its renewal. Finally a bill restoring the suspension passed in the House but received a tie vote in the Senate. Vice President Stephens cast the deciding vote against the bill, and took advantage of the occasion to deliver a diatribe against the Davis administration.

In North Carolina the opposition to the suspension of the writ was perhaps more disastrous to morale than in Georgia. On February 9, 1864, Governor Vance wrote to Davis earnestly urging him to refrain from suspending the writ in that state, because it would accelerate the growth of the peace sentiment. The Chief Justice of the North Carolina Supreme Court, Richmond M. Pearson, discharged many men arrested by conscript officers by granting them writs of habeas corpus. Vance supported him in resisting the arbitrary arrest of citizens by the military officers. Kean noted in his diary, May 3, 1863, that General W. D. Pender, a commander of North Carolina troops, revealed "disgraceful desertion of North Carolina troops as a result of Judge Pearson's decision on conscription."[54] However, when Pearson held that the Confederate Congress could not change the terms of exemption, he was overruled by his Associate Justices. In various other parts of the South, suspension of the writ of habeas corpus was violently attacked as an infringement on constitutional liberty.

[53] Rabun, *op. cit.*, 300-321.
[54] Kean MS Diary, II, May 3, 1863.

The initiative for peace negotiations, however, came from the North through an unofficial visit of Francis P. Blair, Sr., to Richmond. Blair advocated reunion on the basis of a joint war against the French in Mexico to enforce the Monroe Doctrine. A conference between the two governments was finally arranged for February 3, 1865, on the *River Queen* at Hampton Roads. Here Lincoln and Secretary of State Seward met Vice President Stephens, Senator R. M. T. Hunter, and former Justice of the Supreme Court John A. Campbell, representing the Confederate government. Stephens urged the wisdom of the two nations concluding a peace treaty and then together enforcing the Monroe Doctrine. He pointed out that history showed examples of nations at war laying aside a quarrel and cooperating in matters of mutual interest. Lincoln replied that he knew nothing of history: "You must talk history to Seward."[55] Brushing aside protocol, he insisted on the restoration of the Union of all the states and the abolition of slavery as indispensable peace terms. Such proposals, the Confederates refused to consider; and peace negotiations thus ended in failure.

[55] *Ibid.*, II, Feb. 5, 1865.

CHAPTER THIRTEEN

THE DYNAMICS OF THE SOUTHERN MIND

THE MORES of a people have been considered so tenacious, at least from the days of William Graham Sumner, that they supposedly change at a glacial pace. But David Riesman has shown in *The Lonely Crowd* that this is not always true. The impact of the recent accelerated growth of population on the United States has changed the American character, particularly in the large cities. This generation has also witnessed within a few climactic years a remarkable overturning of the folkways of large parts of the South in respect to the Negro. Sumner's thesis therefore applies more authentically to an isolated, rural community such as existed in the Old South than it does to modern America. Yet even in the Old South some of the mores changed appreciably in the time between Thomas Jefferson and Jefferson Davis. This chapter is an attempt to probe the social dynamics of the region and to discover those aspects of the Southern mind that changed between the 1820's and 1860 and those that remained back in the eighteenth and early nineteenth centuries.

It is to the aristocracy—the country gentlemen—of the South that one must look for the most marked differences between the North and the South. They cherished a set of values that were different from those of the North and which have virtually disappeared from our modern society. William Faulkner in "An Odor of Verbena" has described some of these archaic virtues, notably a deep sense of obligation to the family and a willingness to put one's life in jeopardy for the sake of honor. A striking example of this latter characteristic is found in the record of a court of honor held in 1836 at the University of Virginia (manuscript in the Huntington Library). At a dance given by Professor Bonnycastle a student from South Carolina, Louis Wigfall, felt insulted by the refusal of a Southern belle, a Miss Leiper, to dance with him. Believing that he was "elevated by wine," to use her expression, she took the arm of another student and hastened precipitately away. Wigfall was a youth of high mettle and fiery spirit and accordingly sent a challenge to Miss Leiper's escort for uttering language during the altercation "that I could suffer from no one."

When the civil authorities prevented the duel, a court of honor was appointed by the students to adjudicate the question whether Wigfall had been insulted. The court acted scrupulously according to legal forms. Miss Leiper's testimony, presented in a letter, informed the court of honor that she was mistaken in thinking that Wigfall was under the influence of wine when he insisted upon dancing with her. The court of honor reported that the affair between the two students had arisen out of "a delicate sensibility" which each party displayed, and because of a misconception. It ruled that there was no point of honor involved and that Wigfall's conduct in the presence of a lady was not rude or due to alcohol but was owing to "a natural impetuosity" which Miss Leiper had wrongly attributed to intoxication. Thus the matter ended without bloodshed and with the honor of both students preserved. Louis Wigfall lived to become a secession leader in Texas and a senator in the Confederate Congress.

Southern pride was displayed in various other ways than in quick resentment to insult. Many Southerners had a high sense of pride in regard to money matters; they did not wish to appear petty or mean in financial transactions. When James Atherton was touring Kentucky in 1832 he noted how different the Kentuckians were from New Englanders in money matters.

"To offer a Kentuckian cents in change," he wrote to his father, "would be deemed almost an insult" (manuscript in the University of Kentucky Library). Indeed, the values of Southerners were not those of sharp-trading Yankees. Horace Holley, who came from Boston to be president of Transylvania University, observed in 1832 that the people of Kentucky and Tennessee were influenced in their manners and character by slavery and the subtle forces of an agricultural interior. "Commerce," he remarked, "makes a different sort of population from agriculture."

A keen sense of personal pride and honor was, of course, not peculiar to the Southern people of the ante bellum period. The Japanese, for example, have had until recently a code of conduct which exalts honor to fantastic extremes and seems to be the vestigial remains of a feudal society. The Southern sense of honor, too, had a feudal background, but it was powerfully nourished by the institution of slavery. Although Southerners as a whole did not display much vanity about personal appearance, they were overwhelmingly proud of standing up for the rights of their section. Southern pride, indeed, had an important role in bringing on the Civil War.

Honor and personal pride were part of the code of a gentleman in the Old South. Another obligation of the code, affecting even the humblest farmer, was the practice of hospitality. One visitor in the 1850's, the Northern journalist Frederick Law Olmsted, was not impressed by Southern hospitality. He was refused lodging for the night by planters both in Virginia and Mississippi; and often when he was accommodated, he paid for his meals and lodging. When Edmund Ruffin was making his agricultural survey of South Carolina in 1843, the great planters who knew of his reputation entertained him hospitably, but he found that when his route lay through the region of small farms, the inhabitants accommodated travelers for the money. Even a state senator who lived near the Salkehatchie River was not too proud to charge him for lodging and meals, whereas Ruffin assumed that he was receiving hospitality and that it would be an insult to his host to offer payment.

Quite different, however, were the experiences of most travelers in the Old South. Henry Barnard, a Northern schoolteacher who traveled in this region in 1833, was touched by the many evidences of Southern hospitality, especially among the Virginians. "These Virginians," he noted, "won't take anything for their hospitality." For example, on his way to the scenic Peaks of Otter, he spent the night in the home of an intelligent farmer who refused to accept any compensation for lodging and food. "This is the way they do things in Virginia," Barnard commented. A Scottish textile worker, William Thomson, who traveled through the Southern states in 1840-42 and wrote *A Tradesman's Travels in the United States and Canada,* commented on Southern hospitality and sense of honor: "The character of the southern states, for hospitality, stands high, and it is not overrated. They are quite a distinct race from the 'Yankees.' They have a high sense of honour; treating every white man as a gentleman, but rigidly exacting the same respect in return; and although many young men carry bowie-knives, sword-canes, or pistols, after I knew them I felt myself as safe from injury or outrage as in my own house. In short, the society in this part of the country was the most agreeable I ever associated with—Ladies are treated on all occasions with great deference and respect."

The plantation society of the Old South exhibited a strong patriarchal character owing to its isolation and to slavery. These same influences, young Charles Darwin discovered, produced a similar characteristic in Brazilian plantation society. He visited a Brazilian plantation in 1832 while the *Beagle* was in port. His description of it, except for the great pile of coffee beans drying before the residence, bears a striking similarity to accounts of some Southern plantations of the same period: "The house was simple, and, though like a barn in form, was well suited to the climate. In the sitting room gilded chairs and sofas were oddly contrasted with the white-washed walls, thatched roofs and windows without glass. . . . This profusion of food showed itself at dinner, where, if the table did not groan, the guests surely did: for each person is expected to eat of every dish. One day, having, as I thought, nicely calculated so that nothing should go away untasted, to my utter dismay a roast turkey and a pig appeared in all their substantial reality. During the meals, it was the employment of a man to drive out of the room sundry old hounds, and dozens of little black children, which crawled in together, at every opportunity. As long as the idea of slavery could be abolished, there was something exceedingly fascinating in this simple and patriarchal style of living: it was such a perfect retirement and independence from the rest of the world. . . . On such fazendas as these I have no doubt the slaves pass happy and contented lives."

The plantation society of the Old South emphasized the family to a much greater degree than was done in the North. Family graveyards were a familiar sight in the landscape of the Old South; the family altar was a part of its religious mores; and the devotion to kin was expressed in the phrase "kissing cousins." Southerners tended to evaluate people not so much as individuals but as belonging to a family, a clan. This characteristic has survived into the twentieth century in many villages of the Deep South, as Harper Lee's recent novel *To Kill a Mockingbird* has demonstrated. Here, far from the industrial world, the villagers judged people within the family context, as displaying hereditary characteristics. They were accustomed to lump all the Ewells together as being no-account for generations; the Cunninghams could always be trusted to pay their debts; "all the Burfords walked like that"; the Penfields had a "flighty streak"; the Crawfords, a "mean streak"; and the Goforths, a "stingy streak."

John William De Forest, who observed society in the

upcountry of South Carolina at the close of the Civil War, compared Southerners with his fellow New Englanders. "They are more simple than us," he wrote, "more provincial, more antique, more picturesque; they have fewer of the virtues of modern society, and more of the primitive, the natural virtues; they care less for wealth, art, learning, and the other delicacies; they care more for individual character and reputation of honor."

The traits of the Southern people were brightly illuminated during the Civil War. Von Clausewitz, the great German student of war, has argued that a nation fights the kind of war that the nature of its society determines. By 1860 the upper class of Southern society had developed the habit of command and a remarkable sense of pride. They were not accustomed to subordinate their wills to a central authority. Mrs. Chesnut's description of her father-in-law, in 1865—old Colonel Chesnut of South Carolina—points up this characteristic. "Partly patriarch, partly grand seigneur, this old man is of a species that we shall see no more—the last of a race of lordly planters who ruled this Southern world, but now a splendid wreck. His manners are unequaled still, but underneath this smooth exterior lies the grip of a tyrant whose will has never been crossed." Not all Southern planters were like Colonel Chesnut, but many of them were highly individualistic. Most of them, even the well-educated, were provincial in their outlook and in their loyalties.

The higher officers of the Confederate Army (who were not elected) came mainly from the plantation aristocracy, from the professional soldiers, the lawyers, and, surprisingly, from the business class. Ezra Warren establishes in *Generals in Gray* that of the 425 Confederate officers of general rank, 129 were lawyers before the war; 125, professional soldiers; 55, businessmen (including bankers, manufacturers, and merchants); 42, farmers and planters; 24, politicians; and 15, educators. The elected officers below the rank of colonel, however, were often drawn from humble citizens. They nevertheless commanded the sons of aristocratic planters; for example, Kate Stone's brother of Brokenburn in Louisiana served as a private in a company whose officers included a livery stable keeper, an overseer, and a butcher. The Confederate armies were, as David Donald has observed, "a product of the paradoxical world that was the ante bellum South, devoted to the principles of democracy and the practice of aristocracy."

The Old South was also different from our own age in its greater devotion to the classics, which meant a greater devotion to tradition. The whole educational system of the South from grammar school through college was based on the classic tradition, as was also the case in the North, though perhaps to a lesser degree. Hugh Swinton Legaré, editor of the Charleston *Southern Review* and John Tyler's attorney general and secretary of state, advocated that Southern youth should be thoroughly taught in the ancient languages from their eighth to their sixteenth year. The study of the classics, he observed, would form in them a pure taste, kindle their imaginations "with the most beautiful and glowing passages of Greek and Roman poetry and eloquence," store their minds with "the sayings of the sages," and indelibly impress upon their hearts the achievements of the Greek and Roman heroes.

Accordingly, the "gentleman" of the Old South was expected to have a classical education. The lack of such a training gave the novelist William Gilmore Simms an inferiority complex when conversing with the polished gentlemen of Charleston. In a letter to Hammond (1845) requesting that he be called neither doctor nor colonel, he commented: "I have as little claim to be a Dr. of Laws as any literary man in the country. Never was education so worthless as mine—i.e. in a classical point of view. . . . Through painful necessities I have come to the acquisition of an Independent Mind. . . . I must submit to be called Dr. & Col. by that silly class of persons who attach much importance to these things." In advising a young girl on her education Simms wrote (July 13, 1854): "I would have you make yourself familiar with Plutarch, Anacharsis [one of the Seven Sages of antiquity], Froissart, & C." Plutarch's *Lives* was regarded in the Old South, next to the Bible, as the great character-builder and was perhaps the most important single source of the classic tradition.

Legaré was the outstanding champion of the Greek and Roman classics in the Old South. This Charleston intellectual reminds one somewhat of Lord Byron in his temperament and in the circumstances of his life; the lock of hair that he wore over his forehead, his long sideburns, his fastidiousness, and his melancholic temperament were Byronic. Like the English poet, too, his personality suffered a permanent trauma from the fact that he was lame from childhood. In all probability Legaré would have been a literary man had he lived in a different environment. But ambitious of honor, he turned to politics and made literature an avocation. He never married, though apparently he was in love with a South Carolina girl, whom he described as "the most thorough-bred young lady in the country"; she had the same tastes as Legaré but nevertheless married another man, leaving him "alone in society" in Charleston. His affections thenceforth centered on his mother and sister.

The frank letters that Legaré wrote to former Senator William C. Rives of Virginia in 1839 reveal to some degree the paradox of the Southern intellectual of the period—a conflict between classicism and romanticism. He buried himself in the study of the ancient world, especially of Roman law, and wrote to Rives: "I have lately read Greek and German enough to choke ten professors." From 1832 to 1836 Legaré had served as chargé d'affaires at Brussels, where he had cultivated his mind by contact both with books and a continental society, which may explain his discontent with "this humdrum American world." To Rives he described himself as desolate and wretched, like Prometheus on the rock, with a "chained spirit."

His letters are full of romantic longing instead of the serene acceptance of life as it is, typical of classical Greek art and literature. To Rives he also lamented that his mind was preternaturally calm, like the Dead Sea: "I want a tempest, anything that can stir it up to some passionate effort." He found this outlet in politics—at first, in a strong opposition to the Nullification movement; then toward the end of his life, in fighting the "putrid democracy" of Van Buren.

In this last struggle before his early death in 1843 he displayed the spirit of a strong conservative, reflecting some of the characteristics of the South Carolina mind. Lacking the economic basis for the aristocratic life, he nevertheless despised the pursuit of money. "What is there to awaken me," he exclaimed to Rives, "but the sordid love of pelf—which unfortunately does not come to me?" He was disgusted with the vote-getting appeals that the Van Buren democracy made to the common people, which aroused hostility between the rich and the poor, between the North and the South, and between agriculture and commerce. What had these self-styled friends of the poor actually done for them? "Did they encourage them to work as [John Jacob] Astor had done?" Despite such conservative individualism, Legaré rendered an official opinion as attorney general in 1841 that was decidedly liberal for his time, holding that free Negroes were entitled to the same civil rights as white men.

The cross currents in Southern thought that Legaré exhibited were also apparent in the pages of the Southern literary magazines. These reflected a much greater trend toward romanticism than toward a strong and vital interest in the Greek and Roman classics. Their articles on classicism were usually related to practical Southern interests and were often dictated by the desire to justify Southern institutions. The *Southern Quarterly Review* of Charleston, for example, published articles in the 1840's and 1850's on such subjects as "Classical Literature" (July, 1842), "Socrates" (January, 1843),

"Rome and the Romans" (October, 1844), "Cicero's Letters" (October, 1844), "The Roman Law" (July, 1845), "Athens and the Athenians" (April, 1847), "Slavery among the Romans," which justified Southern as better than Roman slavery because of the influence of Christianity (October, 1848), "The Condition of Women in Ancient Greece" (January, 1850), "An Inquiry into Roman Jurisprudence" (April, 1851), "The Athenian Orators" (October, 1851), "Marcus Aurelius" (October, 1853), "Necessity of the Classics" (July, 1854), "Plato's Phaedon" (August, 1856), and "Cicero's *De Officiis*" (November, 1856). Professor Frank Ryan, who has written a doctor's dissertation on the *Southern Quarterly Review,* has found that approximately 5 per cent of the articles in this magazine dealt with the ancient world.

The *Southern Literary Messenger* of Richmond, the most enduring of Southern magazines, showed even less interest in the classics. A considerable number of the issues from August, 1834, the date of its founding, until the beginning of the Civil War contain very little material on the ancient world. In the March, 1836, issue is an article on "The Classics," in which the writer noted a growing neglect of the classics as well as continued attempts of many prominent men "to cast contempt on those studies which were once considered essential to the scholar and the gentleman." The writer defended the study of the classics as providing the best mental discipline for students and the best models of literature. Mathew Carey, the Philadelphia economist and publisher, replied in articles in the *Southern Literary Messenger* (August, 1836 and January, 1837), in which he maintained that too much time was spent in grammar school and college on the dead languages, to the detriment of the study of science and modern languages, which were more useful, especially for youths intended for business.

The issues in the 1850 volume were unusual in the number (six) of articles and translations relating to classic Greece and Rome, including an article entitled "Aristotle on Slavery." In other years the *Southern Literary Messenger* published such articles as "Zenobia, Queen of Palmyra" (May, 1849); "Modern Oratory" (June, 1852), which discussed the differences in style of Demosthenes and Cicero with the conclusion, "Demosthenes is, perhaps, the noblest model of oratory" (p. 371); and an alluring article entitled "Good Eating among the Greeks and Romans" (December, 1855). The general tone of the Southern literary magazines indicated a waning influence of the classics in Southern life after 1830 and the overwhelming dominance of the Romantic movement.

Especially significant, however, was the influence of the classics on the development of Southern oratory. Demosthenes and Cicero were held up by schoolmasters as the supreme models. Hugh Swinton Legaré, while a student at South Carolina College, displayed a passion for the classics that reminds one of a Renaissance scholar; he fashioned his style of oratory upon classic examples and like many other Southern boys practiced the art of declaiming in secluded places with appropriate gestures. Calhoun used the example of the Roman consulate to bolster his proposal of a dual Presidency for the nation, and he modeled one of his major speeches on Demosthenes' "Oration on the Crown." Thomas Hamilton, the supercilious British traveler, observed in *Men and Manners in America* (1833) that one heard more Latin quoted in Congress than in the British Parliament but that it consisted of hackneyed phrases and revealed no deep acquaintance with classical literature. Northern speakers as well as Southern orators engaged in this lip service to the classics, but in the rural South, oratory derived from Periclean Athens and imperial Rome could not compete successfully with romantically styled speeches.

The interest in ancient history and the classics might very well have been a liberating force on the Southern mind. Instead of emulating the liberal side of the classical tradition, however, Southerners of the ante bellum period were attracted to the conservative elements. From the examples of Greek and Roman society, Southerners drew some of their strongest arguments for justifying slavery. They regarded their own society as an extension of a Greek type of democracy, which had been based on slavery. Yet writers in *De Bow's Review* and the literary magazines, taking note of the fact that the Southern states gave little support to literature, considered the Southern character to be closer to the Roman than to the Greek, for Southerners prided themselves on their genius for government, their military exploits, and their practical ability.

Although Legaré was probably the outstanding classical scholar in public life in the South, the classically trained individual who may have most deeply influenced the Southern mind was Professor Thomas Roderick Dew of William and Mary College. Born in 1802 on a stately plantation at Dewsville, Virginia, he received a splendid classical education, including two years of study in Europe. When he returned to America he was appointed professor of history, political economy, and metaphysics at William and Mary College. Very early he became the subject of jealousy on the part of his less gifted colleagues. They harassed him by influencing the board of visitors to mutilate his course in ancient and modern history. In this course, as he himself observed, he did not go much into the dry details but concentrated on the philosophy of history. Though it was not required for a degree, his history course was exceedingly popular with the students. Moreover, Dew was receiving state-wide acclaim for his pamphlet opposing a protective tariff, which he used as a text in his course in political economy.

Dew's greatest fame came in 1832 when he published his *Review of the Debate in the Virginia Legislature of 1831 and 1832,* later to be included in *The Pro-Slavery Argument* (Charleston, 1852). In this work Dew emphasized the practical objections to the emancipation of the slaves and using his knowledge of Greek and Roman history and of Aristotle, he justified the institution as the natural order of life. His essay was the first important polemic in the development of the proslavery argument in the South, and its seeds fell on fertile ground, for the Southerners were ready to be convinced that they were doing nothing wrong in holding slaves. Few in the South controverted his ideas publicly, but one brilliant contemporary, Jesse Burton Harrison of Lynchburg, Virginia, who was also a student of the classics, published a noble refutation of the proslavery argument—*Review of the Slave Question by a Virginian* (Richmond, 1833). Dew was rewarded in 1836 by being chosen president of William and Mary College.

In the struggle between the classic tradition and the romantic spirit for supremacy over the Southern mind, the victory went decidedly to romanticism; even classic culture was viewed in a romantic and unhistorical light. The ante bellum South was filled with neo-classic architecture. Greek Revival colonnades decorated courthouses, churches, banks, theaters, and mansions. Yet behind the imposing facades there was little to suggest the classic tradition except perhaps for libraries representing an accumulation of several generations; occasionally the mantels were of marble and the wallpaper derived from classical motifs, as in Andrew Jackson's Hermitage. The spirit of the architecture of the Old South, both the Greek Revival and the Gothic Revival, was indeed romantic. As Oliver Larkin has phrased it, "under the colonnades and pediments they had created something which the Greeks never knew."

In no aspect of Southern life during the ante bellum period was the romantic vogue carried to greater excess than in the treatment of women. "Years ago," said one of Faulkner's characters in *Absalom, Absalom!*, "We in the South made our women into ladies. Then the War came and made the ladies into ghosts." The ladies of that old time did not walk on their legs beneath their crinoline dresses, Faulkner observed—they floated. It was not always so in the South, for the mores had changed greatly in respect to woman's role from the days of William Byrd II of Westover. The Romantic movement had intervened, so that Southern society of the nineteenth century frowned upon the realism with which Byrd regarded his wife, and women in general. Travelers from Europe between 1830 and 1860 were impressed with the politeness of American men, particularly in the South, who gave up their seats in stagecoaches and railroad cars to women. And in the South men were far more gallant in making compliments to ladies—and still are—than was the custom in the North.

The attitude toward women in the Old South was highly romantic, but actually not many Southern women lived according to romantic standards. Maria Louisa Fleet, the mistress of Green Mount in Tidewater Virginia, seems to have well represented the superior type of Southern "lady" on the plantation. Her letters in 1860-65 and the diary of her son Benny reveal that she was so busy being the mistress of a plantation of fifty slaves and rearing a family of seven children that she had little time to be a romantic lady. Nevertheless, she was strongly influenced by the romantic vogue of her society; she displayed a taste for sentimental songs and novels that were flavored with a moral or religious ingredient. On June 16, 1863, she wrote to her son in the Confederate Army: "I wish you would do a favor for me the next time you go to Richmond, if you can—I have still a hankering after Northern newspapers, illustrated ones particularly. Books and papers are the only things that I want from Yankee land and England."

Maria Louisa Fleet held the Victorian idea that woman's place in society was definitely subordinate to the male. Yet she also believed that most men were easy to manage, "*if you go about it in the right way,*" and she seems to have had great influence in making family decisions. She shared the spirit of *noblesse oblige* that elevated the Southern gentry and scorned those men who, lacking courage and the martial spirit, failed to volunteer to fight for "their country" (the South). At various times she reveals in her letters her aristocratic prejudices; she belonged to an ardent Whig family, who made a distinction between "gentlemen" and other people. When she heard that an effort was being made during the early part of the war to array the poor against the rich, she wrote to her soldier son, "Ah! my child too much democracy will ruin this country." Yet the mistress of Green Mount was a kind and generous woman; she treated the slaves maternally, taught her children high ideals of character, worked unceasingly for the Confederate soldiers (sewing and knitting and sending them food), and practiced a cordial hospitality.

Very different from Mrs. Fleet in personality was Louisa McCord of Lang Syne plantation and Charleston, South Carolina; nevertheless, the two women were both ardent Southerners. Louisa was the brilliant daughter of Langdon Cheves, a prominent Southern nationalist. He sent her North to Miss Grimshaw's School in Philadelphia, but Louisa also learned much from the politicians and planters who came to her father's home. She studied the Greek and Latin classics, and they made such a great impression on her that she tried to mold her life on that of the Roman matron Cornelia; in middle life she wrote a five-act drama entitled *Caius Gracchus.* Like the lady of Green Mount, she worked hard at being a good mistress of the slaves. In articles in the *Southern Quarterly Review* she passionately defended slavery, and Simms therefore selected her to write the review of *Uncle Tom's Cabin.* She advocated the philosophy of conservatism, condemning the "isms" of the North, such as feminism, which she believed took women out of the sphere assigned to them by divine law.

When war came, Louisa McCord became the embodiment of feminine heroism and Southern patriotism. At her own expense she raised a company for her son, and after he died in battle, she worked day and night in the hospitals caring for wounded soldiers and served as president of the Ladies Clothing Association of South Carolina for the benefit of Confederate troops. In her famous diary Mrs. Chesnut recorded: "She has the brains and energy of a man." But Louisa also had the passionate spirit of defiance that animated the women of New Orleans before the surrender of the city in the spring of 1862. The *Southern Literary Messenger* of July, 1863, celebrated their patriotism in a poem by Tenella entitled a "Lament for New Orleans." These heroic women were compared to the cowardly men who had bartered their honor to save gold; the anonymous poet declared:

> In wrath and defiance they boldly arose
> And scorned to concede one inch to their foes.

In Louisa McCord's view there were no blemishes on the "Christian slavery" of the South. Her friend Mrs. Chesnut, though she supported Southern institutions loyally, had her doubts and wrote in her diary (with great exaggeration) on March 14, 1861: "I wonder if it be a sin to think slavery a curse to any land. Men and women are punished when their masters and mistresses are brutes, not when they do wrong. Under slavery we live surrounded by prostitutes, yet an abandoned woman is sent out of any decent house. . . . Like the patriarchs of old, our men live all in one house with their wives and their concubines; and the mulattoes one sees in every family partly resemble the white children."

Mrs. Mary Minor Blackford of Fredericksburg, Virginia, also recognized the evils of slavery and in 1832 began to keep a journal entitled "Notes Illustrative of the Wrongs of Slavery." Mrs. Blackford became an ardent colonizationist and taught her children to hate slavery and worship God devoutly. She and her family were strongly unionist in sentiment, but after Virginia seceded, her sons became devoted Confederate soldiers. Mrs. Blackford, Mrs. Chesnut, Mrs. McCord, and

Mrs. Fleet all belonged to the aristocratic strata of Southern life, and though differing in many respects, they displayed certain common characteristics—intense regional patriotism, romantic tastes, strong religious feeling, and a conservative philosophy of life.

Another powerful agent of change in the South that paralleled the Romantic movement was the rise of Jacksonian democracy. This great uprising of the common people altered the political mores of the South very decidedly. Fletcher Green in an article entitled "Democracy in the Old South" (*Journal Of Southern History*, February, 1946) and Charles S. Sydnor in *The Development of Southern Sectionalism* (1948) have shown the existence of a large measure of political democracy in the Old South. The Jacksonian movement gave poor men the opportunity to become politicians, but the yeomen, though voting in large numbers, never really developed a leadership responsive to their needs. In most instances the members of this class who rose to party leadership forgot their early background, went over to the side of the aristocrats, and became vociferous advocates of planter interests.

Such was a familiar pattern in the history of the Old South from the time of Davy Crockett of Tennessee to the era of Joseph E. Brown of Georgia and Albert Gallatin Brown of Mississippi. J. D. B. De Bow in a pamphlet on *The Interest in Slavery of the Southern Non-Slaveholder* pointed out the ever recurring absorption of the ambitious sons of yeomen into the ranks of the planters: "The sons of the non-slaveholders are and always have been the leading and ruling spirits of the South in industry as well as in politics—[he himself was one of the examples]. In this class are the McDuffies, Langdon Cheves, Andrew Jacksons, Henry Clays, and Rusks of the past; the Hammonds, Yanceys, Orrs, Memmingers, Benjamins, Stephens, Soulés, Browns of Mississippi, Simms, Porters, Magraths, Aikens, Maunsel Whites, and an innumerable host of the present; and what is to be noted, these men have not been made demagogues, but are among the most conservative among us."

The extent and depth of democracy below the Mason-Dixon Line may be gauged by examining the power structure on two levels—the county courthouse rings and the legislatures. The apportionment of representation in the legislatures was the most significant indicator of democratic or aristocratic control. The most democratic method of determining representation was the white basis, defined variously as "free white males," as in Arkansas; or "qualified voters," as in Tennessee; or "free white inhabitants," as in Mississippi. The most aristocratic arrangement was the counting of total population, slave and free, which was done only in Louisiana and Maryland (after 1852). Between these extremes were the federal basis, where slaves were counted at three-fifths of their number, and the mixed basis, which was a combination of taxes and population. The states of the Mississippi Valley, with the exception of Louisiana, belonged in the first category, that of white democracy; North Carolina, Georgia, Florida, and Maryland (until 1852) used the federal basis; and South Carolina and Virginia adopted the mixed basis. South Carolina unquestionably was the most aristocratic, and Mississippi—according to the judgment of Professor Charles S. Sydnor—the most democratic of Southern states. In the latter state the people elected even the judges, high and low.

But the existence of democratic political machinery is, of course, no guarantee that democracy will prevail in the functioning of government. No one can tell, for example, if rich and powerful men in the local communities intimidated poor men as a result of the viva voce system of voting that prevailed in the South (Louisiana, one of the aristocratic states, however, elected its officers by ballot). Nor is it possible to determine the weight of courthouse rings or of family influence in politics, which in colonial days had been so powerful. A former source of aristocratic control, the appointment of the justice of the peace, was undermined greatly by the middle of the century, for only a few of the Southern states, notably Virginia and Kentucky, kept the old system; eight of thirteen Southern states elected all of their county officials. Moreover, the cause of democracy was advanced during most of the period from 1828 to 1856 by the existence of a genuine two-party system. It is ironic, nevertheless, that during this time of ever expanding democratic practice, the political theory of the South became more antidemocratic—a repudiation of Jeffersonian liberalism by such leading proslavery writers as Calhoun, Hammond, and George Fitzhugh.

The Jacksonian movement changed the common man's psychology toward government. Government became no longer a province to be administered by men of the upper class but was a possession of the "sovereign people." After the 1820's most of the leading politicians of the South were not of aristocratic lineage but sons of yeomen. Stump speaking, florid oratory, violent partisanship, the instruction of the senators by the legislatures, and demagoguery were characteristic of the new politics. The Jacksonian movement also brought with it a wave of anti-intellectualism and increased the intolerant atmosphere in the South that the abolition movement had stirred up. The wide use of the vigilance committee and of mobs, representing the direct action of the people, became the order of the day, seriously threatening freedom of speech and of the press.

The Southern mind of the ante bellum period exhibited a great deal of homogeneity because the South remained deeply committed to agriculture. Manufacturing was cautiously emerging when the Civil War arrived, but it was not extensive enough or significant enough to affect the main currents of Southern thought. In 1860 the states of the South that seceded manufactured only 10 per cent of the nation's goods. The overwhelming rural nature of Southern society gave greater significance and influence to the individual and to personal leadership than did the industrial society of the Northeast. I have, therefore, woven my chapters about representative personalities. In so doing, I have sought to find a clue to the role of personality in a society that offered a far greater opportunity for individual influence than in the highly mechanized and impersonal society of America today. Nevertheless, I concluded (very reluctantly) that the history of the South in the thirty years preceding the Civil War, instead of being the exciting drama of the great man or great men creating masterful ideas and the masses docilely following their lead, was largely a story of its representative men themselves being bent and warped by powerful economic and social forces. Calhoun in the field of politics, for example, despite his brilliant mind and strong personality, could not withstand such forces, and William Gilmore Simms in the domain of literature also succumbed. Yet both men seem to have been unconscious of these social forces, and both sincerely believed that in their public life they were guided by great ideas and noble principles—certainly, not by opportunism.

In trying to glimpse the Southern mind as it was in 1860, I have studied fifteen men whom I think represented the major points of view of Southern society. Only four of them—Simms, Thornwell, Polk, and Yancey—clearly favored secession in 1860, and on that single issue this study of the Southern mind may be a minority report. Also, only four—Hammond, Clay, Wise, and Yancey—practiced the code duello. Simms contemplated sending a challenge to an insulting Northern critic and went so far as to submit the question of whether or not his honor was involved to Hammond, who dissuaded him from making a fool of himself. On the other hand, in regard to deeper issues, religion for example, only one—Cassius Marcellus Clay—could be classified as unorthodox, and he was reticent about his religious opinions. In respect to another fundamental issue, the preservation of slavery, only three differed from majority opinion; and, with the possible exception of Hinton Rowan Helper, they seem to have been affected in varying degrees by the Romantic movement. All but two owned plantations, thus setting them apart from most Northerners, and upon the Southern mind of the ante bellum period, the way of agriculture left deeper traces than did the more limited issue of slavery.

Virtually all of them, moreover, were powerfully influenced by their varied economic environments. John Hartwell Cocke, born in 1780, grew up in Virginia during the sunset of the Enlightenment when the decline of the tobacco industry and the consequent unprofitability of slavery predisposed Virginians toward liberal ideas. Hammond was *nouveau riche,* as were many cotton planters in a society that found slavery profitable and planter control of the government necessary to protect their property interests. He was a Hamlet type who changed his ideas and wavered often over the means of "saving" the South but was consistent in his devotion to slavery. Maunsel White illustrates the evolution of the successful businessman into the planter, the economic goal of Southern society. Wise represents the divided mind of Virginia that revealed itself so clearly in the secession crisis. The western half of the state was dominated by the interests of the yeoman farmer; the eastern half, by the old aristocracy. Wise tried to pour new wine into old bottles in seeking progressive reforms in his state. He had one foot in the East and one in the West, a personality half Jeffersonian and half demagogue.

On the surface, Cassius Marcellus Clay and Hinton Rowan Helper seem clearly eccentrics. Yet on closer view Clay appears to have represented a crosscurrent in Kentucky life. From the days of David Rice, the father of Presbyterianism in the West, who published his pamphlet *Slavery Inconsistent with Justice and Good Policy* (1792) to the Pindell letter of Henry Clay in 1849, Kentucky had nourished a sizable group of emancipationists. In 1860 less than one-fifth of the people of the state belonged to slave-owning families, and these were concentrated largely in the Bluegrass region. Hinton Rowan Helper also represented a diverse element in Southern society. The German settlers in the South from whom he sprang had a background of opposing slavery. In the Piedmont section where he lived, slaveholding was a minor interest, and the section had produced other critics of slavery, notably Dr. Henry Ruffner, also of German extraction.

The three men whom I chose to represent the religious mind came from different economic and cultural levels of society. Yet they were in remarkable agreement on the essentials of their theology; they illustrated indeed the typical orthodoxy of the South. A crosscurrent of skepticism, started by the iconoclastic Dr. Thomas Cooper of South Carolina and the discoveries of the new geology of Sir Thomas Lyell, was overwhelmed by the powerful force of orthodoxy. The scientists Maury, Rogers, and Le Conte were all devout religionists who did not permit the critical spirit of science to invade the religious realm.

The career of William Gilmore Simms especially revealed the great changes that came over the Southern mind—changes that converted a realist into a romanticist, a natural democrat into an apostate, and a liberal young man—enthusiastic for nationalism and Southern leader of the Young America movement—into a very conservative older man and an ardent sectionalist. His career was paralleled in some respects by that of William L. Yancey, who as a young man also fought against nullification and for the idea of the Union but in later life used his matchless power of oratory to destroy the Union. On the other hand, Jeremiah Clemens changed from an ardent sectionalist in 1850 to a strong unionist in 1860, apparently influenced strongly by the sentiment of the southern Appalachian area that he represented.

The lives of these fifteen men were encompassed by the

powerful mores of Southern society. Extraordinarily potent, because entrenched in an isolated and beleaguered society, Southern folkways and attitudes were based on tradition and deep folk feelings as well as on economic interests. Consequently, the method of studying only the economic interests of leading men—the technique adopted by Charles A. Beard in interpreting the origin of the Constitution—is inadequate to explain the nature of the Southern mind in 1860. Indeed, beneath the play of changing economic conditions and political opinions, the ways of the Old South altered very slowly—not fundamentally until the coming of the Industrial Revolution to the South in the twentieth century.

What then were these regional mores that set the South apart from the more plastic North, two sections that shared the same general American culture? The unities that emerge from a study of the fifteen individuals presented in this volume indicate these salient characteristics of the South on the eve of the Civil War: (1) an exaggerated sense of honor, based on the cult of the gentleman; (2) a profound religious orthodoxy; (3) an intense local attachment or patriotism that was supported by a strong feeling for family (including blacks and whites)—Calhoun said that the North was an aggregate of individuals, the South of communities; (4) an extreme conservatism (South Carolina, for example, was the only state in the Union that did not permit divorce); (5) an intolerant spirit in regard to the discussion of certain sensitive subjects, notably slavery and heterodox religious ideas; and (6) powerful but mysterious and incomprehensible to liberal Americans today—race feeling.

Regionalism rests on geographic and economic realities and to some degree on history, but it is also based on little things—the nuances of civilization. These little differences, such as accent in speech, racy colloquialisms, different food (grits and hot biscuits, for example), different ways of building houses, different styles of men's hats, are not to be discounted, for the sum total serves to identify regions in America as in Europe. Regional traits are usually not something different —a striking mutation or a pronounced deviant—from the character of the nation to which the region belongs. Rather, they are an exaggeration or an understatement of certain aspects of national character, arising from the peculiar conditions of life within the smaller unit. Tradition has played a strong role in the South; the Southerner, as William Faulkner has observed and illustrated in his novels, has had a more vivid sense of history than the Northerner; the family has meant more to him; the warm climate has affected his mode of life in subtle ways; he has perhaps valued honor and politeness more; he has viewed race relations differently from the non-Southerner. Whereas the Northerner tends to consider social problems in terms of the abstract, the Southerner views them more in terms of personal relationships.

Nevertheless, regional characteristics, like those of nations, do not remain fixed and unchanged. Boyd Shafer in an article in the *American Historical Review* entitled "Men are More Alike," (April, 1952) has observed of nations, and his insight also applies to regions, that there is no such thing as "a constant or ever-present national character, unless it is invented by historians." He has adduced striking examples of how the stereotypes of the English, French, Germans, and Italians have changed from one historic period to another.

Today the high sense of honor of the Old South seems to have largely disappeared from Southern society; also virtually gone are the old politeness, the chivalrous attitude toward women, the delight in florid oratory, and the romantic outlook. Many characteristics of a rural society, such as a warm-hearted hospitality, local attachment, and neighborliness, are rapidly disappearing as industrialism is changing the economic life of the region. Certain traits remain, at least the vestiges of them, in large parts of the South; the religious orthodoxy of an earlier age survives; Southerners are even now in comparison with Northerners, a conservative people; much of the traditional feeling that the Negro is an inferior race and that segregation is necessary to avoid the ultimate fate of amalgamation dominates Southern thinking; and the ghost of Calhoun with his doctrine of "state interposition" stalks through the lower South. Still survives also the martial spirit, which the New Englander John William De Forest found characteristic of the Old South (a conclusion that the Negro historian John Hope Franklin in a recent study has corroborated).

Nevertheless, a great revolution in folkways and thought is now proceeding below the Mason-Dixon Line as a result of the rapid growth of industry and, especially, the dramatic rise of the Negro. The question that concerns the future of the region is: Will the modern South be able to develop new and better qualities to take the place of those that differentiated the ante bellum Southerners from the Northerners? De Tocqueville asked the eminent Baltimore lawyer John H. B. Latrobe in 1831 what was the principal characteristic that distinguished the South from the North; the Marylander replied that the North was the land of enterprise, the South, the land of chivalry. Subsequently, the spread of Jacksonian democracy lowered the tone of "the high-toned Southern gentleman" as well as his influence in politics so that Beverley Tucker commented bitterly in a letter to William Gilmore Simms just before his death in 1851 that Virginia was "sunk in the slough of democracy, which has no sense of honor." This fine old Virginia gentleman would have been saddened even more, if he had lived to see the rise of demagogues after the Civil War, extending to our own time.

But with the settlement of the integration problem, the progress of education, and the attainment of a higher standard of living for both the white and black inhabitants, the Southern states may yet use their democratic institutions and new prosperity to breed a type of Southerner who combines the virtues of the bygone South with those of modern living. Then in this region there may arise an enlightened and responsible society, envisaged by Thomas Jefferson, that elects to office its best men—the natural aristocracy of talent and virtue.